POLITICALLY

INCORRECT

GEORGE JONAS

POLITICALLY
INCORRECT

Lester Publishing Limited

Canadian Cataloguing in Publication Data

Jonas, George, 1935–
    Politically incorrect

ISBN 1-895555-04-3

I. Title

PS8519.052A16 1991   081   C91-094733-3
PR9199.3.J65A16 1991

Lester Publishing Limited
56 The Esplanade
Toronto, Ontario
M5E 1A7

Printed and bound in Canada.

  92 93 94 5 4 3 2

A Note about the Title

You won't find the phrase "politically incorrect" anywhere in this book. The title comes from the realization—brought home to me by my publishers, editors, critics, and friends—that nothing I've ever written has been in tune with the temper of our times. Much as I regret this (I'm a closet conformist at heart), it's probably too late to do anything about it.

The pieces in this book have originally appeared in the *Toronto Sun*, the *Ottawa Citizen*, *Canadian Lawyer*, *Toronto Life*, *Maclean's*, *Saturday Night*, *Ego*, *Elite*, *Manstyle*, *Books in Canada*, and *The Idler* between 1971 and 1991. I'm grateful to editors Barbara Amiel, Michael G. Crawford, John Downing, Robert Fulford, Don Hawkes, Burt Heward, Brandusa Manu, Stuart Morrison, Peter C. Newman, Don Obe, Gerald Owen, Michael Posner, Marq de Villiers, and David Warren for having invited me to write them.

George Jonas

CONTENTS

1.

AVOIDABLE
GOVERNMENT

Notes on Liberty

THE LAST WORD

It is likely that Canada will soon have a new, patriated, amended constitution. Inevitably, such a reformed constitution will curtail provincial powers. It is almost certain that entrenched in this constitution there will be a charter said to be "guaranteeing" Canadians certain "freedoms and rights."

Is this happy news for a person of traditional liberal beliefs, such as I flatter myself to be? The answer is, probably not. Of course, taken at face value—or perhaps viewed thoughtlessly—the features of our new constitution seem desirable. Patriation symbolizes national independence; the entrenchment of a Bill of Rights appears to secure important freedoms. There is nothing wrong with the bait, but my fishy glance is riveted on the hook.

It being a commonplace that our system of government is derived from the English tradition, this may be a good historic moment to ask what this English tradition is. Many nations have a passion for law and order; what has distinguished the English is the passion they seem to have for law and liberty. When a nation feels compelled to specially legislate liberty and justice, there is a chance that it has neither. Certainly English custom assumed both to be inherent in the common law. They did not need to be spelled out. They were not constitutional concessions conferred on the people by the grace of the authorities.

True, this English passion for law and liberty may have had one anomalous result. In seeking to curtail the power of the Crown—in other words, the executive State—the people of England felt obliged to give more sovereignty to Parliament than they had ever yielded to their king. As the constitutional scholar E.C.S. Wade noted, "The plea that an Act of Parliament was contrary to natural justice failed as far back as the seventeenth century." Parliament now had the power to legislate even "in derogation of the principles of the common law."

Until recently this may not have been a fatal flaw from the liberal perspective. The sovereign parliaments of England or of Canada did have one natural limit on their sovereignty: the spirit of the times. Though there were other forces in the society, the spirit imbuing Parliament from the mid-seventeenth century until the beginning of the twentieth has itself been liberal. It did not fancy that the State is better or wiser than its citizens, or that any public good might result from regulating individual conscience.

Liberals began to be worried when the spirit of the times changed from classical liberalism to the neo-feudalism of the welfare state—not to mention benign or malevolent forms of socialism. Suddenly the spectre of, in Wade's words, "the unscrupulous use of power by a Government which finds itself in command of a majority" became very real. Entrenching individual freedoms and other fundamental liberal values into a written constitution along the American model began to seem more attractive. Sublime as the ideals of an unwritten constitution, as expounded by the great constitutional scholar A.V. Dicey, might have seemed, by the end of the 1960s many, including myself, had concluded that an entrenched Bill of Rights may be the only way to preserve liberal values in our society. It was all very well for Parliament to have the power to declare a man a woman—but when Walter Bagchot used this example a hundred years ago it probably never occurred to him that one day Parliament might just do so.

Why then, now that entrenchment is around the corner, are old-fashioned liberals not cheering? Simple. The new medievalism of the authoritarian state has caught up with our Bill of Rights, which has become infused with the very spirit it was supposed to guard against. The draft charter does affirm individual liberties, but cautiously, hedging them with escape clauses of policy considerations and discretionary powers. In the same breath, it embraces profoundly illiberal ideas of group privilege and special status. The charter spells out protected interests and ambitions in unnecessary detail, but it is much more coy about general liberal principles and it pointedly refuses its protection to the enjoyment of property or the position of the family. So is a great unwritten constitution—in Dicey's phrase, "not the source but the consequence" of our inherent liberties—reduced to the narrow blueprint of social engineers outlining their current policy objectives.

As for the idea of federalism—well, it is clearly not streamlined enough for the engineers of the modern state. All our provinces seem to behave as if they took seriously their tradition of being "coordinate and independent authorities." And this is in fierce conflict with the tenets of statism, which holds independence in very low esteem. The net result, at best, is a false dichotomy, like Ontario Premier Davis' brave remark about being a Canadian first and an Ontarian second. It would be interesting to see how the premier hopes to accomplish this, since to be a Canadian at all one has to be an Ontarian, an Albertan, or a Nova Scotian first.

The provinces are not alternatives to Canada; they are its constituent parts. That's federalism—and of course that's why it's a roadblock in the way of the planned, centralized, coercive nanny state. It's also why real liberals ought to view with grave misgivings any reduction in provincial independence, even if it comes in the guise of compulsorily entrenched "human rights."

The bottom line? It is not to be found in the words of the constitution, whatever they may be, but in the moving spirit behind them. For a traditional liberal, Dicey's comments on the aftermath of the French Revolution express it best: "The Constitution of 1791 proclaimed liberty of conscience, liberty of the press, the right of public meeting, the responsibility of government officials. But there never was a period in the recorded annals of mankind when each and all of these rights were so insecure...."

1981

FAMILIAL CHOICE

To put it mildly, I've never had blind faith in the good sense of the authorities. Even in civilized places—never mind such farcical societies as Iran or Uganda—I've always suspected an embryonic Idi Amin or Ayatollah Khomeini lurking inside many prosecutors, bureaucrats, judges, politicians, and policemen, waiting for an opportunity to get out and run amok. If this be a bias, let me declare it at the outset. It has always been my view that the authorities are a necessary evil to be tolerated only because the alternative—complete anarchy—would be even worse.

Still, until recently in Canada and other liberal democracies, the authorities seemed to have a relative grip on sanity. Whatever their inner feelings, they were tempered by a sense of proportion. Much as they might have wished to have everything their own way, in practice they acknowledged the existence of other legitimate rights, loyalties, desires, and interests. They accepted that a citizen is entitled to put his own life, family, property, and dignity first, except maybe in wartime. They did not entirely confuse morality with their own administrative ambitions. In fact, what distinguished free and civilized societies from tyrannies was the assumption that the State existed for the protection and comfort of the citizen, and not the citizen for the comfort and protection of the State.

One example of how this has been changing comes to us from the friendly province of Alberta. It is by no means a rare example—one wishes it were—but it is a pretty extreme one. Near Peace River, a farmer named Nibs Foster was recently convicted in criminal court of failing to assist a policeman in the arrest of Foster's twenty-year-old son, Kevin, for a driving offence.

To make the facts crystal clear, Daddy Foster did not resist the officer in his attempt to put the handcuffs on Foster Junior. He did not even say, "Buzz off, cop," to the guardian of the law. Nor did he stand by with a smug smile while his son wrestled with the policeman. No, Daddy Foster went as far as to tell his son: "You'd better do what the man says." He instructed his son to obey the police. The only thing he failed to do was to physically involve himself in the fisticuffs on the side of the cop against his own flesh and blood.

Now let's stand back for a second and review the issues calmly. In common law the citizen has never been under any obligation to physically aid the authorities. He has never been legally obliged to denounce other citizens or to bodily assist the *gendarmerie* in the apprehension of their quarry. The citizen's sole duty used to be not to help fugitives and not to obstruct the police. No court has ever questioned a person's right to say "that's none of my business" when it came to a dispute between another person and the boys in blue. A citizen's moral obligation in such cases was a matter solely between the citizen and his or her own conscience. As for legal obligations, there were none.

Under common law no court would dare say to a person: "Never mind your own security. Never mind any of your personal loyalties. Your first duty is to protect the authorities, even if it kills you or breaks your heart."

At the same time, it used to be taken for granted that a citizen is entitled to use reasonable force to protect himself, his family, or his property—and "reasonable force" used to be interpreted liberally in such cases. Trespassers foolish enough to make themselves at home in a farmer's orchard could easily expect to find themselves looking down the business end of the farmer's shotgun—and, until recently, the trespassers' complaints would not have found much sympathy. Nowadays, of course, the authorities think nothing of hauling citizens into court for offering armed resistance to trespassers, rapists, burglars, and muggers. There have been dozens of cases in recent years in which citizens have been charged with offences ranging from assault to murder under circumstances that indisputably involved defence of self or property—though juries, much to their credit, have generally been reluctant to convict the citizens. I'll never forget the case of a woman in Ontario who, having temporarily blinded a would-be rapist, instead of being given a medal found herself charged with the illegal possession of a can of Mace.

But while the authorities are blatantly discouraging the tradition that allowed us as free citizens to protect ourselves, they are attempting to put us under a brand new obligation to protect *them*. Let the thief have the run of your house, they say; hand over the money from your till to the holdup man without a murmur—but risk life and limb when it comes to helping the police.

This is the crux of the matter, because the usual justification for discouraging people from defending themselves is that it is not safe for them to do so. Don't resist the robber; you'll only get hurt. But don't worry about being hurt when it comes to helping the policeman. In the view of Mr. Justice W. G. Egbert, who upheld the conviction of farmer

Foster, even if Foster had been afraid of his son (there was no evidence that he was), his fear for his own safety would have been no excuse. Apparently in the Alberta Court of the Queen's Bench it is the policeman's, not the citizen's, safety that comes first.

There are societies, of course, where such an attitude would not raise an eyebrow. In China or Russia, for instance, it would be taken for granted that the comfort and security of the organs of the state would take precedence over the comfort and security of ordinary men and women. For that matter, children in such societies would be expected—would have a legal duty—to denounce their parents, and parents their children. Such, however, used not to be our tradition.

Our tradition and ideals used to take into account duties and loyalties much higher than those we owed to the police. A principal one among them was the loyalty we owed to our families. We would have regarded it as base beyond words—unnatural even—to oblige a father to raise an arm against a son for the sake of the State. Our tradition had great respect for the community, of course. It's just that we recognized that the interests of the community would not be served by such inhuman obligations—certainly not the kind of community in which we wished to live. We envisaged a land of free and dignified human beings, not one composed of mute subjects devoid of any moral sense and feelings except those imposed on them by the authorities.

However, we have allowed the authorities to take their cue from the worst examples in the world around us and they have. By now they are gradually going berserk. Following the Alberta decision, a senior crown attorney in Ontario Attorney General Roy McMurtry's office announced that crown attorneys in this province will "look seriously" at the section of the Criminal Code used by the police in the Foster case, "with an eye to laying the charge more frequently in future."

Far be it from me to talk Mr. McMurtry's crown attorneys out of looking seriously at a lot of things. On the contrary, I think they sorely need to look seriously at a great many fine decisions made by outstanding British, U.S., and Canadian jurists in the last one hundred and fifty years. I think they might even profit by looking seriously at the writings of such authors as Thomas Jefferson, Alexis de Tocqueville, and John Stuart Mill. For that matter, they might wish to look seriously at their own underlying reasons for wanting to look seriously at Mr. Justice Egbert's Alberta decision.

I would take some convincing that the outstanding social problem in this country is that not enough parents are rushing to the physical aid of the police arresting their children. Or that crime is rampant because not enough old ladies are leaping out of their wheelchairs to answer the cops' calls for assistance. I would doubt that what we need is a new legal duty for citizens to protect the police.

What we might need is a wiser use of prosecutorial discretion when citizens choose to protect themselves. That would be a help. And it would also help if, instead of crown attorneys, our usually vocal civil libertarians were to look seriously at the decision of the Queen's Bench in Alberta.

1982

AVOIDABLE GOVERNMENT

It is difficult to be critical of Toronto after one has just spent a few days in Detroit, as I did earlier this week. Our city is a veritable paradise compared to the Motor City. Perhaps the simplest way to put it is that Toronto continues to exist as a city, while Detroit no longer does.

This, at least, is the perception of the white, middle-class suburbanites who have spoken to me on the subject. Detroit proper, they say, is an area occupied by about a million people, mainly poor and black. About three million people, mainly middle-class and white, live in the surrounding suburbs. The two groups hardly ever mix. The suburban communities have become largely self-contained, with their own shopping and recreational facilities and municipal services. Metropolitan Detroit is really a series of fortified villages, connected by expressways.

My own impressions bear this out. Around 11 p.m. downtown Detroit is almost completely deserted. In a little restaurant, serving

Motown's famous Coney Island hot dogs, my friend and I are the only two white customers. "Hey what are you?" asks a young black good-naturedly at a neighbouring table. "Marks or narcs?"

The fact is we are simply Canadians from a not-too-distant city that has not been forced, or seen fit, to establish *de facto* apartheid within its boundaries, either of class or of colour.

I don't believe we should be too smug about our good fortune: I think we owe it more to accidental developments in history and demographics than to good government or plain decency. The question is, how can we hang on to what we've got?

I suppose one answer is, by maintaining a sense of community. But not a community of hostile groups held together by the political vision of city hall bureaucrats, pressure-group representatives, social planners, and the strong arm of the law. This can only bring about the "tranquility" of a police state. To my mind, a sense of community comes from the tradition of free individuals living together by choice within a liberal democracy.

It goes without saying that this means fair government—but it also means as little government as possible. In a modern community "little government" still means quite a bit. Probably the government of an entire country would have taken fewer people and a smaller budget fifty to sixty years ago than the government of a city today. We can't help that. We must have the government that is unavoidable. The point is, we mustn't have avoidable government.

By avoidable government I mean municipal politicians involving themselves in the enforcement of their own social visions, or the social visions of whichever pressure group captures their attention, at the expense of the legitimate economic, recreational, social, or aesthetic choices of the free individuals who make up a city's population. When politicians do that, they engage in avoidable government, which is always detrimental to the community. It makes little difference whether the things they want to enforce or outlaw are in themselves "good" or "bad." What matters is that it ought to be none of their business.

Admittedly, the lines are at times hard to draw between proper municipal concerns and pig-headed bureaucratic or ideological interference into the personal or business choices of ratepayers and citizens. In a few cases there may be room for argument, but most such interference is blatantly, obviously wrong.

For instance, it's ludicrously wrong to take away someone's fundamental property rights by an unwarranted denial of municipal permits for building or demolition. To then disobey a court order as some Toronto aldermen did recently—and expect taxpayers to pay the fine for it—is arrogant, arbitrary government of such magnitude as to leave one speechless. The finest humanitarian purpose cannot justify it.

The aldermen who defied a court ruling are clearly incapable of understanding the limits of their authority in a free society. They are incipient dictators, and should never be permitted to have a hand in the community's affairs—certainly not until they discover the error of their ways. And, of course, they should pay their contempt-of-court fines themselves.

The same is true of the politicians who would force restaurant owners to abide by their new anti-smoking by-laws. Small as the example may be, it is a perfect illustration of avoidable government. The issue is not smoking or non-smoking. That, pardon the pun, is a mere smokescreen. The issue is people being free to run their businesses as they see fit in their own economic interest. If many customers demand no-smoking areas and stay away from restaurants that do not provide them—as one day they might—ordinary business reasons will force restaurants to provide them. Some, indeed, were already beginning to do so. It was simply none of the government's business to try to impose the rule on the rest.

It is not my right as a member of the public to force businesses to be as I like them. It is my right to patronize only the ones that are. In a free society I vote with my wallet—and it's a pretty effective vote. If I don't like wearing a tie and a jacket to honour the overdone steak a fancy place serves me, I don't darken its doors. That's my right. It's not my right to demand that they set aside tables for my sartorial preferences.

Sergeants are often more important than generals for a private's quality of life in the army. The same is true in politics. If our municipalities become tyrannies, no federal constitution can give us back our freedom.

1984

HOORAY FOR THE SUPREME COURT

I enjoyed the weekend for two reasons. Spring has finally arrived, and the Supreme Court of Canada has made an extremely sensible decision. It would be tempting to say that both were overdue, but it would also be much too glib so I'm not going to say it.

What the Supreme Court did just before the weekend was to throw out two silly contentions. One was the government's contention that the court has no power to review cabinet decisions to see if they conform to Canada's Charter of Rights and Freedoms. The other was the contention of a "peace" group called Operation Dismantle that the cabinet's decision to allow testing of the cruise missile interfered with the constitutional right of Canadians to be secure in their persons. Both contentions deserved to be thrown out. It is, in fact, a sad comment on our disheartening times that they were raised in the first place.

Let's begin with the government. In allowing the cruise missile to be tested, the cabinet made an executive policy decision regarding the defensive needs of Canada and the western alliance of which our country is a member. The cabinet had a perfect right to make such a decision. It even had a duty to do so.

It also happened to be the correct decision, though for the purpose of my argument, this is neither here nor there. If I or anyone else thought that it was the wrong decision the government would still have had a right to make it. We elect governments to make such decisions.

Our government, however, not content to advance this perfectly legitimate position, immediately used the opportunity to grab for a blank cheque. It tried to tell the court that the sacred, omnipotent State, as exemplified by its highest executive branch, has some unreviewable prerogative to rule in any way it pleases on any subject, forever and a day, amen. This regardless of the Constitution, the Charter, or any other consideration in law.

Not much to ask for, is it? Our democratic governments these days only want enough authority to make Henry VIII look like a busboy. I'm elated that, for once, the Supreme Court put on the mantle of Lord Acton and saved our leaders from the absolute corruption that would flow from the absolute power they seem to crave.

As for the dear souls who comprise Operation Dismantle, they are the true children of our pressure-group times. They genuinely believe that it is, or ought to be, unconstitutional to disagree with them. They have absolutely no qualms about wanting to see every one of their political, historical, or social positions entrenched in law. No wonder they pin their hopes for peace in our time on the benevolence of the Central Committee of the Soviet Communist Party, whose members have a similar faith in the pre-eminence of their own philosophical views.

Pressure groups—not only peaceniks but many feminists, environmentalists, and other "human rights" activists—frequently believe that being entitled to one's own opinions means being entitled to impose them on others. If they believe, as Operation Dismantle does, that western nuclear defences only invite nuclear war, they have no trouble concluding that any contrary position must violate Canada's constitutional guarantees for personal security. After all, they argue, in a nuclear war no one is secure.

It apparently never occurs to Operation Dismantle–types that, if the courts endorsed their approach to constitutional law, any other group that happened to believe that building up western nuclear defences is the best way to avoid a nuclear war could challenge a future government's decision to *ban* the testing of the cruise missile. What would they argue then? That the Peace-Through-Strength group is mistaken? But, mistaken or not, believers in defence are as entitled to claim their "constitutional guarantees" for security as members of Operation Dismantle. *If* that is the way the Constitution really works.

It isn't, of course—otherwise the political process would deteriorate into one group dragging the other into court over every conceivable issue, with unelected judges trying to pick and choose between competing policies, while the elected government was twiddling whatever part of its anatomy happened to be handy. And since this would mean the end of democracy, some judges might try to forestall it one day by throwing up their hands and ruling that they have no right to interfere in any cabinet decision, whether it really offends the Constitution or not, because at least the cabinet was elected. It would be the lesser of two evils.

Luckily, thanks to our Supreme Court, it is a choice we do not yet have to make.

1985

A Tale Told in Clarkspeak

I wanted to cool down a little before writing this. A columnist has no excuse for gut reactions; he doesn't have to be first with the news. It's better for him to use his viscera for digestion, as the good Lord intended it.

All right. The news is now about ten days old. What happened was that the *Globe and Mail* published an ad promoting tourism in South Africa. The ad was paid for by the Toronto office of the South African tourism bureau.

External Affairs Minister Joe Clark hit the roof. No problem so far; hitting the roof is a human right. He did not like the ad, which is also okay. I didn't much like the ad myself. The ad invited people to join a "study and fact-finding tour" and to "see the real South Africa." That's probably pure bunk. Far from finding facts and seeing the real South Africa, tourists would be exposed to two weeks of carefully orchestrated government propaganda.

At least that's what an organized tour of any tyranny is likely to be. We know it from experience. Communist dictatorships have been offering tours of this type for decades. The Soviet Union offered them long before Joe Clark was born. A lot of western politicians and liberal intellectuals have formed or reinforced many of their silly opinions on such tours. But our External Affairs minister, having hit the roof, proceeded to do something that was no longer okay. In fact, it was reprehensible.

What Clark did was to announce that his ministry would close down the South African tourism bureau in Canada "as soon as possible." Why? Well, because it didn't comply with an earlier Canadian government request to companies and individuals to voluntarily refrain from promoting tourist visits to South Africa.

I can't blame anybody for blinking twice. Is Clark upset at the South African bureau of tourism for promoting tourism in South Africa? Where does Clark suggest a South African tourist bureau should promote tourism—in Uganda? And is he now going to close them down? Gee, that's a big punishment. I wonder why the South African tourism bureau risked it? Let me think. Maybe because if they are not allowed to do business it matters little to them whether they are not allowed to do business closed or open.

Also, the last time I looked it up, the word "voluntary" in English meant that it was up to you whether you did something or not. In Clarkspeak it seems to mean that you do what he says or else he closes you down. That concept in the dictionary seems to be expressed by the word "involuntary." And calling an involuntary thing voluntary is what is called, in plain English, a lie.

The next thing Clark did was to write a letter to the publisher of the *Globe and Mail*, expressing his dismay over the *Globe* not having been sufficiently voluntary. He said that the ad printed in the paper was "defiant of the Canadian government policy." Presumably the minister felt it was not just the South Africans, but also the *Globe* being defiant for running the ad. And it appears that being defiant of government policy is what newspapers must never do in a free country. No sir! Either they toe the line or we have ways to deal with them to make them more voluntary.

Maybe as voluntary as the newspapers in some Third World countries, the countries that really know how to deal with involuntary journals and journalists. Not to mention defiant ones. Of course, those fine countries can promote their tourism in Canada as much as they like. As can such well-known bastions of humanity, civil liberties, and political freedoms as Cuba, China, and the Soviet Union. But not South Africa. Perish the thought. Promoting tourism there is being defiant of Canadian government policy.

At the risk of boring those readers who are acquainted with my views on the subject, I'll repeat that I loathe apartheid. (Who doesn't? South Africa's own government has doubts about it these days—too little, too late.) But I loathe tyranny and repression everywhere, and relish being defiant of hypocritical and arrogant politicians and governments.

So, at the risk of being closed down by Clark for habitual involuntariness, I urge every Canadian who has the time and interest to travel to South Africa—though preferably not as part of a South African government package tour. You won't find out much about the truth on government package tours. I'd urge everyone not to travel to China that way either.

The truth about South Africa is probably in between the official positions of Ottawa and Pretoria. Is Ottawa's position closer to the truth? Not so much closer as to justify closing down everyone else.

Canada is not a Third World country yet and I'm not a foreign travel bureau, so Clark can't even threaten to close me down. What he can do is to send my publisher a dismayed letter. And then? I never speak for publishers, but if the paper is fine enough I promise to put my copy to good use.

1986

THOU SHALT NOT SELL RETAIL

Most politicians are not people of luminous intellect. This has never surprised nor annoyed me. Most people in *any* profession, including journalism, are not of luminous intellect. A luminous intellect is not necessary for people to function in their jobs, unless they work in theoretical mathematics. Most jobs require only some common sense.

Ontario's new solicitor general, Joan Smith, whatever her intellect, did not seem to be totally lacking in common sense so far. Neither did—at least to all outward appearances—the particular journalists questioning her on a recent CBC panel show about the changes in Ontario's Sunday shopping laws. That's why the terms in which they discussed these changes did surprise and annoy me.

As everybody knows, retail merchants have until now been severely restricted from pursuing their ordinary business on Sundays under some provincial variant of the federal Lord's Day Act. The original religious intent of this law was to prevent all citizens from working for gain on the Lord's day, excepting only those who were engaged in jobs of "necessity" or "mercy."

For better or for worse, Canadian society used to be pretty religious. The State was not completely separate from the Church. It tried to enforce a day of exercise in Christian piety and devotion on all of its citizens. However, by 1987 virtually all classes of citizens could work for gain on the Lord's Day without the slightest interference from the law—all except retail merchants. No one tried to stop developers (or politicians) from making their deals, or fiction writers from writing their novels. No one tried to stop lawyers from using the Lord's Day to prepare for court, instead of exercising themselves in the Christian duties of piety and devotion.

On the contrary. Crown attorneys could use their Sundays to work out how to prosecute retail merchants for the crime of working on Sundays. Since prosecutors do get a salary, whenever they prepare for court, they work for gain. Often it may suit their convenience to prepare on Sundays, but this choice can hardly be described as an act of necessity or mercy.

Anyway, as our country was becoming less and less puritanical, it seemed sillier and sillier to most people that in a free and secular society they should not be able to engage in their lawful, ordinary business whenever they wished. They could not understand why, if they wanted to buy something on Sunday and someone was willing to sell it to them, they should not be able to do so.

The majority of those trying to prevent them were, of course, no longer *religious* by this time. They were simply busybodies or do-gooders of various types, who found it distasteful, as such people always do, that others should be free to do as they pleased every day of the week. In their view, it was bad enough that they couldn't interfere with the rest of us for six days; surely they were entitled to the seventh.

Our modern busybodies could no longer rely on piety or devotion to keep the rest of us from buying or selling on Sundays, so they cast about for some other reason. What they came up with was the "unfairness" of requiring sales clerks to work on Sundays. They said it was terrible that these poor souls in retail sales would have to do this or risk losing their jobs or their promotions. They suggested that it would endanger their family lives. They said that working on Sundays would lead to delinquency, wife-beating, and divorce.

The amazing thing isn't that our do-gooders came up with this nonsense, but that virtually no one challenged them on it. No one said: Oh, come on! What about airline crews, bus drivers, ushers, projectionists, maître d's, weathermen, ticket agents, jockeys, disc jockeys, game wardens, judges, cipher clerks, entertainers, or telephone operators? These people all work the occasional Sunday. Do they beat their wives more frequently than people in retail sales? Do they experience a greater rate of divorce?

Can no person have a decent family life, except Monday-to-Friday civil servants at Queen's Park? Are sailors, soldiers, and head waiters condemned to having delinquent children? And, especially, what prevents people in retail sales who don't like working on Sundays from taking another job? What mental or physical fragility requires sales clerks to be protected in a way no one else in the country has to be protected?

But no reporter asked anything of the sort. The CBC panelists (most of whom work on Sundays) solemnly questioned the solicitor general about this new menace to the families of sales clerks, and Joan Smith solemnly answered that, as an individual, it caused her great concern. And I could only wonder if we had all gone completely, irrevocably nuts.

1987

LIBERTY, EQUALITY, REALITY

Social philosophers have often commented on the incompatibility between the two great slogans of the French Revolution: Equality and Liberty. (The third great eighteenth-century slogan, Brotherhood, has always sounded a little too abstract for people to bother about.) Liberty and equality, however, had fairly concrete meanings. It seemed possible to foster them through social arrangements of one kind or another. Laws and policies could be designed for and measured against the ideals represented by them.

The trouble was that the two ideals didn't seem to work in tandem. On the contrary, they appeared to be destined for a head-on collision. When people were left to their own devices—as required by liberty— they did vastly different things. They had different backgrounds, talents, and luck. They conducted their affairs in different ways.

So people neither started nor ended as equals. They were still sharks or guppies. "If we're all supposed to be equal," some people asked, "why does Henry have so much money, prestige, or power, when Jim has little or none?" One reply was that Henry was fortunate, smart, and daring, while Jim was unfortunate, lazy, and timid. However, this sounded callous. Sometimes it wasn't even true: Jim could simply be a dreamer, while Henry might be a crook. Anyway, even when true, it still didn't look like equality.

Perhaps the answer was that society had been unfair. It had somehow stacked the deck in favor of Henry. The solution was a New Deal. Take away some of Henry's aces and hand them to Jim. However, this caused a lot of trouble. Henry hated having some of his aces taken away, while Jim grumbled that Henry still had too many left. Also, when Jim couldn't parlay even a new deal into a winning hand, he complained that Henry had been cheating, whether Henry had been or not. So the dealer suggested that whenever somebody won a game, he would personally assess penalty points against him.

This sounded good to Jim—except it meant that the game no longer had any rules. If the dealer can redistribute the stronger hands, then as- sess points against the winning players, his own judgment becomes the only rule. The skill, daring, or luck of the players counts for nothing. The dealer is king. The trick is to bully or bribe him into stacking the deck in *your* favour. Or to hand you part of the pot, regardless.

In social terms, you go back to the Middle Ages. Or forward to socialism, if you prefer. (The two are really the same, except for tech- nology. Middle Ages + electricity = socialism, to paraphrase Lenin's famous equation.) You may get equality—everyone becomes the dealer's pawn—but liberty is lost.

At this point some social philosophers suggested that the architects of the French Revolution had been naïve. They had picked two incom- patible ideals. What we must do is to *choose* between equality and liberty. We can't have both. Minimally, we must give up a great deal of one in order to get more of the other.

I think these social philosophers are mistaken. The French Revolution didn't choose incompatible ideals, it's just that we have misunderstood the meaning of the word "equality." To us equality means that people should start with equal cards and have equal (or near-equal) results at the end of the game. To eighteenth-century thinkers it meant that people should be allowed to play by *equal rules*. They objected to people being excluded from the game just because they were commoners rather than blue bloods. They objected to having one set of rules for people born in a hut and a different set for people born in a castle.

At the time of the French Revolution there were no general rules. Different rules applied to every player. None had any rights, only some privileges according to his status at birth. Some groups were assured of winning and some couldn't even sit at the card table. The French Revolution demanded the same rules for all.

In this sense, equality has never been incompatible with liberty. One couldn't even have liberty without it. But instead of demanding the same rules, we've started demanding the same cards before the game and the same results at the end. We're asking for parity rather than equality. And that's why we run into a problem. We cannot have *parity* and liberty at the same time. Or even parity and equality. Our neo-medieval idea of statism means saying goodbye to general rules once again. The dealer doesn't pick the cards *equally*, but according to his social plans or pressures. Players still win or lose, only not by their skill or by chance, but at the dealer's whim. They are neither equal nor free.

Henry, incidentally, is still ahead of the game. He's usually better at bullying or bribing the dealer than poor Jim.

1988

TOWARD THE RESTRICTIVE SOCIETY

Let's talk for a minute about social cost. Everyone knows the expression, of course. It's often used in sentences such as "the social cost of unemployment" or "the social cost of crime." Such phrases generally describe the cost of something undesirable. They're rarely employed in a neutral way, as in "the social cost of education."

Whenever "social" is coupled with "cost," the speaker usually wants to convey a negative feeling about whatever society is paying for. Obviously any public (or even private) expenditure is a "social cost," but since we rarely feel upset about sending kids to school, we tend to simply say "the *cost* of education." We reserve the phrase "social cost" for things of which we disapprove.

In the last number of years it has become common for people not only to express unhappiness about certain undesirable things—say, accidents, illness, or family breakups—but also to emphasize their "social cost." We say that broken homes or mishaps on the roads, apart from being tragic, cost the economy so many millions a year. I find this a dangerous habit.

Dangerous, first of all, because it's inaccurate. Even if we could precisely calculate certain costs—say, hospital treatment for accident victims or repair bills for damaged cars—equating this sum with "social costs" would be erroneous. Hospital workers, chemists, mechanics, insurance brokers, and God knows how many other people are employed by what one might call the accident industry. What would be the "social cost" if all these people suddenly became un- or underemployed?

This doesn't make accidents (or crime or illness) desirable. Far from it; they're terrible things, but now we're talking about *costs*. Even terrible things result in economic activity. Lawyers, judges, pathologists, social workers, and policemen make and spend money. One can fight against terrible things but one cannot, without being simplistic, put a dollar figure on their "social cost." To be precise, one would first have to calculate and deduct the social benefit of the economic activity they generate.

But there's an even greater danger. From these arbitrary dollar figures comes the following suggestion: since certain activities or lifestyles are related to undesirable things, at least statistically, everyone's lifestyle is public business. After all, the public is required to pick up the tab for them.

Why shouldn't we ban human activities if they are linked to social costs? Why shouldn't we outlaw such frivolous and risky things as mountaineering, skiing, smoking, drinking, parachuting, or riding motorcycles if they can be shown to result in medical bills or lost man-hours? Why shouldn't we start regulating sexual behavior if it's tied to venereal disease, family instability, divorce, and crime, all of which have a "social cost" of so many millions a year?

I remember writing in opposition to State medicine many years ago. I opposed it then (and oppose it still) for a variety of reasons, but one of the reasons was (and is) that whenever the government pays the piper it tries to call the tune. It might say that since people fall off their bicycles and require medical attention, they shouldn't be riding them. A lot of people pooh-poohed my fears back then. They called them paranoid. I wish I had a dollar for every time I've heard someone argue since that this or that activity, from smoking to motorcycling, ought to be restricted because of its alleged medical-social costs.

We've not yet started banning lifestyle choices, but the handwriting's on the wall. (We're all but doing it to smokers already.) Here's my three-point warning, just for the record:

1) Once freedom is lost, you'll discover that nothing, not even life itself, is half as valuable.

2) You may start regulating *my* lifestyle first, but *your* lifestyle will be next. I guarantee it. You may not care about smoking or motorcycles, but you'll discover that skiing or sweets or sex or anything you do care about is also on the list.

3) Everything has social costs. If we ever managed to eliminate all hazards in life, from cancer to traffic accidents, *that* would have a social cost, too. In fact, the cost would be incalculable.

If everyone lived to be one hundred and fifteen, it might bankrupt the country. If we still retired at sixty-five, our children would have to support us for half a century. And if we retired at eighty-five, our children would be grandparents before they could get their first job. I suspect the same people who are now worried about social costs would then start demanding that everyone take up smoking when they reach retirement age. Preferably while riding motorcycles.

1989

THE WIMPIFICATION OF THE WEST

The recent attack on a twenty-eight-year-old woman jogger in New York's Central Park has galvanized America. The press coverage, compared to coverage given to similar attacks, has been unprecedented. There's been an outcry from just about every quarter of American society denouncing urban crime. Donald Trump took a full page ad in the *New York Times* urging, amongst other things, a return of the death penalty.

I'm not sure why this particular assault is acting as a catalyst on a society that has been selling its Kentucky Fried Chicken from behind bulletproof glass for a long time now. True, the victim has been described as a "petite, blonde" Yale graduate from a wealthy Pittsburgh family, with "beauty and brains." What's more, she was "a promising Wall Street banker." Still, while most victims of rapes, shootings, and muggings haven't had quite as much going for them, this jogger is hardly the first upper-middle-class victim claimed by street crime in North America. Yet, until now, North Americans have taken street crime—like most other indignities—in their stride.

Perhaps, once the furor over the "wilding" of the Central Park jogger abates, people will return to their usual state of equanimity. After all, equanimity is the state of mind that has characterized most of our citizens for decades. "Equanimity" is actually an understatement. "Bovine docility" would be more accurate.

I think if a visitor from outer space (or from a different century) wrote a letter home to describe our place and times, he'd say that our society is split into two groups: a vast, passive, compliant majority and a tiny, vociferous, militant minority.

The visitor would explain that most people in contemporary western countries are law-abiding, civilized, and mature. They're civilized and mature to an extent unknown and even unimagined in other places and periods. In fact, they're civilized and mature to a point beyond virtue and approaching the borderline of vice.

This isn't expressed only by our society's tolerance of crime, though it serves as a dramatic example—dramatic, but hardly surprising. This type of tolerance flows almost inevitably from our acceptance of intrusions and indignities of every other kind.

The extent to which most western citizens of the late twentieth century allow themselves to be bullied, intimidated, expropriated, and regimented—internationally, nationally, and even municipally—is almost without precedent, except in a few tyrannies. Actually, even in celebrated tyrannies there have been private areas which the tyrants considered off-limits. For instance (with the exception of out-and-out slaves), the lowliest serf could count on some sovereignty over his own family. He'd also retain a right of self-defence against marauders, according to his own judgment. He could arm himself with an axe or a pitchfork. What's more, he'd rarely pay more than a tithe of his income—in other words, ten per cent—to the ecclesiastical authorities or to his liege lord. On his own land he could generally build a shack or a pigsty without asking for permission from any higher authorities.

Though tyrants or marauders often used brute force to raid a citizen's home, they could seldom count on his "mature" or "civilized" compliance when robbing him of his property—to say nothing of taking away his wife or children. Today our tax authorities; social agencies; family courts; municipal officials; environmental, labour, or "human rights" boards; house- or home-breakers; muggers, rapists, and other terrorists can safely rely on our quiet compliance when they hand us their hold-up notes.

In the past, bandits, dictators, officials, or seducers had to fight, at some risk to themselves, for what they can now take from our mature and civilized citizenry with a flick of a pen. Today a person who isn't ready to hand over fifty per cent of his income to social engineers, or who contemplates adding a window to his own attic without official approval, runs the risk, in addition to being fined or jailed, of being viewed as antisocial. And if he threatens to look cross-eyed at someone who is after his wife, or if he keeps a shotgun in his bedroom to make things a little tougher for burglars, he'll be considered a Neanderthal.

I don't think it surprising that street crime flourishes in a climate where people run as great a risk of a criminal charge if they defend their property as they would if they tried to rob somebody else. Or where, statistically speaking, people are less likely to find themselves before a tribunal for snatching a purse than, say, for smoking in a taxi, taking a prolonged glance at a pretty girl, or spanking their own children.

The same climate that has ensured the general wimpification of the West has simultaneously given rise to a miniscule minority of hardened militants. These desperadoes, whether they're criminals who prey on joggers or simply political (or religious, environmental, feminist, animal-rights, etc.) terrorists, think nothing of disrupting, threatening, or mobbing any person, institution, or business to extort their demands. As a result, our society has split into two distinct groups.

The first is a majority intimidated into believing that giving up their property, opinions, traditions, or habits is a sign of maturity and civilization. The second is a small, vicious minority convinced that "wilding" peaceful citizens is a sign of commitment and justice. We're truly reaping what we have sown.

1989

SIDING WITH THE SENATORS

People say the darndest things. Take, for instance, the suggestion that by threatening to kill the Goods and Services Tax the Senate is thwarting the democratic process. If only Prime Minister Brian Mulroney and his troops made this suggestion it could be filed away as an inaccurate but understandable partisan shot in the GST wars. However, some neutral observers have also picked up on the theme in the media, including commentators who don't like the proposed tax any more than you or I do.

I find this irksome because it shows an inability to comprehend the system of government under which we live. It is one thing for high school kids to have difficulty with the concept of democracy, but it's scary when fully grown pundits exhibit the same syndrome. I think I'll vent my spleen by reiterating a few elementary points on the structure of democratic government.

Many democracies have upper chambers, some elected and some appointed. They exist for a plain purpose. Contrary to popular belief, it's neither a ceremonial purpose nor the purpose of giving good pensions to aging party hacks. It is most emphatically not a purpose that runs counter to democratic ideals. An upper chamber serves democracy in ways similar to those in which other democratic institutions serve it. Just like independent courts, a free press, or the Constitution itself, upper chambers exist to check and balance the powers of the government of the day. They are to ensure that the government does not go berserk, does not exempt itself from the rule of law, and does not use its democratic mandate to turn itself into a tyranny.

Without checks and balances, any party with a parliamentary majority could, in theory, become a tyranny. In a democracy it would only be a temporary tyranny because the party would have to stand for re-election, but it would be a tyranny nevertheless because, while in office, its powers would remain unbridled. (As a matter of interest, in ancient Greece a tyrant was often an *elected* official. In some ancient city-states, politicians who wanted to rule could ask their fellow citizens for tyrannical powers for a period of time. Their powers were "democratic" enough—eventually they could be thrown out of office—but also quite uncontrolled. That's why they were called tyrants.)

As the concept of democracy developed, people came to realize it was not enough to elect their rulers by popular vote or to limit the time during which they could govern. They also had to ensure that their rulers, even during their legitimate terms of office, would not govern in unlawful, unresponsible, or arbitrary ways. Hence (among other checks and balances) the notion of an upper chamber or senate.

It is true that our Senate is not an elected body. It is also true that, by long and wise tradition, it rarely rejects proposed legislation by the elected government in its entirety. It is especially careful not to interfere with matters relating to budgets and taxation, not even by extensive amendments. This is because our upper chamber recognizes the primacy of elected government in all legislative areas. It is *not* because it does not have the power or the democratic right to amend or reject legislation.

It obviously has the power, otherwise the whole question wouldn't arise (and Mulroney wouldn't have to consider asking Her Majesty to let him stack the Senate with his own boys). But it also has the democratic right—even the duty—to do so, as long as it exercises its powers judiciously and in good faith. It is when a senate becomes so "judicious"—or cowardly or lazy—that it refrains from exercising its powers under any circumstances that it fails in its obligations to democracy. That's when taxpayers begin to wonder why they should continue paying for it. Until now our upper chamber has been judicious to a fault. Now that it has acted for a change, has it acted in good faith?

That's a harder question. A cynical observer may say an upper chamber that acts entirely along party lines, according to whether its members are Liberals or Conservatives, is just a costly extension of partisan politics. It can't be relied on to balance unresponsive government, which alone would justify the millions spent on it.

Yet if an upper chamber did the right thing only once in a century (and even then only because of fortuitous circumstances) I think it would be enough to justify its existence. The GST is a case in point. It's a bad tax which the government proposes to collect through costly, cumbersome, and confusing methods. Canadians hate it—and love the Senate for trying to stop it. What can be more democratic than that?

1990

2.

THE
LURKING
AYATOLLAH

Notes on Censorship

IMPROPER CHANNELS

I suppose the reason I'm not on the dinner party list of either camp in what passes for our political spectrum is that I've never been able to see much difference between the left and right. Not being on the list, incidentally, bothers me very little. If it did, I guess I'd embrace the left because, except for some Mexican dishes, its dinner parties are marginally better.

To try and get back to my topic, when I say I don't see much difference between left and right, I have in mind the only kind of difference that matters: a difference between human beings reared in the western tradition of individual liberty from those reared under coercive tinpot bigots. In this sense, left and right invariably meet, however much they may differ in their ostensible social and political goals. Such differences may seem like an abyss, but one over which conservatives and socialists, or the Moral Majority and Women's Libbers, can shake hands with amazing agility and ease.

This is the sense in which they both differ from my fast-vanishing breed of old-fashioned liberals. Because, as I have vainly attempted to point out to acquaintances who insist on calling themselves liberals, what makes a liberal doesn't depend on how he views homosexuals, unwed mothers, or nudity in art, but solely on what measures he would feel free to employ to make others view them the same way. Which accounts for my unpopularity at "liberal" dinner parties. My unpopularity at conservative dinner parties stems from the fact that I have no strong views one way or the other on gays, common-law unions, or *Milesian Tales*.

Which brings me closer still to the topic of this essay. *Milesian Tales*, since their first introduction by—if memory serves—Aristeides around the second century B.C., have always enjoyed a certain degree of popularity. Their tradition seems to stretch from Petronius' *Satyricon* right to *Playboy* magazine. If people wish to describe *Milesian Tales* as "soft porn," I won't object. That's pretty much what they are.

It so happens that I'm not crazy about porn, soft or hard, ancient or modern. Not only would I not cross the street for it, but I would probably cross the street to avoid it. I think the most tedious evening I've ever spent in Toronto was at—you guessed it—a dinner party in the home of an acquaintance (a gynecologist by profession) who insisted on separating the girls and the boys after dinner and showing the latter a pornographic movie. Hard-as-nails porn, too, close-ups and everything. Talk about a busman's holiday.

For reasons of personal taste, when one of the new pay-TV channels—I blotted out of my memory which—decided to entice its viewers with productions from *Playboy*, it made my choice of which channel not to subscribe to extremely easy. I prefer to take my soporific in pill form where twenty bucks will get me a whole year's supply; and even if I wished to induce slumber through audiovisual means, there would be plenty of programs to put me to sleep on free TV. Going a step further, I might even agree with people who are outraged by *Playboy*-type programming on the basis that it presents or promotes a worthless, misleading view of life—though my outrage would be tempered by the observation that about eighty per cent of everything else on TV (or in print) presents or promotes views just as worthless and misleading. Including—without being limited to—the views of contemporary feminism.

Which brings me to the fulcrum of my topic. As everyone must have heard by now, when the aforementioned pay-TV boys announced their brave new programming plans, militant factions of the women's movement promptly went berserk. They demonstrated, picketed, and called for a boycott of every institution that had the remotest financial connection with the porn programmers, including the hapless T. Eaton Co., whose venerable founder—having been puritanical enough to forbid the sale of tobacco in his store nearly a century ago—must have been turning in his grave. What's more, the pressure ladies half-successfully mao-maoed Communications Minister Francis Fox—better known for his expertise in handwriting than for his moral authority (Fox had once admitted forging the signature of a husband on a document so that the husband's wife, with whom Fox had been having an affair, could secure an abortion)—to censor the offending shows or cause them to be censored by the CRTC.

The fervour with which the ladies of the women's movement (here-inafter the left) besieged the Great Calligrapher was no different in kind from the fervour with which their counterparts in, say, the Christian Decency League (hereinafter the right) might have besieged whatever unfortunate minister of the Crown was accessible to them. Despite the difference in their slogans—Violence Against Women for one, Sanctity of Family and Womanhood for the other—their motives and ultimate aim would have been similar. For one thing, they would have wished to register their sincere outrage against Frivolous and Sacrilegious Treat-ment of Sex, which for women (to a greater extent than for men, anyway) has always been and still remains Serious Emotional Business and, sometimes, a Livelihood. For another thing, they would have taken it for granted, as they would take it for granted in their conservative incarnation, that having a right to their own tastes, emotions, and opin-ions somehow gave them the right to control the tastes, emotions, and opinions of others. By force of law, if necessary.

There is a cast of mind that is genuinely unable to distinguish between fundamental human rights (such as security of one's person and property) and wishful ambitions, such as not having one's tastes or beliefs challenged by expressions of contrary tastes and beliefs. The difference may be self-evident to many people, but they'd find it hell to explain to either the Moral Majority or to the Status of Women types who stormed the Great Calligrapher's office in Ottawa. The more "liberal" of them, sensing a contradiction between their dutifully enlightened stance on censorship in general and their atavistic desire to have their ideas enforced on all pet issues, came up with rationaliza-tions that ran as follows: "There are certain 'freedoms' we elect to forego—like killing each other—and which we legislate against. Insofar as pornography is the 'death' of women, then it must be another 'freedom' we elect to forego." (This quote from the British feminist author Catherine Itzin.)

Of course, such two-cent sophistries shouldn't get Ms. Itzin past the front door of an undergraduate debating society, but nowadays they get her ilk a serious hearing and may result in regulatory agencies such as the CRTC issuing warnings to broadcasters that if they don't clean up their act voluntarily, they will have it cleaned up for them by law. Needless to say, "by law" in this case means censorship, since if the fem-libbers or the CRTC believed for one moment that *Playboy*'s programs were obscene, they could employ the simple remedy of bringing their perpetrators or distributors to court. Obscenity *is* a criminal offence in Canada. But of course even the Women's Movement cannot imagine that any court composed of sane contemporaries would find the proposed pay-TV offerings obscene. No, they're simply something the lady storm troopers do not wish to see on the screen. The reason being—what else?—that they feel strongly about them.

I can sympathize with strong feelings. For instance, I strongly feel that three-quarters of everything militant feminists have been saying or writing in the last fifteen years ranges from the baseless to the base. I find most feminist ideas, at best, inaccurate as they pertain to history and human nature, and at worst, pernicious and spiritually obscene. Far more obscene, in fact, than *Playboy* programs. I believe that no false charges ever levelled against women by men—and there have been some dandies—have been nearly as divisive, as conducive to gender hatred, as "sexist" if you will, as the false charges levelled by feminists against men. However, I'm not banging on the government's doors to have feminist ravings banned—or to establish "guidelines" for my own intelligent, humane, conciliatory, and infinitely more accurate options about the two sexes on the nation's airwaves. Even though I firmly believe that humankind would be better served by the compulsory dissemination of my ideas and the total exclusion of others.

Apart from my distaste for banging on doors, I have another reason for my reticence. I may be a virulent antifeminist—yet ultimately I would sooner be on a desert island with someone who embraced feminism but allowed me to persist in my error than with someone who agreed with me about feminism but plotted to outlaw feminist literature. I'd find such a person too dangerous to live with on an island, and would take measures to protect myself from him. Or her. Typical knee-jerk liberal thinking? Maybe, but outside of it lurks the Ayatollah Khomeini, in whatever guise.

1983

DANGERS OF CENSORSHIP

I don't blame *Toronto Sun* Publisher Paul Godfrey for being upset last week at an ad that ran in his own paper that tried to use a huge swastika—the Nazi symbol—to protest the suppression of the December issue of *Penthouse* magazine. The ad was in despicable taste.

Of course, by now it's almost routine for some people to compare their plight, whatever it may be, to that of the victims of Nazism. When Metro Police raided some homosexual bathhouses a couple of years ago, gay spokesmen immediately screamed "Crystal Night!" in an effort to suggest that a morality raid on four steambaths was comparable to the infamous night in Nazi Germany when tens of thousands of Jewish houses and shops were destroyed, with hundreds of people beaten or killed. Trying to fry one's licentious little fish by the flames of the Holocaust is a tendency as universal as it is disgusting. Good for Godfrey.

Having said this, however, I will add that banning the December issue of *Penthouse* magazine was wrong. This question has nothing to do with the tasteless and misleading ad the publishers of *Penthouse* tried to use in protest against the censors. Certain acts, though they fall far short of the evils of Nazism, can still be wrong. And even tasteless people—which, for my money, the publishers of *Penthouse* are by definition—can have a point.

Their point is that in Canada—and in the U.S. too—we are heading into a new and dangerous era of censorship. The fact is, we are. The December *Penthouse* was ordered removed from the news-stands because of a so-called photo-essay entitled *Sakura*, in which Oriental women were shown in various poses of bondage. In my personal view, in spite of its ludicrous pretensions to "art," the horrid little series was clearly pornographic, catering to the peculiar tastes of sado-masochistic deviants. However—and this is the point—an even lengthier "photo-essay" in the same issue, depicting in stomach-turning detail the delights of lesbian love and, in my opinion, exhausting just as fully any reasonable definition of obscenity, would probably have escaped the wrath of our censors. Certainly they never made any reference to it. They seemed to have found pictures of nude women in poses of oral gratification just fine.

Why? I assume because in our present socio-political climate lesbianism is a protected "sexual orientation," while sado-masochism is not. And this, precisely, is what is wrong with censorship. It is, inevitably, the suppression of some people's tastes or ideas by others who happened to have grabbed enough power to exclude all tastes or ideas different from their own. Such decisions are always arbitrary. There are never any objective standards. Censorship is invariably a capricious line drawn by a politically powerful group between their own notions of propriety and the notions of others.

One person's erotica will always be another person's pornography. I have no doubt that *Sakura* is pornographic, for instance, but I have seen the eminent publicist Arnold Edinborough express a contrary opinion on television. He seemed to think that the half-clad Oriental ladies tied to tree-trunks represented a form of art. If so, I'd be prepared to debate him on television or in print, but that is all I'd be prepared to do. Under no circumstances would I feel entitled to suppress what he believes to be erotic art.

Some customs officers, feminists, or religious pressure groups have no such qualms. They feel entitled to suppress anything, including works the most outstanding representatives of their country's culture regard, rightly or wrongly, as works of art. The justifications of the censors vary, depending on the time and the place, but on close examination they always turn out to be nonsense. Right now, the justification is the need to protect women against violence. The censors' thesis is that verbal or pictorial representations of sado-masochism promote such violence.

There isn't, of course, the slightest evidence for this and there's much evidence to the contrary. A tiny segment of the population happens to have a sado-masochistic sexual orientation. They include both men and women. They enjoy acts of bondage and similar pastimes with one another's full consent and without, on the whole, causing any physical harm to anyone. They are no sicker than adherents of any other sexual deviations—not even fewer in numbers than, say, lesbians—and are statistically no more prone to enforce their tastes on unwilling partners than anybody else. They tend to advertise rather than rape.

I happen to regard sado-masochists, along with voyeurs, exhibitionists, homosexuals, and consumers of any kind of pornography, as rather sick people, but as long as they stay away from juveniles and harm no one I can see no reason to restrict their tastes in a free society. I can especially see no reason to pick and choose between deviations, according to political fashion, and suppress one while endorsing another.

In the great social experiment called World War II the Red Army raped its way across Eastern and Central Europe. Though the Soviet soldiers came from a society where sexual mores were positively Victorian, with no *Penthouse* or *Playboy* magazines and, of course, no television, they were about ten times as likely to commit acts of sexual assault than their American, French, or British counterparts. The western soldiers came from societies where pornography was freely available, even in those days; the Soviet soldiers from a society where total repression extended to sexual matters. Ask any woman who lived through that period which occupying army she preferred.

1984

WHEN LIFE IMITATES ART

The book burners are upon us. The fires are not yet lit, but organized movements at both ends of the political spectrum—from feminists and "human rights" advocates on the left to police associations and Moral Majority types on the right—are gathering wood for the stake. They have already persuaded many branches of government to join the *auto-da-fé*. Under the guise of hate-literature, anti-discriminatory, and anti-pornography laws, censorship legislation of all kinds is being drafted by municipal, provincial, state, and federal governments in Canada as well as in the United States.

Nothing stands between heretic books or films and the New Inquisitors but a thin red line of liberal intellectuals. However, when it comes to censorship, liberal intellectuals have more than the censors to worry about. They also have to worry about a glaring inconsistency in their own position.

I'm not talking about the traditional contradiction everyone faces when, for the sake of freedom, he has to speak out for somebody else's right to say something with which he profoundly disagrees. The necessity of having to defend even obscene or anti-Semitic garbage at times, for the sake of free speech, may be painful but it is also self-evident. The contradiction I have in mind is more subtle and cuts more deeply.

As creators and consumers of cultural products that require the moral and financial sympathy of the community, intellectuals must maintain that books, films, plays, or paintings have a profound and lasting effect on the human mind. Their demand for public support of the arts has to rest on the premise that artistic expression is "good" for the community—that is, it's capable of influencing people's sentiments and behavior in a beneficial way. Lunch-pail philistines might dismiss the written word and the painted image as unimportant frills or idle entertainment. Intellectuals can't do that. The legitimacy of their own occupations and preoccupations as makers, interpreters, or consumers of novels, dramas, ballets, and symphonies has to be anchored in the assumption that these are important things. They have the power to expand the minds and ennoble the hearts of all who come into contact with them.

At the same time, to fend off the censor, liberal intellectuals must try to allay suspicions that anything with enough power to expand human minds might also constrict them. They must attempt to deny that anything sufficiently strong to ennoble can also demean human beings. While fervently confirming the good influence of the arts, proponents of a liberal culture must just as fervently deny their capacity for bad influence. They have to propose that while a book can make someone better it cannot make him worse, while it can induce someone to charity and love it cannot induce him to selfishness or hate. Only by assuming this position can they suggest that the public must support and foster the arts without controlling or censoring them.

But, logically speaking, this is nonsense. The philistine position that the arts don't count for much has relatively more merit than the assertion that a good book is potent but a bad book is impotent as an influence on human values and behavior. One reason—perhaps the main reason—for the survival of some censorship in even the most liberal societies stems from the recognition that both propositions can't be true. If the arts can have social and moral value, they can also do social and moral harm. Intellectual insistence on a direct, one-to-one relationship between artistic expression—or any educational experience—and the minds of those who are exposed to it, makes the periodic upsurge of censorship inevitable. The minute we convince the community that the arts are important and are to be fostered because they exert a direct influence on people, we have, alas, also convinced the community that it must, through laws and regulations, try to exert a direct influence on the arts.

This explains the paradox of the arts flourishing in relative liberty in philistine societies that attribute little or no significance to them, while being stifled in Byzantine tyrannies that recognize their importance only too well. In this sense, the arts councils and the censorship bureaus of a nation become flip sides of the same coin. Does all this mean that I oppose arts councils? No. Does it mean that I endorse censorship? No again. I abhor censorship. Does it mean, then, that I doubt the capacity of books, films, or paintings to influence people either for good or for evil? Yes—except the reality is even more complex.

Though books, films, and paintings do influence people both morally and intellectually, their influence is so indirect and roundabout, so independent of the artist's aims and methods, and is so much filtered through every individual recipient's own consciousness, that its course cannot be charted or predicted. Bad books can have a good influence on some people, good books can have an evil one. This includes the would-be censors. It makes all attempts at censorship seem vain, childish, presumptuous, and futile.

Can literary works trigger some individuals to commit unspeakably horrible acts? They certainly can. In 1956, a man named Stephen Nash murdered and gruesomely mutilated several children in California. In 1970, a man named John L. Frazier massacred the entire family of a Santa Cruz ophthalmologist. In the early 1940s on the Belcher Islands, nine Inuit adults and children were killed by another group of Inuits. Very recently in Ontario, a man and his wife allegedly baked their own little daughter in an oven. Each of these killings was inspired by a book, but not a book of pornography.

In the case of Stephen Nash it was Tolstoy's *War and Peace*. In the case of John L. Frazier it was environmental literature. (In a handwritten note placed on the windshield of the murdered doctor's car, Frazier proposed death to everyone who "misuses the natural environment" or "does not support natural life on this planet.") The Belcher Island and Ontario murderers found their sources of inspiration in Christian literature: the Bible.

It would be child's play to collect hundreds of examples (especially connected with the Bible, the Koran, Marx, Marcuse, Fanon, Nietzsche, etc.) of literary and philosophical works that served as inspiration for murder. Interestingly, it would be far more difficult to come up with examples of worthless pornographic junk serving as direct triggers for criminal acts. More difficult, but probably not impossible: very likely anything, including a pop album, as in the case of Charles Manson, is capable of inducing horrendous impulses in some twisted minds.

Such examples should humble both intellectuals and censors. Intellectuals, because it ought to indicate to them how much like the sorcerer's apprentice they are in the face of all the mysteries in which they profess to be connoisseurs or experts. And censors, because they aren't even apprentices, only futile, conceited, and clumsy bullies.

1985

WHAT IS CENSORSHIP?

Earlier this week a friend asked me to take a look at a list of books. It was a lengthy list, containing well over fifty titles. These books—so my friend was told—had been censored in Canada. My friend, a lawyer and a civil libertarian, was being asked to read from one of the books at Toronto's Harbourfront, where a group of people were gathering to protest censorship. The event, called Freedom to Read, was a repeat performance from previous years.

My friend is a busy man, and he is used to being accurately briefed. When he received the list with a letter asking him to participate (over the eminent writer Margaret Atwood's signature) he didn't think it necessary to question the premise on which the exercise was based. He just wanted me to recommend a book for him to read.

I hate censorship, as would any person who spends most of his time reading and writing. As a reader or writer, any book censored could be mine. As an old-fashioned liberal, I react to the word "censorship" like a warhorse does to the sound of the bugle. I looked at the list. There were many excellent books on it by first-rate writers from Alice Munro to George Orwell. Had he picked any of them, my friend would have been reading from the best of our civilization. There was only one problem. Most of those books hadn't been censored. They had only been subjected to *choices*, or attempts at choices, by school boards, libraries, parents, or educational authorities.

The choices, or attempts, were deplorable. They were obtuse, sectarian, and at times moronic. I wish to give no comfort to those who made or tried to make them. They are, in my view, not fit to be in charge of a turkey farm. But just as I'm entitled to my view, so is the person who'd remove George Orwell from his library. To be an idiot is, alas, a fundamental human right.

I suggest that in Canada we've had so little experience with censorship that we have become confused about the meaning of the word. Some of us seem to believe that it is simply a synonym for ignorance or poor literary taste. But that's not what censorship is. Censorship is a government authority banning the publication, importation, sale, or distribution of written material to the public at large. At its worst, censorship is prior censorship: a board of officials to whom you must submit a book or article before you are allowed to print or distribute it. There is, at present, no such censorship in Canada—except, unfortunately, for motion pictures and videotapes.

Another form of censorship is Canada Customs preventing the entry of books into the country, or police officers marching in to remove them from bookstores or libraries. Such arrogant acts foist the customs or police officers' taste on every citizen—without any due process of law.

But three-quarters of the books on my friend's list were neither prosecuted nor censored. They were objected to—in many cases unsuccessfully—by parents, school trustees, or ministry officials. As a result, some were removed from certain reading lists or libraries. They were not banned from the community; they couldn't be banned. Anybody could buy or borrow them across the street.

It is the job of certain people to choose books and make up reading lists for the children in their charge. That's why they have been hired or elected. The rights of parents, of course, are natural rights. If we find some of their views moronic, what are we to do? Deny them their freedom to choose—or even to protest? People who'd exclude Solzhenitsyn from their reading lists are unfit; I can't put it any stronger. But I don't pay their salaries. If those who pay them are happy with their choices, what can I do—except to pillory them and call them names? As a writer, I can't demand the "freedom" to be put in everyone's list or library, whether he wants me or not. I can't say I'm "censored" if someone fails to select my book. And as a reader, unless the State stops me by real censorship, I can buy or borrow any book somewhere else—for my child or for myself.

"Oh all right," my friend said, "what about the other books on the list? The books genuinely censored? Which is best? Which should I read from?" The best? Well—there is *The Anarchist's Cookbook*, a manual from the turbulent '60s with recipes for home-made explosives. There is an anti-Semitic treatise claiming the Holocaust never happened. There is *Show Me!*, a trendy picture book with photographs of little girls looking at their parents' genitalia. And there is *The Joy of Sex*.

These books have been genuinely censored at one time or another—by the police, customs, the government. They should not have been, of course. Nothing should ever be censored. But which one would you care to stand up and read from in front of an audience?

1986

BABY, BATHWATER, AND ALL

It would seem unnecessary to add one's voice to the increasing clamour over the wretched Bill C-54, Ottawa's pig-headed attempt to interfere with what people may read and write (or watch or listen to) in Canada. Unnecessary, because this asinine piece of legislation has virtually no supporters among Canada's opinion-makers. Editorial writers have condemned it. Author Pierre Berton has called it "monstrous," adding that it would "make us the laughing stock of the world." Civil libertarian Alan Borovoy has successfully roused the nation's librarians against the proposed law. I can't think of a person or group of the slightest intellectual respectability who supports Bill C-54, at least as it's drafted. By now, only Justice Minister Ray Hnatyshyn and his bureaucrats seem to think that it's okay.

Joining a choir is not my strong suit, not even when I like what they are singing. I guess I'm a soloist by nature, even a voice in the wilderness, enjoying the advantages (and griping about the disadvantages) that such a choice entails. I won't go on about this since I'm not paid to analyze myself; I raise the topic only to explain why I'm joining a chorus in this instance.

Actually, I have two reasons. The first is that, notwithstanding all the clamour, this hideous bill may yet become the law. The government has not given up on it. Hnatyshyn and his troop of would-be censors figure that they can withstand an attack of enraged librarians, led by Borovoy on a pink charger. They may even be right. Good as it is to have Berton on the side, it's far from being decisive in this battle. The second reason is that long before there are laws, there is a *climate*. And before there are any hideous laws, there's usually a hideous climate. Hideous laws do not appear out of the blue.

Hold the Nobel Prize: I'm not the first to have discovered this—though I may be among the few who can actually absorb it. There haven't been many journalists who bothered to scream about (or even simply to report) an unholy alliance developing between our pressure groups of the left, our pressure groups of the right, and Canada's government. I was among the few who did scream, maybe to the point of appearing something of a crank. I didn't particularly mind: the company was select and the cause was good. Simply put, it was (and remains) the cause of liberty.

In particular, I suggested that old, rickety, arch-conservative Mrs. Grundy and young, shiny, radical-feminist Ms. Grundy were about to join hands to enforce their tastes, values, and ideas—to the total exclusion of all other tastes, values, and ideas—on the entire nation. They did not merely want to be free to act as they wished; they desired no one else to be free to act any other way. The handwriting for Bill C-54 has been on the wall for years.

I repeatedly suggested that even the noblest cause, such as the protection of women and children, can serve as a Trojan horse to penetrate the autonomous family, the staunchest bulwark of a free society against the intrusive state. The worthiest measures directed against rape or wife-beating or child-abuse can become tools of tyranny given some excessive, trend-blinkered, or unscrupulous people. The protection-racket of the state begins with bills like C-54, then often leads to Chairman Mao or the Ayatollah Khomeini.

I also suggested that, if our incipient commissars have gone past all common sense, so have our libertines. It's one thing to decriminalize sexual deviations, but quite another to entrench them as human rights. There's a huge distance between tolerating promiscuity, adultery, or homosexuality, and promoting them as "alternate lifestyles."

I said the artist's freedom is to be cherished—but silly, trendy hacks using words in public that they would never dream of using in private (as they seemed to do throughout the '60s and '70s) would do nothing for artistic freedom. All it would create is a backlash, in the course of which the baby would be thrown out with the bathwater.

Behold Bill C-54.

For my friend Borovoy I borrow from the German poet Friedrich von Schiller: "Late you come, but still you come!" Glad to have you aboard. It may have been easier to draw the line some time ago, but at least you're drawing it now. To paraphrase Lord Tennyson, there's cannon to the left of you, cannon to the right of you, but perhaps the Charge of the Light Librarians can still lead to victory.

1987

SEE NO EVIL, SHOW NO EVIL

A PBS television program last week explored the subject of news censorship in South Africa. The program suggested that, from the government's point of view, censorship worked. It even led to a degree of self-censorship by the big networks and newsmagazines.

The PBS show documented that, since the official clamp-down, the flow of apartheid-related items has diminished in the western media. South Africa hasn't exactly dropped out of the news, but it no longer has the primacy it once had. Today, one can actually watch an evening newscast without seeing any footage about the wicked regime in Pretoria.

The PBS show speculated that there were two reasons for this. One, the big networks did not want to risk expulsion. They felt that trying to circumvent the law and sneak a film clip of demonstrators being brutalized by the police past the censor wasn't worth jeopardizing their chances for some big news break. Two, without "dramatic" photos or film footage the news value of apartheid stories dropped. South African reports became tame. They were no longer front-page items, or perhaps news items at all.

PBS didn't set this out in exactly the same terms as I'm setting it out here, but this was the essence of their conclusion. I think it was accurate. Government censorship does work up to a point. To some extent, it works for the very reasons outlined on the PBS show.

At editorial meetings news items compete for the front pages. This competition is even more intense for air time on TV. Reports with so-called dramatic pictorial content (in plain language, shocking and violent items) generally have the inside track. In most such contests intrinsic news value comes second. A bus falling off a cliff in India killing fifty people is ordinarily a back-page item in western newspapers, and it's unlikely to make TV news at all. However, add some dramatic photos and you may get it on the front page. Add a film clip of the bus as it actually plunges, and the same story might be read by Dan Rather on the *CBS Evening News*.

If, whether by censorship or other means, you reduce opportunities for violent items, you'll reduce coverage. Reduce all opportunities for detailed reports on controversial events—even without shocking pictures—and all reporting might stop. At the very least, they will be reduced in bulk as well as in prominence.

This fact has never escaped totalitarian tyrannies. They might never have had a good press in the West, but they knew that by censorship and news management they could escape a lot of bad press. For a reporter to file adverse, let alone shocking, reports about the Gulag (or whatever) he first has to get there. He has to be able to shoot pictures, and he has to be able to send them back. Minimally, he has to be allowed to conduct some interviews.

It was because repression was *total* only in totalitarian countries—communist countries, since the end of World War II—that an anomalous situation developed. Semi-repressive authoritarian dictatorships received a far worse press in the West than their fully repressive big brothers. North Americans heard more about one student being beaten in South Korea than 1,000 people being tortured in the communist north. One victim in South Africa, Argentina, Israel, etc., could be imprinted into the West's consciousness far more deeply than millions massacred in Cambodia or "re-educated" in China during the reign of the Great Helmsman Mao.

I have tried, God knows how often, to point out this simple fact and so have a few other commentators. Most journalists, however, have been too entranced with what they've read in their own papers or seen on their own TV programs. They seemed to forget completely that if South Africa appeared to be a greater violator of human rights than, say, Romania, it was because of South Africa's relative freedom—freedom of press, freedom of movement, freedom of assembly. For journalists and for protesters.

Nothing in this should give the slightest comfort to those who favour apartheid, or those who favour press censorship. In my view, both are unmitigated evils. But yes, censorship does "work." It keeps some of the evidence (and most of the impact) out of view. Now that PBS has discovered this truth about South Africa, will they also discover it about communist tyrannies? (The program gave no indication that they have.)

But wait. Since censorship, while increasing in countries like South Africa, Israel, and even Britain, is decreasing within the Soviet bloc, it may happen that the Soviet bloc will start getting its worst press. Just as *glasnost* begins to improve it, our media may begin to see the Soviet bloc for the evil empire it has always been.

1988

3.

THE
FASHIONS
OF FOLLY

Notes on Social Engineering

FREEDOM MEANS NEVER
HAVING TO SAY YOU'RE HIRED

When sentencing one of the killers of shoeshine boy Emanuel Jaques, Ontario Supreme Court Justice A. W. Maloney made a remark that became the subject of considerable controversy. Justice Maloney was reported to refer to the murderer, Saul Betesh's, "...acknowledged tendency to seek out ever younger homosexual partners. I wonder," said His Lordship, "how common that is among homosexuals. There are those who would seek legal protection for homosexuals in the Human Rights Code. You make me wonder if they are not misguided."

On the face of it Justice Maloney's comment merely seemed silly. It outraged homosexual activists, but even those writers-to-the-editor who had no partisan views found the judge's remarks unfortunate. After all, Betesh's "tendencies" were no more indicative of the tendencies of homosexuals in general than a heterosexual child-molester's tendencies would be of heterosexuals, etc., etc. It would be a "gross distortion of justice"—in the words of Ontario gay lib spokesmen Michael Lynch and Tom Warner—to use the criminal conviction of three men to deny basic human rights to four hundred thousand Ontario homosexuals.

No doubt. But are we not beginning to confuse basic human rights, such as equality before the law for everyone, naturally including homosexuals, with special human ambitions, such as the "rights" to employment, promotion, or social approval? Is it not a greater distortion of justice for society to pass legislation about an increasing number of personal judgments and values? Are the current pressures to extend the protection of the Human Rights Code to an ever wider circle of special interest groups not demonstrating a basic weakness in the philosophy of the Human Rights Code itself?

Do human rights laws not compel individuals to suspend their own views and beliefs as much as discriminatory laws might? If it were illegal for me to employ a homosexual it would, of course, be a chilling concept, but isn't it just as chilling to make it illegal for me *not* to employ one? Don't both laws curtail my personal liberty in a matter that, insofar as it can be said to involve a question of human rights, also involves my own? Is Justice Maloney's comment, on a deeper level, not a plea for some freedom of conscience in our increasingly regulatory society?

We have absolutely no idea what homosexuality is. We don't know whether it is innate or learned behaviour, or a mixture of the two. Some people believe it to be a moral failing, some think it is a sickness, and some regard it as a normal sexual variation. An eminent Ontario psychiatrist, when I asked him about his profession's current thinking on the subject, reported that of course it was *not* a moral shortcoming, and while some of his colleagues might still categorize it as a sickness, the best view of his profession was that homosexuality is a perfectly normal expression of human sexuality, in no way different from a preference for blondes. When I asked him whether he would be at all disturbed on learning that his own twenty-year-old son had a marked preference for blondes, he said of course not. Being an honest man, however, he admitted that he would be quite disturbed if his son exhibited a similar preference for other men, his profession's best views notwithstanding. This anecdote proves nothing about homosexuality, and it does not intend to. What I try to indicate by recounting it is that there are many areas of life that are not the proper subject of legislation in a free society.

It is one thing for the law itself to discriminate, which it should never do, and quite another for individuals to discriminate according to their own moral imperatives and beliefs, misguided as they may be. The first denies liberty, the second affirms it. Legislating against discrimination can be as bad as legislating for it, from the point of view of surrendering our own judgments to the judgments of the State. This is why outlawing homosexuality is pernicious—but no more than it is to enshrine it into law as a basic human "right."

The question of homosexuality merely brings into focus the much wider question of human rights legislation. Though I would without hesitation sell my house to an Indian, extend credit to a woman, or give employment to a disabled person—and have a pretty low opinion of anyone who wouldn't—I much resent being compelled to do so by law. My reason for this is simple: the State that can compel me to be virtuous today may forbid me to be virtuous tomorrow. It may also compel me to act in a manner it regards as virtuous but I regard as evil or stupid. As long as an activity is lawful—such as selling property, giving credit, or offering employment—its conduct should be my business, not the government's. The private value judgments that motivate me in dealing with one person rather than with another ought not to render my otherwise legal actions unlawful. And no human rights legislation is needed to prevent me from robbing, cheating, assaulting, or wrongfully dismissing anyone.

I have no way of knowing what my views on the matter would be if I were a homosexual myself, but I doubt if they'd be different. For example, I happen to be an immigrant Jew. There are a certain number of Canadians who for this reason alone would prefer not to have me as an employee or a neighbour. This, as far as I'm concerned, is their privilege. As long as they don't make it illegal for me to seek employment or housing altogether—as in Nazi Germany—I would not dream of making it illegal for any *individual* not to house or hire me. If my government does so, it does so without my approval or consent. And while I think that the owners of those factories in the 1930s that stuck "No Englishmen Need Apply" signs on their front gates were indescribably stupid, I believe that the age that permitted them to do so understood the meaning of liberty better than my own.

Liberty has its costs, but perhaps it is necessary to have lived under tyranny to appreciate that it is still a bargain at any price.

1978

WHAT TO DO ABOUT AIDS

As far as doctors can tell at present, the cause of AIDS is the human T-cell lymphotropic virus-III. Not everyone who is infected by the virus will develop AIDS; in fact, it is currently believed that only a minority will. [This was the medical profession's view in 1985. Today the prognosis is far more pessimistic.] However, everyone who has the virus may transmit it to another person, who in turn may or may not develop AIDS. As of this writing, there is no cure for AIDS. People who get the disease are likely to die within a few years.

Most people who are infected by the virus will develop antibodies to it inside of six months. These antibodies can be detected by a test. The test is available in Ontario. Individuals who react to it positively are almost certain to have been infected. The virus is present in their body fluids, certainly in their semen and blood, possibly in their saliva, sweat, and tears. Though they may never develop AIDS themselves, they are potential carriers of the disease. They can infect others. In the language of the Ontario Ministry of Health, taken from its current advice to physicians, "most antibody positive, apparently healthy individuals from high-risk groups are viremic." These are facts. Eventually scientists may be able to tell us much more; they are certainly working at it. That's good. The question is, what are we going to do in the meantime?

The trendy media and the health authorities urge us to be calm. Their chief concern seems to be that we may "overreact" to victims and carriers of the disease. Last week AIDS victim Allan Pletcher's picture appeared on the cover of *Maclean's* magazine along with his plea: "Please do not ostracize us." In the *Maclean's* article on AIDS was another quotation from Pletcher: "It is the hardest disease in the world to catch. You have to work at it."

In the editorial introducing the cover story there's the opinion that the possibility that "a victim might deliberately try to infect others through sexual contact" is too remote to justify the idea of quarantining adults. The magazine also quotes Pletcher's "message of compassion and responsibility"—originally sounded on CBC's *The Journal*—"I am chaste, and I will remain so until I am cured or I die."

Well, good for Pletcher. He seems like a courageous and honest man, whatever his past sexual habits, and I wouldn't doubt his word. Still, I wonder if relying on the promise to remain chaste of people who, in Pletcher's opinion, had to work very hard to catch the disease in the first place, is a sufficient measure of public hygiene.

Remaining chaste is a difficult business for anyone, let alone people who seemed to spare no effort to get infected by a supposedly hard-to-catch disease. In any case, a disease that is transmitted through saliva, tears, etc., in addition to semen, may not be all that hard to catch. While a *deliberate* attempt to infect others through sexual contact may be rare, a disease that can be transmitted by asymptomatic, "apparently healthy individuals"—to use the Ministry of Health's phrase—may be very commonly transmitted through non-deliberate, innocent sexual contact—innocent, that is, of any other desire but to have sex.

We know that AIDS is deadly. Some scientists suspect that, as the virus attacks the immune system—the very system, in other words, that normally produces defences against disease—a vaccine may not be developed against it even in theory. A.D.J. Robertson of the Research Testing and Development Corporation has expressed the view in the *Wall Street Journal* that the virus may become "incorporated in the genetic material of brain cells." Let's hope that all pessimistic scientists are wrong. One day we may prevent and cure AIDS—but today it is the leading cause of death among males between the ages of thirty and thirty-nine in New York City.

At this point, therefore, isolation and identification seem to be our only defence. But is this our chief concern? No. Our chief concern seems to be protecting the "human rights" of victims and carriers.

The Ontario Ministry of Health tells physicians that their "seropositive" patients—people who have no symptoms themselves but appear to carry the virus in their body fluids—should be advised to "use condoms during intercourse" and "avoid deep, intimate kissing." I asked Dr. A.I. Malcolm, a leading forensic psychiatrist, if he would so advise his seropositive patients. His answer: "Certainly not. I would advise them to refrain from any sexual contact."

On the whole, it is great to be calm. However, when a 10-ton truck is bearing down on you, remaining calm is insufficient. The intelligent human reaction is to jump the hell out of the way. Jump calmly, by all means, but jump. AIDS is fatal and is spreading. Under such circumstances to write about "human rights" and "compassion," mainly in relation to those who are helping to spread it, is only possible because the paper can't blush.

1985

WHAT'S LEFTER THAN LEFT?

It was a fun week, what with a couple of government studies and papers, both on the provincial and federal level. I wonder if I'm the only one in town who's glad it's Monday. Last week was boisterous, and I'm not even counting the skies over Greece or Libya. The skies over Ottawa and Toronto were enough.

Not that they came rushing down on the heads of Ontario Premier David Peterson and his worthy Health Minister, Murray Elston, because the skies are notoriously patient. More patient anyway than wounded New Democratic leader Bob Rae, who rose to the threat of being outflanked on the left by the Liberal government. On the left, if you please! Some pundit should tell us if it was the first time in NDP history that one of its provincial leaders felt impelled to speak out against a contemplated new tax on the "rich." I certainly can't remember another occasion.

I'm putting the word "rich" in quotation marks, as you've noticed, because the contemplated tax, which even upsets Bob Rae, is to kick in at around $40,000, the annual income of high school principals, who must be surprised to learn that they have joined the ranks of the plutocracy. It seems that in our society it will soon be possible to share the burdens of wealth without reaping any of its benefits.

The tax being considered is the one that would add the cost of medical services used to the taxable incomes of individuals who use them, if in the government's view they are affluent enough. On the basis of the figures that are being bandied about, this means that if you are a plumbing contractor, industrial designer, police inspector, or some such magnate of the realm, and if you have spent $4,000 on doctors in a given year, you'd have to pay an extra $1,500-$2,000 a year in taxes. In addition, of course, to your "universal" OHIP insurance premiums. The "rich" will have the privilege of paying insurance without being covered by it. I wonder how a private insurer would fare if it offered such policies.

A private insurer couldn't, of course, because nobody would buy, but the government can compel its customers. If you, being a wealthy school principal, were to say: "To hell with it, I'm not gonna buy expensive government insurance if I have to pay for half my medical bills anyway," you'd soon discover that you could not be treated in Ontario at all. Your money would not be good enough. Remember, doctors won't be permitted to "extra-bill" if our current government has its way, which is only a step from not being permitted to bill, period. If you're sick, you either pay the government, or let nature take its course.

I think the reason Bob Rae wishes Peterson and Elston would shut up about their contemplated schemes is because it permits a glimpse too soon into the world of a state-run, socialist system. The silly, greedy Liberals are tugging on the line before the hook has been firmly set. Let's get the ban on extra-billing in place first, says Rae, before we let the people of Ontario see what it will cost them. We had better not let the middle class know yet that we are about to tax them if they get sick.

Oh, it's just a study, it's just one of the things we're considering, say Peterson and Elston, beating a dutiful retreat. Actually, I don't doubt their word. They're only studying options. "Question: How to avoid bankruptcy? Answer: (1) Spend less; (2) Earn more; (3) Rob your sick neighbour." Right? They're all just options.

After all, some options our federal government is looking at go even further. They're spending public funds on feminist lawyers whose study last week suggested that it should not be unlawful for the "poor"—and especially for "poor women"—to steal and cheat. Yes. I didn't make it up. It's the recommendation of a study you paid for, dear reader. I'm surprised the feminists don't go further still. Why not simply say that: (a) it should not be unlawful for anyone who has less to steal from anyone who has more, and (b) it should not be unlawful for any woman to steal from any man. Or from the public. Or for a poorer woman to steal from a richer woman, of course.

Then, when those who had less to begin with have stolen so much that now they have *more*, those who now have less are enabled to steal it back from them. This way society can be kept in a beautiful state of equilibrium. No rich, no poor, no men, no women, only a perfect balance of larceny.

1986

Human Rights Exemption?

Here's an ad from a Canadian medical journal that illustrates the nightmarish ethics of social engineering. In this country it's already part of our world. Unless we wake up to its dangers, it is certain to engulf us completely. The ad invites applications from experienced psychiatrists for a position at the University of Guelph. After describing the job and the required qualifications in some detail, the ad goes on to say: "Preference will be given to female candidates. (Human rights exemption number has been applied for.)"

All right. Never mind technical questions, such as how can a publicly funded institution engage in a practice it acknowledges to be unlawful—discrimination on the basis of sex—*before* it receives an exemption in law? The university's application must be supported by reasons. They could, presumably, be either accepted or rejected, yet the institution has already begun practising discrimination by placing its ad.

But quibbling with such details means that one is prepared to accept the premise—and it's the premise that is the real problem. The premise of the social engineer's world George Orwell predicted nearly forty years ago: all people are equal but some are more equal than others. Subject only to a properly issued and duly stamped human rights exemption number.

On the same technical level, one could also object that it is sheer idiocy to practise affirmative action for medical specialists. Not just for the obvious reason that in certain areas—say doctors or jet pilots—*any* consideration outside strict qualifications is not in the public interest, but also because people at certain elite levels of achievement no longer need any help. A fully trained and experienced psychiatrist, such as this job calls for, is competitive by definition, regardless of gender or race. Whatever assistance they may have needed to get there, the point comes where members of even the most "disadvantaged" group can be relied on to make it on their own. Is the University of Guelph suggesting that if it simply took the best of all comers that person would not be a woman? Why? I think it probably would be. Or—even worse—is the university saying that, without a deliberate effort to pick a woman, it would never pick one because of its own bias? A pretty shocking admission, if true.

I'd like to make it perfectly clear that *I'm* not objecting to employers being free to choose their employees on any basis, including sex. It's the "human rights" commissars who object to that. I think an employer should be free to advertise, not only for women, but specifically for handicapped black single mothers—provided that he can also advertise for able-bodied white family men if he chooses. (I also believe that any employer who bases his selection on such extraneous grounds as sex, race, religion, etc., rather than individual qualifications, is a silly person who will soon go bankrupt and deserve it.)

I think being considered for a job is a very legitimate human ambition, but hardly a human right. However, *if* we regard it as a fundamental right and so enshrine it in law, it follows that it must truly apply to everyone. That's the whole point about human rights. A "human right" that can be taken away by an application for an exception number is a joke.

A sick joke, actually; a terrifying joke. A government that can issue exemptions from human rights, that can take away, for some temporary purpose of social engineering, something it regards as fundamental, can obviously do anything. Such a government becomes a law unto itself. Such a state serves notice on all of us that its actions will be guided by administrative convenience before anything else, and that it will dispense privileges on certain groups, or disadvantages upon others, solely according to its own lights and interests. In short, such a state intends to act as Roman emperors acted in the past.

I repeat, it's not *my* view that it is a fundamental human right for male psychiatrists to be considered on equal footing with female psychiatrists (or vice versa) by the University of Guelph. That is the Human Rights Commission's view. However, when it runs counter to their current ideas of social engineering, they feel entitled to take away the human rights of male psychiatrists by issuing an exemption number. The State giveth, the State taketh away.

Sorry. A state that is exempt from the observation of any human rights has none. A state that is exempt from its laws is exempt from its legitimacy.

1986

MORE EQUAL THAN OTHERS

A great writer of antiquity, looking at his society, summed up his view in a sentence that has survived for two thousand years. "It is difficult," he said, "not to write satire." If this was true in Roman times, what should we say about our own? Probably what the French say: the more things change, the more they remain the same.

It is difficult not to write a satire about our times, but it is equally difficult to be satirical. How do you satirize something that is already a joke? Just recounting it in a straightforward manner should be funny enough. Or sad enough, for that matter.

This particular story comes from a freelance public relations man. He does not want to be identified—naturally—for he could lose a lucrative contract. The federal bureaucracy is one of his major clients and they would not appreciate him telling tales out of school. The job for which the PR man is about to be hired by a government department is to help officials to identify women, visible minorities, and disabled people.

Help to identify them? You mean our government officials can't tell a woman from a man, or a black person from a white one? They can't count up to four to tell if someone's missing a limb?

Okay, maybe in the case of the disabled the bureaucrats do need some help—you can't tell at a glance if someone's deaf or claustrophobic. But surely the whole point about visible minorities is that they are visible. As for women, until now all humanity managed to be fruitful and multiply by relying on its ability to tell women from men, at least by and large.

Ah, but the matter is not so simple. You see, the government has certain programs for women, visible minorities, and disabled people. There's special training, benefits, affirmative action. There are jobs and budgets set aside for these groups, and there are bureaucrats with offices and secretaries to allocate and administer them. The trouble is, there aren't enough clients. Lots of people may be eligible, but they don't know about the programs and the officials can't call their attention to them. Unless the potential clients identify themselves.

Wait a minute. You mean an official can't say to someone who comes into the office: "Excuse me, madame, but I couldn't help noticing that you are a woman. And/or a Pakistani and a paraplegic. Well, we have some wonderful benefits and programs we can offer you. Would you care to take advantage of them?"

Exactly. The official can't say that. The official is not allowed to notice that the client who comes into the office is a woman because that would be *discrimination*.

Get it?

In the government's view, it is *not* discrimination to have special programs and benefits for certain selected groups. Oh no, perish the thought. But it *is* discrimination to tell an individual member of the group about it. Unless he or she asks first. Except they can't ask if they don't know.

That's why the government wants to hire a freelance PR man. To create posters, ad campaigns, and film commercials that urge women to identify themselves as women to the government. And/or as Pakistanis or paraplegics. Women are not women in the government's eyes until they so identify themselves. Then they become women and the officials can discri... pardon me, tell them about all the wonderful government programs.

There is, of course, a little problem here that may not have occurred to our bureaucrats. Before they spend another chunk of my money on a study or a task force, let me quickly outline it to them. Free of charge.

If there are benefits attached to being a member of a certain group, but it's discrimination for officials to notice who does or doesn't belong to it, it follows that any person can belong to any group he or she wishes. A white man can walk into an office and say: "Hey, fellow, enrol me into one of your programs for black women." The official can't possibly reply: "Nothing doing, chum, you're a white man." This would be noticing a person's race and gender, which is discriminatory. In fact, by noticing, the official would be depriving the client of something, which is obviously a worse discrimination that noticing it in order to confer something on him.

Yes, I'm afraid there's no way out—if the government wishes to stick to its own principles. We must all be whatever we say we are: men, women, black, white, able-bodied, or disabled. At least for official purposes. It's our choice. And if there are benefits, privileges, preferential treatments accorded to one group, who will be crazy enough to identify himself as belonging to any other?

It's all right by me. I'm rather looking forward to a society composed entirely of disabled black women, so far as the government's records are concerned. Then, maybe, the government can really start treating all of us equally. Maybe we have to reach this point before our bureaucrats can grasp the meaning of the word "equality."

Meanwhile, let my PR friend make a bundle on his commercials. He and I will toast old Juvenalis, who saw it all two thousand years ago, with a glass of the best Roman grape.

1986

HUMAN RIGHTS OUTLAWS

In one sense I don't have any strong feelings about last week's amendment to the Ontario Human Rights Code, the one that makes sexual orientation another prohibited ground of discrimination in housing, employment, or services. In another sense, however, saying that my feelings are very strong is putting it mildly.

I maintain, as I have for some time, that so-called human rights advocates who use the law to prevent others from making choices according to their own lights and conscience do not understand the meaning of human rights.

I don't have strong feelings about a law that would stop me from refusing to employ, house, or (dare I put it this way?) service a homosexual because I would not refuse to do so anyway. I wouldn't refuse, whether required by law or not, just as I would not refuse anyone because of his or her gender, race, ethnic origin, or religion.

It's not only that "some of my best friends are homosexuals"—they are, in fact—but it is my considered opinion that sexual orientation alone tells nothing about a person. I have known brilliant and reliable homosexuals (or, for that matter, foot fetishists) as well as stupid and despicable ones. I would consider just about any aspect of a person's moral makeup more important than his or her sexual tastes.

Only—and this is the crucial difference—I believe that those who don't think as I think are also entitled to their opinions and beliefs. This is where the current "human rights" crowd and I part company. They think that their creeds, their socio-political or, indeed, their scientific views should be binding on everyone. They are prepared to make outlaws of all persons who have different opinions. They regard their own judgments as "human rights" and the judgments of all others as punishable offences.

Nothing illustrates the point better than sexual orientation. Personally, I attribute even less significance to sexual orientation than I do to gender or ethnic origin—and, trust me, I attribute very little significance to those—but the fact is that sexual orientation, unlike some other prohibited grounds in our so-called Human Rights Code, intrudes on two specific areas that should never be subject to legislation in a free society. One such area is scientific inquiry, the other is religion.

Medically speaking, at present we do not know much about homosexuality—not to mention voyeurism, exhibitionism, sado-masochistic behavior, necrophilia, or other fetishistic forms of human sexuality, all covered by the term "sexual orientation." For instance, until about fifteen years ago medical science classified homosexuality as a mental illness. Possibly medical science was mistaken, but the point is that when doctors changed their views in the mid-'60s, they did not do so for scientific reasons. They discovered nothing new about homosexuality. They simply stopped classifying it as a sickness because of political pressure and a change in social fashion.

Fashion and politics may be bad for science, but there isn't much we can do about them. However, when we reinforce their impact by legislation, we simply put science into chains. We turn inquiry into heresy once again, as we did in the Middle Ages.

Today it is unfashionable for psychiatrists to inquire into the relationship between lesbianism and total personality, or to suggest that pederasty may not be as natural a sexual variation as a preference for blondes. By 1987 it may also be unlawful. Even more importantly, it may become unlawful for a researcher in the field of venereal disease to look into certain measures of public hygiene because to do so might discriminate against members of a protected group.

As for religion, it is such an obvious matter that it should be unnecessary to waste words on it. There is no human right more basic than that of a person to practise his or her religion, follow its moral teachings, be governed by it in his or her daily conduct, and act on its commands according to his or her conscience. This goes back to the *Mayflower*: this is why the pilgrims came to America. It also happens to be the cornerstone of Canada's new Charter of Rights and Freedoms. Our entire society is founded on the unfettered ability of every person to judge right and wrong, not according to my lights, or Attorney General Ian Scott's lights, but his or her own lights. And this human right, unless it includes freedom of association, freedom to choose one's neighbors or teachers, has no practical meaning. Yet this is the very right the recent amendment to Ontario's Human Rights Code would deny.

Ironically, the legislators who voted for it (or for most of the other provisions of the code) share all my personal values. Except the most important one: an ability to resist outlawing other people's personal values. In the end, this value alone separates liberals from autocrats or fascists.

1986

Why Affirmative Action isn't the Answer

I attended a debate not too long ago in which the resolution was phrased (as it often is) as follows: *Is Affirmative Action Reverse Discrimination?* I guess one could say affirmative action isn't "reverse" discrimination because the reverse of discrimination is not to discriminate. Affirmative action is plain, old-fashioned discrimination.

When you "single out one individual or group, etc., for special favour or disfavour," as the greater Collins dictionary has it, you "discriminate." This is the first meaning of the word. Still, this is an uninteresting truth. Every selection process involves discrimination between people on some grounds. The question is—on what grounds?

In the case of affirmative action, the answer is self-evident. Affirmative action is discrimination based on sex or race—in Canada, mainly on sex. Honest supporters of affirmative action readily admit this, not only because it's undeniable, but because, in their view, it doesn't settle the issue. They think it's possible for a degree of sex or race discrimination to be socially desirable and necessary.

This question can be legitimately debated if we recognize it challenges a number of our basic assumptions. Our society—a liberal democracy—takes it for granted that any discrimination based on sex or race is wrong (unlike, say, discrimination based on qualifications). Liberals assume this because they consider the line of social progress to have been, in Sir Henry Maine's well-known phrase, "from status to contract."

This assumption may be rebuttable, but it's fundamental to the liberal view. It puts the onus on those who would argue against it. The liberal view opposes discrimination based on "status"—factors such as race, ethnicity, sex, or class—preferring instead purely individual differences such as commitment, character, education, or training. This is precisely why classical liberalism has always favoured the equality of women (or any other group) before the law.

Of course, a liberal state wouldn't outlaw *individual* discrimination, even on the basis of such illiberal grounds as race or sex (much as it would discourage it through education and example). What the liberal state would forbid is for the law or the government to discriminate. If the law itself were to discriminate, even in the "best" of causes, the state would cease to be liberal.

Therefore, people who favour affirmative action actually depart from the liberal view in four basic ways. One, they propose to have the state discriminate between groups. Two, they propose to have it discriminate on the basis of such status factors as race or sex. Three, they'd *forbid* individuals to discriminate in ways of their own choosing. Four, they'd *oblige* them instead to discriminate in ways prescribed by law or edict.

This, in effect, is turning the liberal position around. It's saying to fellow citizens: "You may not discriminate, but the state must. Moreover, while you're not at liberty to discriminate in your own way, you've an obligation to discriminate in ways the state sees fit."

This may not bother those who don't wish to be thought of as liberals, but many proponents of affirmative action do. It's their resulting discomfort that has given rise to euphemisms, such as calling quotas "goal-oriented timetables." Most intellectual debates on this subject are nothing but attempts to reconcile liberal self-images with illiberal social positions.

These illiberal positions include the replacement of individual freedom with social planning, and the replacement of the ideal of equal opportunity with the ideal of group parity. Abandoning freedom may not disturb those who think of parity as the greater good, but not being able to think of themselves as liberals disturbs them. This is why they use certain verbal devices, such as "pay equity," to mask their regression from contract to status without injuring their illusion of progress.

But status preference and group parity are regressive—indeed, medieval—notions, whether the people who hold them like to think of themselves as progressive or not. One could argue that this alone may not be enough to dismiss such ideas if they can be shown to avert some grave injustice or social emergency. The next question (if one accepts this argument) is: what's the injustice? And where's the emergency?

In the case of sex, the disparity affirmative action seeks to cure amounted in 1982 to an income differential of 8.7 per cent between single male and female workers with university degrees, and 6.6 per cent between single males and females with post-secondary educations, according to Statistics Canada. In other words, if we don't cook the books, don't compare apples and oranges, and adjust aggregate statistics for such relevant factors as education, age, and marital status, the difference shrinks to less than ten per cent.

These examples aren't unique: for instance, in 1971, single women in their thirties who had worked continuously since leaving school earned over nine per cent *more* than single men of the same age. In 1982, never-married women over 55 earned eighteen per cent *more* than never-married men of the same age. (In fact, there's compelling proof that total parity of income between men and women could best be achieved not through "pay equity" or affirmative action, but through abolishing marriage.)

Human disparity isn't caused by human prejudice alone. A denial of equal opportunity (past or present) rarely accounts for all of it. When it comes to wage disparity between men and women, it's our failure to control for certain statistical factors—such as a woman's decision to interrupt her education or career for her family or to choose a more congenial but less remunerative career for herself—that results in statements such as "women earn only fifty-two per cent of what men earn" in the labour force.

Some people may concede this, but still feel that society should induce women to make different choices for themselves. Such social engineering or "re-education" is one of the goals of political feminism. But no matter what one thinks of feminist goals, or the general idea of social coercion in the service of any ideology, the fact remains that the real disparity—the actual current pay differential between those men and women who are similarly committed, qualified, and experienced—is closer to being under ten per cent than over fifty per cent. In certain age groups, the difference *favours* women.

Is a disparity of this kind a grave social emergency? Does it require a repudiation of basic ideals? These, in my view, are the only relevant questions in the debate. Unless one can say yes to them, it's difficult to say yes to affirmative action.

1988

THE ERRORS IN EDUCATION

Here is an item to illustrate the squishy left's mind, from a recent issue of *The Nation*, America's venerable voice of democratic (more or less) socialism. The subject is education.

The Nation's editorial criticizes U.S. Education Secretary William Bennett for his report entitled "American Education: Making It Work." According to the editorial, Bennett does not know his history. Bennett thinks that there is a crisis in education. He does not realize "that at no time in our past have Americans in any numbers been well educated."

"Any healthy inquiry," admonishes *The Nation*, "must start by asking why this has always been so." *The Nation*, of course, knows the answer that any "healthy inquiry" would produce (and would find no inquiry healthy that does not produce this answer): Americans have never been well educated in any numbers because America has been a capitalist (racist, sexist, etc.) society.

The Nation finds this so self-evident that the editorial doesn't even bother to spell it out. But what escapes *The Nation*'s attention is that this isn't what we mean when we talk about a crisis in education. People may not have been well educated in America (or elsewhere) in any numbers, but that was because people never went to school in any numbers in America or anywhere else.

Not going to school is a crisis of non-education. It may be a problem worth addressing, but it's totally different from a crisis in education. A crisis in education occurs when people remain uneducated in great numbers in spite of going to school for fifteen years or more, as they have done in the last three to four decades.

When we're spending mountains of money on schools and universities; when B.A.s and M.A.s outnumber brunettes in the population; when we hand out degrees like candy to graduates who then can't tie their own shoelaces, academically speaking, that's when we have a crisis in education.

And we sure have one today.

The Nation says Bennett's answers to this crisis are "more discipline, tougher standards, more tests, more homework." This makes the editors unhappy. They consider such answers old-fashioned and regressive, the products of a small mind.

Why? Well, because in the editors' view an educated person should have "the capacity to make judgments." He should have "the ability to learn independently, the wits to detect problems." In short, an educated person should learn "the use of the mind." Loads of homework or multiple-choice tests won't help students learn the use of the mind, no matter how much Secretary Bennett increases them in frequency or toughness.

So speaks the squishy left, and it's easy to agree with part of what it's saying. Persons who can learn independently and detect problems have probably not achieved this blissful state through lots of homework and multiple-choice tests. Right.

But would tougher tests or standards have *prevented* such persons from learning to use their minds? Why would students learn to use their minds better through an "open" education, such as value-free studies, ungraded rap-sessions on "socially relevant" issues, creative toilet-training, or "minority" history?

Have they in fact learned to use their minds while our faddish educators have been going to bed (or at least heavily petting) with such educational subjects and methods? Well, no. That's why we have a crisis in education.

It offends the good social engineers of the left that education has limits and that the very thing it can rarely teach by any method is "the use of the mind." They won't accept that schools must teach spelling precisely because they can't, or at least can't be counted on, to teach thinking.

Alas, a capacity to learn independently and to make judgments do not come from a good education. They come chiefly as gifts from God, who hands them out quite sparingly under any educational system. (The left bristles at this notion, of course. In the left's view there's nothing that nurture cannot do.)

At the risk of shocking the left, there are limits to nurture—which is not to say that schools can't do a lot. They can hand out chunks of knowledge. They can hand out degrees (deserved or undeserved). We can make sure that they hand out knowledge, not garbage, and that their degrees are honestly earned. Maybe that's all we can do, but it's more than we have done of late.

Our old rote-learning educational system may have erred by treating all students as if they were morons. Our modern system has erred by treating them as if they were all geniuses. For my money, the modern system has made the bigger error.

1988

PLAYING FOR BIG BROTHER

When the Edmonton Oilers traded Wayne Gretzky to the Los Angeles Kings, in all the sensational media coverage there was one sentence that stuck with me. According to press reports, "In Ottawa, NDP house leader Nelson Riis asked the government to block the trade."

Maybe this sentence stuck with me because I was reading about the great trade in something of an emotional vacuum. I'm at best a casual spectator of hockey (as I am of any sport whose object is to hit or carry a puck or any other small, elastic sphere across, over, or into a net). I knew, of course, that Gretzky is a spectacular player, but it made little difference to me whether he'd be wearing red, green, or purple colors when he appeared on my TV screen next.

Sooner or later, though, the sentence dealing with the NDP would have leaped out at me even if the Gretzky trade had affected me as deeply as it affected thousands of hockey fans from coast to coast. That one little sentence, lost among scores of seemingly more important sentences in the news reports, revealed something essential about our times.

We live in an era where some people would use the power of the State—the law, the government—to coerce other people about every human act. Maybe even every human thought, sentiment, or word. Such people would not allow anyone to do or believe (or omit to do or believe) anything that did not coincide with their own opinions, desires, or tastes. Whether it was by the remotest stretch of the imagination any of their bloody business or not. In party politics, the chief exponent of this trend is the NDP. It carries the ball for statism.

The NDP is a party of socialists (or social democrats, as many prefer to call themselves). "Progressive" NDP intellectuals often accuse people like myself—people who have experienced communism and fascism—

of being paranoid about socialists. We have the delusion, these left-libbers say, that there's a straight line between minimum wage laws and the Gulag.

I can't speak for others, but I have no such delusions. I certainly don't think the line is straight: I think it's pretty convoluted. I do accept that most social democrats abhor the Gulag as much as I do. (They should, anyway, as many of their comrades perished in it.)

However, if not a straight line, there's at least a strong nexus between coercive social legislation and the Gulag. I don't have to dislike socialists for those consequences of their beliefs they do not intend or that, with luck, may not come about in this country anyway. It's enough for me to dislike them for those consequences they do intend, and that would inevitably happen if they ever came to power.

Such as the consequences of saying to a young athlete and his wife who for whatever personal, professional, or financial reasons decided to switch clubs: "You can't do it!" Such as declaring that an athlete (or an artist or a scientist) is not a free individual but government property. Such as telling a businessman like Oilers owner Peter Pocklington that he has to let the bureaucrats run his business and his team. All he is permitted to do is to pay his taxes. These are not matters of conjecture or delusion. The NDP itself rose to make them clear. They are now a matter of the parliamentary record.

Never mind for a moment that house leader Riis may have been politicking or grandstanding or that Canada's government would probably have no authority under the law to block such a trade. This is immaterial. What matters is that the NDP's request was proudly put on the record. The government should interfere. An athlete should no longer play for the club he wants to play for. He should no longer live in the city where he and his new wife might spend more time together. He should live and play only where the NDP's social engineers decree—or not play and not make a living at all. Presumably that's exactly what would happen if the NDP ever came to power in Canada.

Whether the Gulag would or would not follow, whether we would suffer the worst consequences of social coercion or only the mildest, may be matters of conjecture. For argument's sake, let's assume the best. All that would happen is that a Wayne Gretzky would have to play where the NDP tells him to play.

This is the most optimistic scenario. For me it's enough to want to throw up.

1988

QUESTIONING THE EXPERTS

In February 1987, a girl of six was examined by a consulting pediatrician to the Cleveland County Council Social Services Department in England. The pediatrician, a Dr. Higgs, had previously been impressed by the works of Drs. Hobbs and Wynne in Leeds who became noted for their observations on a phenomenon termed "reflex relaxation and anal dilation" for the diagnosis of sexual abuse in children. On the basis of anal dilation, Dr. Higgs diagnosed that this little girl was sexually abused. During questioning, she indicated her grandfather had been responsible.

The grandfather was arrested, charged, and removed to a bail hostel. About a month later, Dr. Higgs examined the six-year-old again. She found that the signs had reappeared and diagnosed further abuse. The grandfather, on this occasion, couldn't be the perpetrator. "Did I say grandfather?" the little girl responded, in effect. "I meant to say father."

In the language of Madam Justice Butler-Sloss, who chaired the inquiry into the so-called Cleveland Crisis in England, "the police were embarrassed by this revelation." They dropped the charges against the grandfather and asked that their senior police surgeon, a Dr. Irvine, examine the child. According to the police, Dr. Higgs wouldn't allow the police surgeon to do so.

This was the beginning of the Cleveland Crisis which, within the space of a few months, saw a total of 129 children removed from fifty-seven families in the area and placed into "care." The reason for their removal was Dr. Higgs' diagnosis of sexual abuse, based either partly or solely on anal dilation. The diagnosis was confirmed by her mentor, Dr. Wynne of Leeds, and by a colleague named Dr. Wyatt. When allowed to see the children, other pediatricians and police surgeons rarely agreed with Dr. Higgs' diagnosis. Many questioned the reliability of anal dilation as a test and the observations of its pioneers, Drs. Hobbs and Wynne.

I'm not going to trace the story of the Cleveland Crisis in detail. Suffice it to say that it split the community, with the social services bureaucrats and pediatricians on one side, and the police, independent physicians, hospital workers, children's families, and the weight of public opinion on the other.

In a carefully balanced 700-page report handed down this summer, Madam Justice Butler-Sloss concluded the Social Services Department's pediatricians "[had] a responsibility...to consider whether their practice was always correct [and] in the best interests of the children." And she said, "[they] are to be criticized for not doing so, and for the certainty and over-confidence with which they pursued the detection of sexual abuse in the children referred to them." The High Court judge also chastized the bureaucracy of the Social Services Department and its newly-appointed child abuse consultant in similar terms.

However, she strongly cautioned against "misplaced adverse criticism" of social workers generally. It could result, she felt, in a failure to take seriously the problem of child abuse. "Social workers need the support of the public," the judge wrote. "It is time the public and the press gave it to them."

With great respect to this judicial recommendation, I doubt that I'd be willing to support social workers (or any other profession) in the abstract. The test, to my mind, isn't whether a profession is performing a potentially useful service, but whether its members are doing a good job of it in specific instances.

It's easy to agree that the sexual abuse of children, when it actually happens, is a grave problem. What's much harder to agree on is: a) what is "abuse"; b) who is a "child"; c) how often or how badly are children sexually abused; d) how reliable are methods used to detect sexual abuse; and e) how is society's interest in preventing sexual abuse to be balanced against other social interests that it may conflict with— such as, the rights of parents, due process, limits on administrative or "expert" powers, and the real interests of a child.

Unfortunately, in this area, sober reflection has given way to hysteria. Those caught up in the witch-hunts (or growth industry) of sexual abuse are rarely assailed by any doubts. For example, a 1981 Canadian Human Rights Commission study defines abuse to include "sexual remarks or teasing" or "subtle sexual hints and pressures," and even "leering or suggestive looks." Nor do such people doubt that anal dilation (or whatever else catches their fancy) is a near-infallible indicator of sexual abuse.

Since they have no doubts, people caught up in this trend are no longer interested in discussion or inquiry, only in legislation and indoctrination. They dismiss those who question their methods or values as either ignorant or uncaring. They accuse their scientific critics—as Drs. Hobbs and Wynne did in a recent paper—of being guided by a different social "philosophy."

This may be true, but it cuts both ways. The Social Services Department in Cleveland county certainly appeared to be waging its battle more along ideological than scientific lines. Closer to home, the recommendation in a 1984 Canadian study by Professor Robin Badgley, namely that the age of criminal responsibility for boys accused of sexual misconduct be *lowered* from fourteen to twelve, also denotes a different philosophy. Neo-Victorian may be a good word for it.

Social workers aren't necessarily caught up in this trend more than other groups. But they're in a position to give it more clout. Nor, being human, are social workers immune to the allures of power and empire. A monarch might have thought twice before trying to remove a child from its parents. Now, it's a snap for any twenty-three-year-old with a Master of Social Work.

So the momentum gathers. The political right feels benign about the witch-hunters of sexual abuse because all moral strictures appeal to it. Indeed, Professor Badgley's recommendations under the report heading of "abuse of position of trust," would put a nineteen-year-old camp counsellor away for a ten-year prison sentence for engaging in some heavy petting with a perfectly willing seventeen-year-old girl. For Mrs. Grundy, it's a dream come true.

As for the political left, anything that extends the power of the State's experts and bureaucrats is good. Why, what new prospects for social engineering lie ahead if the magic words "sexual abuse" can open doors formerly sealed by custom and law! What a way it would be around legal safeguards or for breaching the walls of the family! The family...that outpost of autonomy...that hotbed of reactionary notions. The last barrier in the path of the triumphant State. What a lovely idea to have the very children monitor their parents. Savonarola might have envied it.

1988

4.

From
the Baseless
to the Base

Notes on Feminism

GREASING THE SQUEAKER SEX

Nothing has proved the folk-wisdom of the proverb about the squeaky wheel getting the grease more in the last couple of decades than the women's movement. They have been squeaking relentlessly and greased regularly as a result. Here, however, the parallel ends. Wheels, when greased regularly, stop squeaking. Metal is reasonable. When it has no legitimate complaints, it no longer makes any noises. Unlike the women's movement.

I imagine the reason for this is partly institutional and partly psychological. The institutional part has to do with the fact that, by now, a fair number of people depend on feminism for their living. Righting the perceived wrongs of women has become a career choice, like dentistry. There are professionals, specialists, indeed experts in the field, who would have to be retrained if business ever dried up. Feminism has become an industry. Employing many women and even some men, it is by now an actual part of the economy.

There are lawyers, bureaucrats, academics working in organizations devoted to the "status of women" and "women's studies." Governments on all levels have entire branches; crown corporations and even some of the larger private businesses have entire departments churning out studies, directives, and programs in the same field. They employ secretaries and janitors. Researchers, librarians, and inspectors staff permanent or *ad hoc* government commissions. Journalists and pundits specialize in covering or commenting on "women's issues." There are ministers responsible for the status of women, and where there are ministers there are ministries.

The squeakers as well as many of the squeaked-at are salaried or receive professional fees. Feminism has long ceased to be a volunteer cause like protecting baby seals. It is now a living, and a good living for many. For some, it is the only alternative to answering phones or digging ditches. Squeaking is the only job for which they are qualified.

Institutional pressure is not in itself proof, of course, that a problem is artificial. Crime and sickness, for instance, are not artificial problems, though policemen or doctors make a living from them. But institutional pressure is a factor, and when the perpetuation of a problem is tied to an economic interest there is a greater chance that the problem will be perpetuated, whether it is genuine or not.

The psychological factor is self-evident. When you condition an entire generation to the idea of a fundamental wrong, some individuals will become sensitized to it to the point of fanaticism. They will perceive a wrong where it has never existed; they will perceive it where it has long ceased to exist. For them, any ambition unfulfilled will take on the appearance of a right denied; any disparity, whatever its cause, will seem to be the result of discrimination. A few will identify every problem endemic to the human condition as being caused by deliberate enmity to their group, and may feel exploited and prejudiced by all frustrations right down to the pangs of unrequited love.

Such people will see all of their impulses and interests as legitimate, while the impulses and interests of others will appear to them intrinsically selfish and wrong. They will seek to enforce their ideas by law, and try to outlaw any position contrary to their own.

This psychological state of being ill-done-by forever and in every sphere is, of course, not exclusive to feminists. There are many other groups conditioned to feel the same way. But no group has managed to squeak as loudly and to capture the attention of the State so completely as feminists.

This has often resulted in legislation or other social action costly and counterproductive to society as a whole or unfair to men in particular. More interestingly, however, it has also resulted in unfairness to women. The treatment of the interests of second wives (and, of course, children) in divorce proceedings is a good example.

While husbands are being increasingly hounded for support payments to their first families, there is virtually no legal machinery in place to determine the needs of second families. The law that may at times enforce luxuries for the first wife will simply not address itself to necessities when it comes to the second. Alas, the second wife is also a woman. She realizes that you can't squeeze blood from a stone. For her, feminist-inspired family law is not working out too well.

As a result, second-wives' associations are being formed all over the country. Somewhat feebly as yet, but they are beginning to squeak. It will be interesting to see how much of the grease will go their way.

1985

A Kiss is Just a Kiss

It is a fair guess that every day in Canada at least a thousand men will touch, kiss, or put their arms around a woman. They will do it in homes, offices, movie theatres, lobbies, parks, or streets. Some will make the great move for the first time in their relationship with a particular lady. Not one of them will be breaking the law.

Touching, kissing, or putting one's arm around a woman is not a crime. At least, it has never been regarded as a crime, whether a man did it at the first encounter or after the thousandth, provided the woman was not under age or feeble-minded. When done with sexual undertones such acts have always been regarded as a "pass," which could be either welcomed or rebuffed by the recipient. Only if a man persisted after a rejection did a pass run the risk of becoming sexual assault.

The law has not changed. Touching, kissing, or putting one's arm around a woman is still not a crime—but the interpretation of the law seems to have undergone an important change. The point at which a pass runs the risk of becoming a sexual assault has been brought forward by one subtle step. A subtle but extremely dangerous step, in my opinion.

As shown by some recent criminal charges (I'm not going to add to the embarrassment of the people involved by naming them), the law is being interpreted as if a pass became a sexual assault the minute a woman rebuffed it. The difference is clear. By this interpretation, if a man kisses a woman she had better respond to him warmly, because if she turns her head away the courts might find him guilty of sexual assault. Even if he did nothing to persist.

I must repeat, this is not a paranoid flash in my mind. Charges of sexual assault have recently been laid in cases where the complainant's evidence indicates only that a man made a move which she did not welcome. There was no second move, on the complainant's own story.

Sorry. This is not a sexual assault in my books—but never mind my books, in any book of Canadian law. Much as one sympathizes with the women's movement or the terrible lot of women in our society, it's a bit much to ask for a legal guarantee that only men whose passes they welcome will make passes at them. (The next step, I suppose, can only be to oblige any man whose pass a woman does welcome to make a pass at her, whether the man wants to or not.)

By cultural tradition, possibly by nature, in our species it is usually the male who initiates sexual moves. This has been so in virtually every society throughout human history. True, the male ordinarily does so after he has received some sign of sexual receptiveness from the female. These signs may range from the extremely subtle to the all-too-blatant, depending on the class, culture, age, or nature of the people involved. Generally, the male interprets them correctly. This is why a thousand Canadian men can touch or kiss a woman every day without being hauled into court.

These signs, however, are often less than certain—partly, I suppose, because a woman, owing to her own sexual nature, may not be sure herself whether she'll like a move until after it's been made. These things depend on a lot of variables, as we all know. Hence the pass, which can be welcomed, tolerated, or rejected.

The law cannot guarantee to women that the pass will be enjoyable. If it isn't, a woman can pull away or say: "Kindly keep your hideous fingers to yourself." The law can, should, and does guarantee that after this point her person is inviolate. The law has no sympathy for men who press on regardless, and neither have I. (Not even when a woman, before the actual pass is made, gives every sign of receptiveness. She has a right to change her mind.)

But blaming a fellow for trying—blaming him criminally—is ludicrous. All men, as all women, are sexual beings according to their own lights, and their own lights vary a great deal. Some men have a poor sense of timing. Some are crude or uncouth. Many are not romantic experts. But being uncouth is not a criminal offence. The solution for such men is to gently pair them off with uncouth women, of whom there are also quite a few.

There are common-sense exceptions to all this. A first "pass" can be so brutal as to amount to sexual assault. Obviously, a man can't tear off someone's blouse or jump at a passerby from the bushes and then say: "Oh, gee, I was just making a pass." But the recent cases in court are not remotely of this type. They arise out of social situations, and involve nothing more than a kiss or an embrace—a tolerated kiss or embrace at that.

Which gives rise to a further point. Clearly, a kiss or a touch is not an assault if the woman consents to it—but lately "consent" is being interpreted by some as if it were a synonym for "enjoy." It is not. Consent means acquiescence for whatever reason (other than a threat). If you consent only to avoid hurting the fellow's feelings—it happens sometimes, I suppose—you still consented. You can't change your mind about it later, or charge him with assault if he comes back for seconds. The guy's not a mind-reader: if he were he would not have kissed you.

In sexual situations men make moves. The fact is, they have always been, and still are, *expected* to make moves. So-called verbal passes have been, and still are, regarded as somewhat wimpish. Romantically skilled men should know when to make their move, but asking for permission is considered a turn-off by many women. Frankly, only extreme feminists or lesbians would consider a pass by a man so intrinsically offensive as to bring it into the ambit of criminal law. It's a pity that prosecutors are responding to such extremist pressures. The law's proper function should not be to prevent men from starting, but to show them where to stop.

1985

RADICAL CHICK HISTORY

One of the more innocuous myths spawned by feminist chic is the sincere and oft-repeated belief that the world for women began around the 1960s. Before that date women were supposed to be on the outside, excluded from the great affairs of humanity. (I mean *business* affairs, of course.) The circles of real power, the circles of movers and shakers, were closed to them according to this myth. It was only when feminism began raising everyone's consciousness during the last two decades that women started doing a little moving and shaking themselves.

This kind of "you've come a long way, baby" view of history crops up everywhere, from schooltexts to articles in the popular press. Maybe I shouldn't call it "innocuous" because it's no less dangerous and misleading than any other falsehood. But I enjoy being amused—who doesn't?—and feminist "history" does give rise to some real howlers.

One of my phantom clippers sent me an item from the *London Times* the other day. "These days," begins writer Liz Gill, "the finger that pulls the trigger or sets the detonator is almost as likely to be female as male." The article goes on to give examples of women who "have risen to the top" in the gory field of contemporary terrorism.

What I find amusing is not the aggressive, success-oriented attitude that displays pride in any "rising to the top," in any "achievement," with almost no reference to what the achievement, so-called, consists of. To be frank, I find this kind of amorality (as typical of the women's movement as of any other power-seeking group) more chilling than amusing. The amusing thing is that it's terrorism, of all things, in which the involvement of women is singled out as being a new phenomenon. Sorry, baby: you haven't come a long way in that field. You have been there all along. You've had your cute little finger on the trigger throughout recorded history.

At an educated guess, today about one out of eight persons involved in terrorist or terrorist-support activities is a woman. Women are political assassins in roughly the same proportion. I doubt if this proportion has either increased or decreased since Attila the Hun was assassinated by Mrs. Attila the Hunness. The person who did away with one of the French Revolution's great leaders, Jean Paul Marat, by stabbing him in his bathtub was named Charlotte Corday. The year, if memory serves, was 1793. (I know it was 1921 when Dora Kaplan shot and very nearly killed Lenin.)

Nineteenth-century terrorist ladies included the Russian "Jacobin" groupie Maria Oshanina, or Sofia Perovskaya who organized the assassination of Czar Alexander II in 1881, or the legendary Vera Figner.

Historian Nikolai Tolstoy tells an amusing story about Vera Figner. Somewhat like the contemporary German Baader-Meinhof group's co-founder Ulrike Meinhof, Figner came from an upper-class family, being a general's daughter. Considered a leading intellectual in nihilist circles, Figner was visited in jail by one of Nikolai Tolstoy's ancestors, the Czar's education minister Dmitri Tolstoy, for a little philosophical chat, Russian-style. They had a great time, and at the end of it Tolstoy said: "If I had two more hours, I'd convert you to loyalty to the government." Replied Figner: "If you could stay for two more hours, I'd convert you to *my* ideals."

The point isn't that women are particularly bloodthirsty as a group, only that it has required no "liberation" for a small minority of them to become attracted to political violence, nor to be accepted and welcomed in that role by male comrades.

The real historic fact, in case anyone's interested, is that society used to be split along the lines of class-hierarchy far more than any other factor, including gender. Until this century, if you belonged to the aristocracy by birth you had a chance to be a mover and shaker; if you didn't, you had almost no chance—whether you were a man or a woman. Although there *were* some rare exceptions, like Napoleon. Or Joan of Arc.

If you did belong to the upper crust, were you excluded from the exercise of power just because you were a woman? Don't ask me. Ask England's Queen Elizabeth I, the Austrian Empress Maria Theresa, the Dowager Empress Tzu-Hsi of China, the Byzantine Empress Theodora, the late Roman Regent Galla Placidia Augusta (who sought alliance with the aforesaid Attila the Hun), the Egyptian female Pharaohs Hatshepsut and Cleopatra, or the Renaissance Mantuan princess Isabella d'Este. Or maybe ask Russia's Catherine the Great.

1987

THE TROUBLE WITH HARRY

In late May-early June, 1987, a minor furor erupted over the fact that a man was appointed to the deanship of Osgoode Hall Law School. The trouble seemed to be that a qualified woman, the current associate dean, had also sought the position. Since she was unsuccessful some feminists not only hurled charges of sexual discrimination, but apparently laid a complaint to this effect before the Human Rights Commission against York University's selection committee and its head, Harry Arthurs.

I did allude to the incident in one of my columns, but there seemed to be little I could add by way of comment. Knowing next to nothing about the candidates, I had no opinion on whether the selection committee had made the right choice or not. In any case, it was none of my business. When people have the authority to make appointments, it is hardly anyone else's concern how they exercise it (unless they exercise it incompetently or corruptly).

As for the feminist critics, their tone made it evident that the only "right" choice for them would have been the appointment of any woman who wanted to become the dean of Osgoode Hall Law School over any man similarly inclined. There was no comment I could make on that position. More precisely, I have made so many comments about it over the years that the thought of making another one would have put me to sleep.

The reason I'm raising the subject now is a reader's letter to the editor, which a friend kindly clipped for me a couple of weeks ago. It is written in defence of Harry Arthurs, in the wounded tone of the unjustly maligned. It certainly came close to moving me to tears.

The correspondent is evidently a progressive and enlightened fellow. He takes great pains to point out that it is "important that every effort be made to right the under-representation of women in senior positions in the legal profession, including the law faculties. There can be no objection to strenuous efforts to persuade universities to appoint women at all levels. Even the argument that women should be given preference will, in certain cases, be a respectable one."

Well, one might ask, in that case what is the letter-writer's problem? The feminists who complained to the Human Rights Commission against Arthurs are clearly making "strenuous efforts to persuade universities" to appoint women.

The letter-writer may not think that the deanship of Osgoode Hall Law School is one of those "certain cases" where women should be given preference, but the feminists do. Since the machinery for sex-discrimination charges is in place, they use it. What else can they do, unless they do nothing? If the correspondent considers the position that "women should be given preference" to be "a respectable one," what objection can there be to people trying to give effect to a respectable position?

Oh but you see, the charges are laid against not just anyone but Harry Arthurs, a man as progressive as the letter-writer himself. Arthurs, too, is likely to consider the position that women should be given preference, in certain cases, to be a respectable one. (Which "certain cases"? Let's slide over this one for the moment.) Anyway, as the correspondent puts it: "There can be no one who knows Harry Arthurs who can fail to agree that he is incapable of an act of sexual discrimination."

Hmm. I know Arthurs, only through his public utterances, but I would have fancied him to be capable of an act of sexual discrimination, even if not the one with which he is charged. I would have thought that he might bring himself to discriminate against a male (or Caucasian, heterosexual, able-bodied, etc.) person in "certain cases." I suspect that Arthurs would find such "affirmative" discrimination respectable enough. That's why the entire affair fills me—I must confess—with such delight.

When the letter-writer, Arthurs, and their progressive friends let the genie of affirmative action out of the bottle they persuaded themselves that, while it would enable them to interfere with other people's choices in what they regarded as a good cause, other people serving dubious causes could never use it to interfere with theirs. They thought that their credentials as enlightened liberals would act as some magic, protective caul. They could pick "certain cases" to practise discrimination in good faith, immune to the natural consequences of this horrible and fundamentally illiberal idea.

This is what they must have believed, in spite of considerable historical evidence that this is not how any form of discrimination works. How it really works is something that they are now beginning to find out. As a connoisseur of poetic justice, I can't say that I'm displeased at all.

1987

FEMINIST PLOT THICKENS

Some years ago fanatical feminists sought to include "leering" and "ogling" in their definition of sexual offences against women. Their hate literature against men these days seeks to widen the definition of domestic violence. The newly included items would come under such headings as "verbal abuse" or "put-downs."

I guess the good news is that no attempt has yet been made to include ordinary disagreements. Who knows, it may be just a question of time. For a husband to respond to his wife's statement: "It's going to rain," by replying: "No, dear, it's not," could soon be a matter for the police. It's next to impossible to analyze all this seriously, but I'll try. Crazy as it is, it probably consists of a relatively rational component as well as a completely irrational one.

The semi-rational component is calculated to back up arbitrary or grossly exaggerated figures of "abuse"—e.g., the contention that "two out of every four girls have suffered sexual abuse." Since these figures would be unsupported by any statistics (including those compiled by people ideologically committed to, and professionally dependent on, the sex-abuse industry) one method of cooking the books has been to include "leering" or "ogling" quite literally in the same breath with violent rape. This way it has been possible to arrive at the desired numbers. It would have been possible to arrive at *any* number. In fact, the fifty per cent figure raises the opposite question: what on earth is *wrong* with every second girl that no one has ever given them a suggestive look?

When feminists attempt to include "put-downs" and "verbal abuse" in the list of domestic violence against women, things become even more anomalous. Never mind for a moment how a sane person can define a put-down as "violence" without doing violence to the language. Assume, for the sake of argument, that he or she can. The question then becomes this: if verbal slights in a domestic situation amount to violence, by what stretch of whose imagination is it *women* who require society's protection? Couldn't a much better case be made out for *men* requiring protection against this form of domestic violence?

It's true, of course, that some husbands are hideously sarcastic, belittling, and unpleasant to their wives. But who would seriously suggest that some wives aren't hideously sarcastic, belittling, and unpleasant to their husbands? If put-downs amount to violence, any random sampling of the population would show more men than women to have been victims of this kind of "domestic abuse." Certainly no less than an equal number.

At least—there are no studies in this area—this is my guess. Assume, however, that I'm wrong. Assume that husbands try putting down their wives much more frequently than wives try putting down their husbands. Even if this were so, in what way would women require social protection against verbal violence? It's easy to see why society has to step in if a husband *beats* his wife. He is stronger. As a rule, she can't physically defend herself. Whoever started the fight, whoever is at fault, once they engage in physical combat a woman and a man are no longer evenly matched. If he resorts to physical action, she needs help.

But who would ever suggest that men and women are not evenly matched in a verbal fight? That women are more tongue-tied? That, as a gender, women have a lower degree of mental acuity or aggressiveness? That they are less willing or able to launch a verbal attack or to put up a verbal defence? (Well, maybe someone could suggest it. There have been many asinine suggestions made about male and female nature or abilities over the centuries, by asses both ancient and modern.) But saying that women, as a group, need the protection of social or legal agencies against their husbands' put-downs is more than just asinine. It flies against the common experience of all humankind.

Why do I think, incidentally, that women engage in verbal abuse more often than men? Only because human beings are rational. When they feel combative, they go for the high ground. They try to have an edge. For men, a possible edge lies in physical abuse; for women, it lies in verbal abuse. The opposite would be counterselective, to borrow a word from natural science.

This is not to condone abuse, physical or verbal. It's just to say that the two are not the same. One requires some careful and judicious social intervention, the other doesn't. Calling a husband's put-downs "violence" may cater to the irrational component of contemporary feminism, but it actually trivializes the very real problems of battered spouses.

1988

THE INCOMPLETE CAD

According to newspaper reports last week, some judges are angry. Their ire is directed at an enforcement agency of the Ontario attorney general, set up last year to collect overdue support payments from debtor spouses. (This generally means ex-husbands, as ex-wives are rarely required to pay such support.)

The judges are upset for a simple reason. The law permits a maximum deduction of fifty per cent of a debtor's net wages to reduce arrears. The attorney general's collection agency for spousal and child support has been treating this ceiling as if it were a floor. As a matter of policy, the agency has been going for fifty per cent of the ex-husband's net wages in every instance.

Predictably, the courts have found this an unreasonable attitude. Maximum burdens or penalties are generally reserved for the worst cases in any dispute, civil or criminal. Rigid policies make no sense because individual circumstances vary. Some debtors fall into arrears because they refuse to pay their debts, and some fall into arrears simply because they can't pay them. Also, when two litigants come before a court, one saying: "Look, judge, I'd like to negotiate," and the other insisting: "No, judge, I want it all," it's a rare jurist whose sympathy would not be with the first litigant, whatever the issue.

As a result, judges have begun to reduce the attached amounts in several cases, even awarding court costs against the attorney general and uttering dark phrases of disapproval in the process. They've suggested that the enforcement agency is wasting the court's time and the taxpayers' money by its pig-headed attitude. This attitude was spelt out by the enforcement program's director, Gail Taylor, who said: "We found it was important to make an impact and to do so right at the beginning."

If you get right down to it, neither the judges' reaction nor the enforcement agency's attitude is surprising. Judges are often judicious and reasonable people in our society, because we try to select judges for these very qualities. Politicized government agencies, on the other hand, are often staffed by injudicious and unreasonable people—logically, since such agencies tend to attract, select, and reward this particular human type.

The attorney general's support and custody enforcement branch exemplifies, at least to my mind, a politicized government agency at its worst. It operates in the ideological mist of blinkered feminism, having been set up in response to its pressure. True, it has also been set up in response to a genuine social problem, but that can hardly be solved by declaring a total war on men.

This social problem has two components: one old and one new. The old component can be described by the old word "cad." Cads are selfish men who leave their families in the lurch, not caring if they live or die. Such men have always existed and no one has ever wasted any breath in their defence. But a new component has to do with families breaking up in increased numbers as a direct consequence of social change—including the changing role of women—and often through no fault of the men involved. Not surprisingly, such men go on living and forming new ties, but many can't afford to support two families.

Job opportunities have increased for women and social programs provide support for single-parent families, so the spectre of deserted children begging in the streets doesn't really arise. While only complete cads let their families go begging, there are some men—incomplete cads, maybe—who are not above letting society sort out the wreckage. (Some have no choice, in fact, unless they either stop eating themselves or marry an heiress the second time around.)

Not to judge the cases of such debtors on their merits is lunacy. The trouble is, lunacy also defines the militant fringe of the women's movement: the very fringe whose ideas (and cadres) have infiltrated many government programs and agencies. I never expect extreme feminists to be reasonable about the plight of men—men are the enemy, after all—but what amazes me is that they don't see the plight of women either. For instance, the fact that a second wife is also a woman should be hard to miss.

Still, as a taxpayer you might feel this is none of your concern. Since you don't want to end up holding the bag for men who default on their support payments for whatever reason, you cheer even the harshest efforts to collect. Hold on, though, because that isn't how the numbers work. Since last July, the new feminist-inspired enforcement branch collected $4.7 million from defaulting husbands—at the cost of $10 million. My calculator tells me that's a bag weighing $5.3 million and you, dear taxpayer, are holding it.

1988

5.

TOTALITARIANS AND TERRORISTS

Notes on Plain Evil

JOHN PAUL II: A REFUSAL TO YIELD TO MARXISM

My first contact with the Catholic Church under communism came in the role of a persecutor. As a fourteen-year-old member of the Young Communist League, I stood by with my comrades, jeering and singing "revolutionary" songs, while a group of nuns were being forcibly evicted from their convent in Budapest. But the shame I later felt for cackling along with a gaggle of Red Guards on that day in 1949 was somewhat balanced by the pleasure of having learned something others are still trying to divine. I learned—and even the Second Vatican Council had vainly tried to divine this until the Holy Spirit came to its rescue—that books of Marxism are not the place from which to borrow leaves in order to retain the Church's moral authority in the world.

Of course Catholic theologians have often argued that the Church, though run by weak and fallible mortals, is always rescued from ultimate error by the Holy Spirit. Now it looks as though the theologians were right. At least, considering the sheer moral brilliance of electing the former bishop of Cracow as the new pope, John Paul II—and contrasting it with the ulterior political motives that are likely to have brought about his election—even sceptics and scoffers like myself are momentarily awed by the kind of end run Providence can make around human affairs.

The observation that man cannot live by bread alone is hardly novel, but it is worth restating in order to grasp a few things about the modern world. For instance, if man lived by bread alone he might never consider any alternatives to free-enterprise liberal democracy. This system clearly produces more bread for more people than any other system in the world. Capitalism is being doubted in the West precisely because it is not equipped to address itself to some of the finer (or nastier) spiritual needs of mankind: fraternity, faith, equality, envy, identity, and the rest. If Canadian man lived by bread alone he would probably seek free trade with the United States—at the admitted risk of being eventually absorbed by it—and French-Canadian man might stop flirting with separatism. However, man wishes to use his mouth not only for initiating the digestive process but for expressing his native self, preferably in his native language.

He may also wish to use it to praise his Creator. If man lived by bread alone he would never insist on being a Catholic in communist Poland or Hungary. Being one of the faithful in those countries is not a good route for getting more of this world's bread. In the recent past it has not even been a good route for keeping out of jail.

While Marxism was not the only question to which the late Pope John's Vatican II addressed itself, it was certainly central to its deliberations. More than anything else, it contributed to the deep schism affecting the post-conciliar Church. In the words of stubborn dissenter Archbishop Marcel Lefebvre: "The refusal by this pastoral council to issue any official condemnation of communism alone suffices to disgrace it for all time."

Of course the pastoral council could not condemn communism because it was more than a little swayed by its appeal. This was quite obvious in the case of some delegates, chiefly from Latin America, who talked openly about exploring "Christian Marxism." But even those churchmen who, like the pope himself, were not remotely tempted by the idea of bridging so fundamental a gap, seem to have been struck by the power of a secular religion that was gaining converts at almost the same rate as the Church was losing them in the West. Could it be that Marxists were tackling important moral questions neglected by the Church? Was it time perhaps to raise the Church's social conscience?

Under the papacy of Paul the gap between the Church's "left" and "right" wing continued to widen, aggravated by such "spirit of Vatican II" acts as the forced resignation of Hungary's resolutely anti-communist primate, Cardinal Mindszenty. Blinded by the seeming success of Marxism in the non-communist world, the left wing of the Roman church had become oblivious to its own success among the very people who have been personally experiencing scientific socialism: the people of communist East Europe. Because, of course, it was among those millions that Catholicism (and other forms of Christianity) had come to represent a moral force once again.

After Pope Paul died the College of Cardinals' chief concern seemed to be to elect a pope with whom both the left and the right could be comfortable: hence the non-political pastor, John Paul I. It is not likely that this concern had abated in the few weeks the new pope was allowed on this earth. Forced to elect another pope, the cardinals scrambled for another compromise candidate in a fashion that came close to being desperate. Though centuries of tradition called for an Italian to be the new bishop of Rome, the church-fathers were willing to depart even from that hallowed usage if only the new pope could be acceptable to both sides. It was at this point, it seems to me, that the Holy Spirit intervened.

The election of a Polish cardinal may have only been the least offensive compromise for the contending factions within the College. Yet, it recalled the Church's most vigorous ages of political genius. It did not give in to hidebound traditionalism but, even though John Paul II is reported to be a "liberal" in social matters, it repudiated more firmly any drift towards mindless "liberalism" in Catholic politics (which, in post-conciliar terms, has come to mean shrill cries about the mote in the Western world's eye coupled with total silence about the beam in Marxist eyes) than the election of even the archest of conservatives could have. It suggested to nearly one hundred million East European Catholics that they are not entirely abandoned. It signalled that the Church was still prepared to teach morality rather than learn it from Marxism. It probably sent a whole contingent of party bureaucrats in Warsaw brushing up on their catechism. It served as a reminder that while liberal democracy does not answer man's spiritual needs, at least it leaves him free to seek his own answers.

And the Holy Spirit accomplished all this independently of the new pope's ideas or actions which, at this point, only a fool would try to predict.

1978

RESIGNED BEWILDERMENT

A group of terrorists invaded the Turkish Embassy in Ottawa recently, killing a Canadian guard and causing the ambassador to injure himself while jumping out of a window to escape the gunmen. The terrorists were quickly captured and are now facing charges of murder.

Canadians noted the event with what can be described as resigned bewilderment. Resigned, because acts of terrorism have by now become almost commonplace in the Western world. Though few incidents have occurred in Canadian cities compared to such places as Paris or Rome, the fact is that in the last fifteen years even our relatively peaceful and dispassionate country has seen bombs exploding in mailboxes, installations wrecked, and at least one politician's body pulled out of a car trunk. We have had diplomats kidnapped and killed—the last one, as it happened, another Turkish official in Ottawa not too long ago.

The reason for the public's bewilderment was different. First, unlike in Asia, the Middle East, or even Europe, our past political disputes have rarely been addressed by violence. Resigned as we are by now to such things happening, we are still bewildered by them. While no country's past is entirely free of gunpowder and the noose, never in recorded history has a larger tract of land been settled by many different groups more peacefully than in Canada. Our tradition includes political violence as an exception rather than as a rule.

Second, we can't help being bewildered by the bitterness that accompanies such conflicts in other parts of the world. Even our full-scale wars have been relatively short, have involved the spilling of relatively little blood, have been followed by relatively fair settlements, and have left behind relatively little residual hatred. After the passage of some years we are more likely—to use a modern example—to appoint a former violent political extremist like Anne Cools to the Senate than to exile her, at least when her political violence involved no threat to life. It puzzles us why, in many other parts of the world, the very children or grandchildren of such a person would be excluded from political affairs, if they were lucky enough not to be resettled in Siberia or its equivalent.

It was in the spirit of this resigned bewilderment that a short news backgrounder was telecast on the Global network the other day. In a few minutes it traced the history of the conflict between the Turks and the Armenians. It noted—accurately, in my view—that in 1915, seventy years ago, a large number of Armenians were massacred and expelled by the Turks. It indicated, also accurately, that to this day Turkey has not really acknowledged the massacre or offered any redress to the victims or their descendants. In fairness to the Turks, the telecast also emphasized the obvious fact that modern-day Turkey is in no way heir to the ideas and practices of the Ottoman empire of seventy years ago, which was responsible for the Armenian holocaust.

Both points were worth noting. The first, lest Canadians—who know little about the history of what, for them, is a very remote part of the world—should think that some Armenians have suddenly gone mad for no reason. The second, to make it clear that the Turks who are being bombed, kidnapped, and shot by the terrorists today bear no responsibility for a massacre that occurred not only many decades before they were born, but also under a system of government that they have long since repudiated.

In other words, while the Turks did massacre the Armenians at one point in history, for a terrorist to assassinate a Turkish diplomat today is no more justified than it would be, say, for a Crimean Tartar terrorist (if there were such a person) to assassinate a Soviet diplomat for what happened in the mass expulsion of the Tartar population of the Crimea. Less justified, in fact, because while the Soviet diplomat, born many decades later, would have no personal responsibility for the expulsion, at least the government he represents would be an heir to the government that caused their displacement. In the case of a Turkish diplomat, there would be no such continuity.

All this being self-evident, the Global telecast ended on the same note of resigned bewilderment on which it began. It could have asked one more question, but it did not. Why have a few Armenian terrorists started shooting Turkish diplomats sixty to seventy years after the 1915 massacre?

This would be completely puzzling, were it not for some known facts. The outbreak of terror coincided with the Soviet Union's drive to destabilize Turkey—and with it, NATO's southern flank—in the late 1970s. As reported both by the *New York Times* and the *Sunday*

Times in London by the spring of 1980, the Armenian terrorists were receiving training and funding through Dr. George Habash's militant Palestinian Marxist groups in Lebanon. The connection between those groups and the KGB has been a matter of record for some time.

Knowing this will not reduce our sorrow and anger over political violence being imported into Canada. It might, however, reduce our bewilderment as well as our resignation.

1985

ENEMIES OF DEMOCRACY

Often the most revealing parts of newspapers are the back pages. A little item tucked away on page 42 can frequently give you a more important message about the world you live in than the headline. Like the wire-service story last week, describing in ten lines how eight soldiers were killed in a clash with communist guerrillas in the Philippines.

Eight government soldiers dead? In a fight with the communists? Last week? But hasn't it been more than two months since dictator Ferdinand Marcos was deposed in the Philippines? Is the government in power today not Corazon Aquino's, democratically elected against all odds after a bitter struggle with an entrenched tyrant who had ruled the Philippines for twenty years? Isn't Marcos, who is strongly suspected of having had a hand in the cowardly assassination of Aquino's husband, living in exile today? Weren't the soldiers killed by the communists last week serving the democratic government of Aquino's widow?

And has it not been the near-unanimous opinion of left-liberal pundits that it is the intolerable repression created by right-wing tyrants, supported by the West, that gives rise to terrorism, communist guerrillas, and "armed struggles of liberation" in the Third World or elsewhere? That if we only supported the political forces of liberalism and reform in those places, instead of right-wing generals and dictators, the menace of communism would diminish or disappear? Tell it to the eight Filipino soldiers who died last week. Or their families.

Let me make absolutely clear that I favour supporting the forces of liberalism and reform against tyranny. I have been writing for many years—as have others who share my views on the subject—that supporting repressive regimes is wrong. It is wrong, apart from any practical considerations, because it betrays the ideals which form the basis of our own societies. We should not be friends with tyrants, we should certainly not prop them up against their own people, whether they fight against communism or not. We should not have made a common cause with a Marcos or a Samoza for the same reasons we did not make a common cause with a Mussolini or a Franco. Even though they, too, opposed communism. The enemies of liberalism and democracy come from many sides, not only one.

This is a far cry, however, from the illusion that the menace of militant Marxism would disappear, or even significantly diminish, with the fall of right-wing dictatorships. Militant Marxists, whether they go by the name of communists or Sandinistas or anything else, are not simply the enemies of fascist or neo-fascist tyrants. They are the enemies of liberalism. They are the enemies of democracy. Though some NDP-types will not see this, until it's too late, they are the enemies of social democracy as well.

The communists do use the real grievances, the real discontent, the real inhumanities or injustices of a people suffering under a right-wing dictator. They would be fools if they didn't. But we would be bigger fools if we believed that this is because they oppose inhumanity or injustice. Insofar as we have believed it, we have been bigger fools.

What the communists want is power. Once they have it, they use it to establish a tyranny of their own. Their tyranny is as devoid of justice, humanity, freedom, or any other liberal and democratic values as the tyranny of right-wing dictators. It brings as little, or less, in the way of general prosperity. Their regimes protect the environment, the safety of the workers, or any other popular (and sometimes valid) left-lib causes no more than any other dictatorial regime.

And to get this power, the communists will try to ambush and kill the soldiers of any government. Whether they are Marcos' soldiers or Aquino's. Whether the soldiers serve a dictatorship in situations which bring them more popular support and, not surprisingly, less resistance from western liberal public opinion. In a tactical sense, in today's world it may be easier to acquire power by overturning a tyrant than by attacking a democracy. I'm glad that this is so; it is a hopeful sign. It may augur well for the future that even the worst enemies of democracy have to pretend to be its defenders. But not realizing that communists *are* the worst enemies of democracy is among the most dangerous illusions of our times. It is the real lesson of page 42. Long after we have forgotten the day's headlines, we should remember it.

1986

ACCOMMODATING EVIL

At a dinner party the other night the talk turned to the Austrian presidential elections. Someone wondered how and why questions about Kurt Waldheim's possible Nazi past surfaced at this particular time. I suggested that he probably started the rumours himself to improve his chances with the voters.

People laughed, taking my remark as a confirmation of their own views, namely that most people in certain Eastern and Central European countries were, and perhaps still are, Nazi-sympathizers and anti-Semites. In fact, that wasn't my point at all.

Of course there were, fifty years ago, many people in Eastern and Central Europe who were attracted, impressed, or influenced by National Socialism. Is it surprising? There were a fair number of such people even in the West. In those days newspapers, the radio, politicians, middle-of-the-road public opinion, respectable citizens at fashionable dinner parties, and so forth all talked about Hitler and his followers in different tones. Even in London, Toronto, or New York. No one has to take my word for it. The library is just around the corner. Newspapers and periodicals from the 1930s are available for everyone to see.

The point isn't that many far-sighted people didn't oppose the Nazi movement right from the start. There were millions of people who did, ordinary citizens as well as writers, pundits, politicians, and opinion-makers. This was certainly the case in the West—where it was quite safe to oppose the Nazis—but was also the case in East-Central Europe or Germany itself where it wasn't. Yet, the opposition was not nearly as universal or as unequivocal then. Today the evils of Nazism are as plain as the nose on your face. Then they weren't, at least not for everyone. Including some western editorialists.

Most people, whether intellectuals or common folk, are probably not cruel or evil. But they can be impressionable, uncertain, or unimaginative. They are not historians, heroes, or moral philosophers. Sometimes, alas, not even when they strike heroic poses or dabble in history or moral philosophy.

When a movement sweeps one of the great nations of the world—as National Socialism swept Germany or Fascism swept Italy—it can impress a lot of people. Does everyone stop to analyze for himself politics or ideas? Many people simply accept whatever is blowing in the wind. In the world nothing succeeds like success; nothing is as trendy as fashion. If something has such momentum, if it gathers so many enthusiastic followers, people might say to themselves: perhaps there is something to it.

Then there is fear and hope, the two great motivators. Fear of conflict and hope for accommodation. In the 1930s the memory of the Great War, with its ten million dead, was still very much on everyone's mind. Even before the nuclear age people didn't cherish the idea of another world war—and who could blame them? Perhaps the Nazis were not all bad. Perhaps we could learn to coexist with them.

And if this was part of the mood of the West—where opposing Nazism was cheap, where it would have extracted no price in terms of personal ambitions—what about the countries where it did? What about the countries where opposing Nazism was costly? Where it could have meant a loss of opportunities, a loss of friends, a loss of business or income? Where for a young man like Waldheim instead of officers' school it could have meant being a conscript in the infantry?

Was it not more tempting, in those countries, to accommodate the Nazis—even in one's own mind? To say that, yes, perhaps they were a little excessive, but what if they did have a point? Or that their bark was probably worse than their bite?

Remember, in the 1930s no one had yet seen the corpses of Auschwitz. Auschwitz hadn't even been built yet. There were only some exclusions, expulsions, or confiscations. A little affirmative action favouring Germans. A little loss of civil liberties or political freedoms.

Many people felt, whether they approved or not, that they could put up with this much for the sake of their careers, their families, their own safety or well being. For the sake of not being out of tune with the times. Sometimes for the sake of ordinary patriotism. This is what happens to people under totalitarianism. This is what happens when an evil idea becomes part of the everyday landscape.

Did such people make a wrong choice, an immoral choice, a destructive choice? There is no doubt in my mind. There may not even be much doubt in their minds, today. But it's not part of people's nature to feel guilty forever about a choice they, or their fathers, made fifty years ago. They'd rather forgive themselves for they knew not what they did. Which is why Kurt Waldheim could count on his past not costing him too many Austrian votes.

1986

TANGLED ALLEGIANCES

Suggesting that immigrants should stop concerning themselves with the affairs of their former homelands would be unreasonable. No effort would enable people to erase from their minds or hearts, from one moment to the next, simply as a result of having journeyed to some other part of the globe, everything that has preoccupied them before. Nor would it be necessary or desirable for them to do so.

Not only immigrants, but in many instances even their children and grandchildren, maintain some emotional ties to their ancestral countries. This is as natural as it is wholesome, to use an old-fashioned word. Nothing should be done to discourage it. Probably nothing could be done. Roots go deep; that's the whole point about roots.

However, Canadians of whatever background, be they naturalized, native-born, or third generation, owe their first allegiance to the country of their citizenship. This requirement is both reasonable and practical. It puts no stress on human rights or human nature. It is simply Canada's due.

Historically, the majority of individual immigrants from all ethnic groups have always recognized this. They or their ancestors came to Canada for the very purpose of becoming Canadians. Far from disputing the need for such loyalty, immigrants have been among its most ardent supporters. On the whole, this is probably as true today as it has ever been. Still, there have been some signs in recent years that I find disturbing—both as an immigrant and as a Canadian.

As everybody knows, a few individuals from certain ethnic communities—for instance, Sikhs or Armenians—have committed violent acts in Canada, or used Canada as a base for committing violent acts elsewhere to protest or avenge the grievances of their former homelands. As a result, Canadian lives have been lost or endangered.

Committing terrorist acts in Canada for foreign causes, or using Canada as a terrorist base, is disloyal to Canada's interests and institutions. This much is self-evident. When immigrants or their descendants use Canada's territory for the commission or preparation of political violence, they commit (in addition to every other objection one might raise to terrorism) a specific act of treachery. They abuse the country that took them in.

Needless to say, such acts usually involve only a handful of people. They are in no way representative of the ethnic group whose name serves as a pretext for their crimes. The rest of their community cannot be held responsible for them. Even when they share some or all of the terrorists' political views or their sense of grievance, most Canadian Sikhs, Armenians, etc., would not dream of committing terrorist acts.

Lately some representatives and spokesmen from these groups, sensing—rightly—the loathing and horror that terrorist violence engenders in this country, and sensing—again rightly—that such acts may lower the esteem in which the entire community is held by other Canadians, set about to rectify their communities' image. However, instead of publicly dissociating themselves from the terrorists and unequivocally condemning their acts, they started exploring different avenues.

Journalists and politicians began receiving newsletters explaining and justifying the aims, causes, and grievances that have served as a basis for the terrorists' acts. Community spokesmen gave statements to the press or appeared on television with similar messages. At the same time, complaints were being received by editors and broadcast executives about the identification of a given ethnic community with terrorism. Lawyers were being consulted to see if the press could be persuaded—or maybe even forced—to stop identifying the suspected or convicted perpetrator of an act of political violence as a member of a given national group.

True, there was no attempt in these statements, pamphlets, or requests to justify terrorist acts. But neither were there any attempts to condemn them. The communities' sole concern appeared to be explaining their national causes (riding, as it were, on the coat-tails of the terrorists) while voicing their indignation about their communities' poor image.

Of course, I don't need to be persuaded that no child should be taunted in school because someone of his nationality or religion put a bomb on a plane. I don't even need to be persuaded that, say, Sikhs vs. India or Armenians vs. Turkey have legitimate grievances: I happen to agree. But neither Sikhs nor Armenians have grievances against this country, and those individuals who use or facilitate violence here are merely being disloyal to Canada. Explaining their motives does nothing to alter this fact.

The answer to the valid concerns of Armenian-Canadians or Sikh-Canadians does not lie in lectures on history, and certainly not in trying to tell the press what and how to report (other than pointing out inaccuracies). Their best answer is to join with other Canadians in the unreserved condemnation of terrorism.

1986

LAST OF THE HITLER GANG

By the time he died, apparently by his own hand, in Spandau prison a few days ago, Rudolf Hess had been a prisoner for over forty-six years. This includes the four years Hess spent in Britain as a prisoner of war after he landed there by parachute on May 10, 1941. Jail was the right place for Adolf Hitler's one-time deputy. Not only because, as one of the architects of Nazism, he deserved to spend much of his life in prison, but also in the sense that the thing Hess hated, feared, and rejected the most was freedom.

Rudolf Hess may have been insane, but only in that he carried his phobia to human autonomy (which is what freedom is) to an unusual, pathological extreme. Otherwise, his sickness was shared by many people who would never be diagnosed as mentally ill by anyone. In fact, if the dominant illness of a century can be characterized by the pathology of one person, the illness of our own century could be defined by the Hess-syndrome. What is it? Simply put, a terror of liberty combined with a sick craving for submission to some absolute, total authority.

By all accounts, Hess was an awkward, painfully shy man, susceptible to every occult or pseudo-scientific notion he encountered, from homeopathic medicine to astrology. Had the circumstances of his life been different, he might have simply become a passionate vegetarian, a Jesus-freak, a Moonie, or some environmental or animal-rights fanatic. What he was looking for was unquestioning faith in some person or cause, the more bizarre the better, into which he could submerge his entire being.

As it happened, in 1920 Hess heard Adolf Hitler speak to some small group. According to the recollections of his wife, Ilse Hess, all he could do after listening to Hitler's speech was to come home, laughing ecstatically and shouting: "The man, the man!" From that moment he had found his guru, the fixed point of his own empty existence. He had found the God-substitute he was seeking, the idol to whom he could surrender in total, worshipful devotion.

The German historian Joachim C. Fest describes Hess as a man "seeking for the strength to utter the prayer used in [Nazi] day nurseries: 'Führer, my Führer, my faith, my light!'" In his neurotic craving for faith, he wanted to be reduced to a child. Having the mental make-up of a true believer, but being born in a secular age where the religious outlets that such personality types seem to require were unavailable to him, Hess embraced the religion of totalitarianism.

According to contemporary observers, both inside and outside Nazi circles, Hess was a man of very limited intelligence. He wasn't even particularly shrewd, ruthless, or ambitious.

Hitler appears to have anointed the brooding maniac his deputy führer several years after their first meeting for no other reason than Hess' complete devotion to him. When, eight years later, in the middle of the war, Hess took it into his head to fly to Britain and offer a personal peace proposal to the Duke of Hamilton, it was probably due to some confused idea in his head that he was carrying out Hitler's secret wishes.

Insofar as the Nazis had an ideology, other than "the will to power," it centred around the twin notions of "race" and "living space." It is possible that in Hess' muddled mind the plan of the Nazis "guaranteeing" the British Empire in exchange for a free hand to conquer enough "space" in Europe for Germany was what the Führer really wanted.

Hitler himself couldn't say this—Hess may have reasoned—partly because of the war and partly because "the Jews have hypnotized Churchill." He felt that it was his task to carry Hitler's unexpressed wishes to the duke. The rest, of course, is history. The British locked up the deputy führer without replying to his "peace plan," and a furious Hitler announced that he would put Hess into a madhouse if he ever laid hands on him again. Apparently excommunicated, Hess attempted suicide twice before his trial at Nuremberg.

At Nuremberg, Hess convinced himself that Hitler, before his death, recognized his loyalty and forgave him. For the next four decades he existed in Spandau prison, with other Nazi prisoners at first, but later alone.

Whether or not there was any point in keeping the old madman locked up after thirty years or so, the Soviets never agreed to his being released. After all, Hess was their enemy. While he may not have had a direct hand in the Holocaust, he sought a separate peace with the

West the better to wage war on the Soviet Union. The Soviets, who *had* made a separate peace with the Nazis only two years before Hess' trip to Britain, might not have thought it was such a crazy plan.

1987

ARCHITECT OF GENOCIDE

On December 11, 1988, the *New York Times* ran a short piece by Janet Heller, entitled "Ceausescu, cultural vandal." "The president of Romania, Nicolae Ceausescu, is playing God with his country's architectural heritage," the article begins. "His disastrous policy of ultimately demolishing six thousand to seven thousand villages in the countryside and destroying the historic centres of forty-five towns…is well under way. The stated purpose of this so-called systematization is to give socialist Romania a modern profile."

The piece goes on to explain that: a) Ceausescu hopes to shift people from their private houses into prefabricated apartment blocks so new types of citizens may be created who "think in collective terms according to socialist principles"; and b) that most villages, churches, and cemeteries scheduled for the bulldozers are in Transylvania, home of Romania's Hungarian-speaking minority.

The *Times* concludes that: "World attention must focus with greater intensity on President Ceausescu's architectural desecration…. The only chance to halt Ceausescu's 'modernization' policy, if any, lies in a loud international outcry that he simply cannot ignore."

Okay. All this is quite true as far as it goes, but considering what has been happening in Romania it hardly goes far enough. In fact, it falls so short as to be rather comic, in a sad sort of way.

I'm trying to think of an example to illustrate how inadequate it is. Picture a man standing in a room holding an antique crystal goblet. As a horror-stricken *New York Times* reporter looks on, an assassin approaches with a pick-axe and is about to bring it down on the man's head. Whereupon the journalist cries out: "In God's name, stop! He'll drop that priceless glass."

I know that genocide has become a shop-worn and abused word, but that's what has been happening in Romanian Transylvania during the 1980s. Hungarian-speaking Transylvanians, a large, distinct ethnic group, about as numerous and distinct as French Canadians, are being systematically destroyed by the mad-hatter Ceausescu family in the heart of Europe. Roughly three million people are being forcibly uprooted and relocated. Their language is being suppressed; their community leaders and intellectuals are being murdered; their schools, libraries, and theatres are being shut down; their towns and villages are being bulldozed into the ground. There is a full-blown genocide going on right under our noses.

Genocide would certainly be the word we'd use, and rightly so, if anyone tried to implement such policies against francophones in Canada (to stick with the same example). If anyone tried to, say, deport French Canadians from Quebec and relocate them in small groups all over the country. Or raze Quebec City and Trois Rivières.

Ceausescu is no mere cultural vandal. He's a kind of mixture between a commissar and a cannibal. He may well be clinically insane. This joke of a human being, this cross between Stalin and Idi Amin, along with his wife, the "scientist" Elena, may suffer from what psychiatrists call a *folie à deux*, a form of madness bonding two people. They torture Romanians as much as ethnic minorities, but lately Transylvanians have borne the brunt of their sickness. And what does the world do? Next to nothing. No headlines, no diplomatic protests, no mass demonstrations (except one in the summer of 1988 in Budapest, Hungary). Or maybe a short piece in the *New York Times* worrying about architecture.

Architecture? After the turn of the century Upton Sinclair wrote a novel called *The Jungle* about the inhumane condition of immigrant workers in the slaughterhouses of Chicago. The book became an immediate bestseller in America. Why? Coincidentally, it also happened to describe the unsanitary conditions under which breakfast sausages were being prepared. "I aimed at America's heart," Sinclair wrote ten to fifteen years later, "and hit it in the stomach." I guess his line can still stand as the last word on the subject.

1989

DEFINITION OF A TERRORIST

Some people say that ordinary, everyday terms lose their definition in political affairs. Words like "terrorist" or "patriot" become meaningless or they mean whatever we want them to mean. This view is often summed up in the cynical phrase: "One man's terrorist is another's man's freedom fighter." It's all a semantic game, based on nothing but political sympathies.

"They're all terrorists," a former hostage said on CBS television last week. He was a priest, held by some Moslem faction in the Middle East before his release. He had obviously been traumatized and saddened by his experience. As far as he was concerned, the Shiites, the Palestinians, and the Israelis were all cut from the same cloth.

This man, needless to say, was no friend of terrorism. On the contrary, he had the dimmest possible view of all terrorist acts. Yet the terrorists would have welcomed his opinion. The terrorists would have said: "You see? Even our victims agree that there's nothing to choose between us and our enemies.

"If you want to call us terrorist, you have to call the other side terrorist as well. Or don't our enemies also shoot, kidnap, and bomb people? Don't they, too, number among their victims some innocent bystanders?"

This has been the standard argument of terrorists for years, and I think we do ourselves a great disservice if we let it confuse us. To say that everyday terms lose their definition in politics, or that one man's terrorist is another man's freedom fighter, is worse than nonsense. It's sophistry of the cheapest kind.

The fact is that words do have ordinary meanings. They are not too difficult to define (though they may be obfuscated on purpose). The difference between cops and robbers is quite plain, even if both cops and robbers are tough guys who carry weapons. Political sympathies don't alter this. For instance, I've never heard a person, no matter how much sympathy he may have had for Israel, refer to a unit of regular Arab soldiers during the wars of 1948, 1956, 1967, or 1973 as "terrorists." Those warriors in the Arab armies also tried to destroy Israel; they also tried to shoot and bomb Israelis, yet they were clearly not terrorists, but soldiers.

Terrorists are not defined by their aims but by their methods. Fighting for the Palestinian cause may be as honorable as fighting for the cause of Israel, but groups that deliberately blow up noncombatants are still terrorists. They're terrorists, whatever their political aims. Groups who kidnap and murder tourists, travellers, shoppers, envoys, journalists, or members of peacekeeping forces are not engaged in warfare but in acts of terror.

Terrorists, of course, may use any national, religious, or political cause. Many causes (including Israel's) have been used by terrorists at one time or another. However, some causes have allowed themselves to be defined by terrorism, permitting terrorists to take them over. This, in my view, has been the tragedy of the Palestinian cause.

As for Israel's response, I certainly don't think it has been beyond criticism or debate. Brutalized by decades of terrorism, vastly outnumbered, and with their very existence at stake, Israelis have responded in ways that have at times been ill-advised, intransigent, or counter-productive—or at least counter-productive in terms of western public opinion and support.

Without doubt, the Israelis have broken international laws by sending forces across sovereign borders—sometimes for impeccable reasons, as at Entebbe, but sometimes for reasons many people in Israel itself have questioned. The recent kidnapping of Sheik Abdul Karim Obeid from Lebanon may be an example.

However, nothing the Israelis have done can be discussed in the same breath with terrorism. It's possible to debate questions of excessive force, such as responding to stones with bullets, or whether it's wrong to murder murderers, but there's nothing to debate about the kidnapping or murder of shoppers and travellers. There's nothing to debate about using one's own wives and sisters as a shield for military bases, as the terrorists have done.

People who purposely attack their enemy's schoolyards (or who purposely set up their armed camps among their own children) inhabit a different moral universe. It's impossible to negotiate with them. Any dialogue implies a shared moral language, and the terrorists do not share a moral language with the rest of the world.

Of course, it's possible to *learn* their language—possible, but tragic. Israel may have begun to feel that it has no choice but to learn it. If so, it may turn out to be the ultimate tragedy of the Israeli cause.

1989

TOTALITARIAN RECALL

Some of the deadliest extremists of our century seem to have suffered a crushing defeat. Gradually, during the last fifty years, they've been discredited militarily, economically, socially, and philosophically. By now the fanatics of race- or class-hatred—that is, most fascist- or communist-inspired societies—have been destroyed, isolated, or reduced to insignificance.

The fascists or quasi-fascists were the first to go, their demise hastened by the defeat of the Axis powers in World War II. By the mid-1970s they existed only in isolated pockets: one country in Europe, another in Africa, two or three in Latin America. As a mass social movement, fascism was finished. Eventually communism followed—though for a while it looked as if it had a stranglehold on this century. But when the collapse came, it was swift. Today China is the only communist power of significance that is not yet in evident retreat.

Can these movements recover? Perhaps, but I doubt it. The memory of the harm they've caused is still too fresh. They've lost whatever intellectual clout they may have had, along with all of their emotional allure. They've lost their trendiness as well as the terror they once inspired. In the near future people are unlikely to turn to fascism or communism either in hope or out of fear.

In the past, each movement could achieve some success just by claiming to stand as a bulwark against the other. Fascists would promise to stem the tide of communism, while communists would undertake to stand firm against the fascist menace. An amazing number of people could rationalize going along with either as a lesser of two evils. However, their simultaneous demise has refuted this option for both systems in the 1990s.

If this makes me sound like an optimist, wait. While I doubt if communism or fascism will threaten us again on a global scale in this century, I'm much more pessimistic about equal menaces in different forms. Communism and fascism may be dead, but the totalitarian impulse is vigorous and very much alive.

I've speculated before about movements that may attract the deadly extemists of our times. To be effective, such movements should have a kernel of truth, a veneer of plausibility, and—like Marxism or racism—offer radically simple solutions to complex problems.

To attract people in sufficient numbers a movement should capitalize not only on the worst, but also on the best impulses of human beings: on altruism as well as on selfishness, on magnanimity as well as on envy, on a wish to dominate as well as on a wish to submit. It should be far-fetched enough to promote a fundamental change, but sufficiently rooted in some aspects of human nature to attract more than a few fringe lunatics.

Nationalism is unlikely to serve as a basis for a global mass movement. Nationalism tends to arise in too many places at once, which makes it self-cancelling in its effect. Virulent patriotism *is* intolerant and deadly, but it's more likely to cause many little fanatic movements than one big one. For similar reasons, I doubt if the next wave of the totalitarian impulse will centre around religious fanaticism (though a kind of theocracy may spread through Moslem countries). But, just like fanatic nationalism, religious fanaticism is also self-limiting.

This makes extreme feminism or environmentalism the best bet. If a new type of totalitarianism arises, it's likely to come from either—or both—of these movements.

A fundamentalist, tyrannical streak is clearly present in both. Hard-core feminists, in the words of one of their philosopher-activists, Sandra Harding, call for "a more radical intellectual, moral, social, and political revolution than the founders of modern western cultures could have imagined." They consider marriage oppressive and "heterosex-ist." (Heterosexism is bad since a truly just society is supposed to be bisexual.) They wish to do away with the family, just as they wish to do away with "androcentric" western science and art.

Sandra Harding wants to "reinvent science and theorizing itself to make sense of women's social experience." As for Simone de Beauvoir, one of the founders of radical feminism, her view is even simpler: "No woman should be authorized to stay at home and raise her children."

And what about radical environmentalists, you ask? Well, they believe that all evil can be traced back to Neolithic times. The trouble started when people began tilling the soil instead of hunting and gathering. So, they propose to lead us back to the Stone Age. By persuasion if possible, by force if necessary.

1990

MORE THAN "US VS. THEM"

If, as we hope, the Cold War has indeed come to an end, our strategic aim should no longer be to contain grim police states like Saddam Hussein's regime in Iraq. Our strategic aim should be to destroy them. Until a year ago such an aim would have been dangerous whether directed against the Baathist tyrant of Baghdad or any other dictator enjoying the Soviet Union's protection. It would have had the potential of bringing the world to the brink of nuclear war.

In the fall of 1990 the situation has changed. The Soviet Union has now joined the United States in condemning Hussein's annexation of Kuwait. Soviet warships are patrolling the Persian Gulf not to oppose but to help the rest of the world enforce an embargo against Iraq.

Destroying tyrants like Hussein is still difficult and costly, but it's no longer dangerous in the same sense. By now it's more dangerous not to destroy them.

Hussein portrays himself as the champion of "the Arab nation." He attempts to unite Arabs behind him by suggesting it's them against us. He argues that America, Europe, and even industrialized Asia are just after Middle Eastern oil, and he's posturing as the defender of Arab riches against the rest of the world. Hussein hasn't been entirely successful in his efforts, but neither has he been entirely unsuccessful. While many Arabs see in him a ruthless, barbaric dictator, other Arabs look to Hussein as a leader who may be able to redress their sense of grievance.

Hussein's appeal to many Arabs is similar to Hitler's appeal to many Germans sixty years ago. Germans also felt impoverished and hard done by the West as well as by "traitors" in their own midst. In Hitler's demonology they included Jews and plutocrats, i.e., the wealthy upper classes of old Germany. In Hussein's demonology Israel also comes first, followed closely by the "haves" of the Middle East, the rulers and people of the oil-rich conservative Arab sheikdoms.

Some Arabs have a genuine dilemma. Being anything but naïve, they have reservations about a tyrant who uses chemical weapons and tramples on the national sovereignty of other Arab states. But they're also impressed by Hussein and argue he may be the kind of tough guy Arabs need to stand up against their enemies. These Arabs tell themselves that once Hussein has played his part they'll be able to control him—which is exactly what some Germans told themselves about Hitler.

Most Arabs are simply waiting to see which way the cat's going to jump. That's why what liberal democracies do in the coming weeks is so important. What we'll do depends on how we define the issues for ourselves. Without clarifying our purpose, it's unlikely we can take concerted and effective action.

The main thing is not to fall into Hussein's trap and define the Middle East crisis as "us against them." This conflict is not about westerners vs. Arabs; it's about a rabid, Neanderthal throwback against the entire civilized (or even semi-civilized) world. Poison gas-throwing military dictators are as deadly to Arabs as to anyone else. More deadly, in this case, since Hussein is running amok in the Mideast.

Nor is this a conflict about oil. True, industrialized nations need fossil fuels, but Hussein's aggression would be just as intolerable if there were nothing but sand dunes in Kuwait. When we're talking about defending the West's vital interests we're not talking about oil alone. We're talking about the principles of the U.N. Charter. We're talking about civilization.

When U.N. forces fought the aggression of North Korean invaders in the early 1950s, they weren't defending oil. South Korea had none. They were defending civilization. Oil only confuses the issue, western guilt about Third World exploitation having become a part of conventional thinking in the postwar years.

But there's nothing wrong with defending civilization against a barbaric threat just because it happens to coincide with defending our vital interests as industrial nations. The fact we have an interest in oil doesn't diminish the legitimacy of our interest in principles. It simply provides an added economic reason for doing what we ought to be doing in any event.

Of course, just because the issues shouldn't be defined as "oil" or as "them against us" doesn't mean that they won't be. If so, it's a pity; but it shouldn't make us hesitate. We still ought to wipe Hussein and his ilk off the face of this Earth. At whatever cost (the cost can only increase if we wait) and for the sake of the Arab world no less than for our own.

1990

THROWING THE FIRST STONE

Did Israeli soldiers "overreact" when Arab rioters began stoning Jewish worshippers at Jerusalem's Wailing Wall last week? The world seems to believe so. The soldiers fired on the mob, reportedly killing twenty-one Palestinians. A United Nations resolution is being drafted to condemn the Israeli action, with the participation of the U.S. and Canada.

The world's unhappiness with Israel has little to do with whether the soldiers' reaction was proportionate or disproportionate to the threat posed by the rioters. It's a safe bet that if an independent inquiry after a meticulous investigation found the Israelis could not have safeguarded the worshippers or quelled the riot any other way, the world would be just as unhappy with Israel. It's probably unnecessary to spell out why this is so, but let me spend a couple of paragraphs on it anyway.

After Iraqi dictator Saddam Hussein invaded Kuwait, he badly needed a diversion. Having grabbed an Arab country, he was facing the hostility of his Arab neighbours in addition to the hostility of the world. Once this became evident, Saddam tried to justify his conquest by posing as the champion of all Arabs against their common enemy, Israel.

Cheap and blatant as Saddam's ploy was, in the volatile atmosphere of Middle East politics it had a slim chance. By somehow connecting his naked aggression against Kuwait with the highly complex Palestinian issue, Saddam could possibly muddy the waters long enough to consolidate his gains. He could try to split the alliance that was forming against him and persuade some Arabs that instead of supporting the U.N. against Iraq, they should support Iraq against the U.N. and Israel.

Noting this, the world was most anxious for Israel to keep a low profile. Everyone believed that Israel could best assist the resolution of the Gulf crisis by keeping out of it. This not only suited Israel, but it was Israel's own considered view. Israelis of different political hues, Israelis who couldn't see eye to eye with each other on most other subjects, readily agreed that any unnecessary Israeli words or action at this time could only play into Saddam's hands.

Naturally, both Saddam and the Palestinians tried to draw Israel into the conflict. They made every effort, albeit for different reasons: Saddam, obviously, wanted to divert attention from himself, while the Palestinians wanted to focus attention on themselves once more. By shooting a score of stone-throwers in Jerusalem, Israel appears to have obliged them both.

Now the world is furious with Israel. What we're saying (in effect, if not in so many words) is that Israel should have chosen to take some casualties rather than fire its weapons and thereby hinder our collective efforts in the Gulf. If we must have riots in Jerusalem, our side can make better mileage out of Jewish worshippers being stoned to death than Palestinians being riddled by bullets. Only Saddam can make any mileage out of dead Palestinians in the Middle East; why can't those Israelis understand this?

That's what we'd say if we spoke bluntly—but, of course, we rarely speak bluntly. Instead, we get on our moral high horse and produce a lot of holier-than-thou speeches, conveniently forgetting the force we have often employed—in Canada or France or Great Britain or the United States—to quell significantly lesser threats to our security than Israel has faced throughout its existence.

Canada is a pacific country, but I'd hate to see it put to the test. I'd hate to think what kind of force we might employ here if, say, native rioters started stoning citizens or police officers in Quebec—especially if, like the *intifada*, they kept it up for a couple of years. I wonder if we'd be prepared to take as many casualties as Israel has before we started shooting. As a matter of fact, I'd say the Mohawk at Oka were prudent not to press their cause much further than they did this summer. Had they pressed it, Canada might have been condemned in some U.N. resolution—but many of the Mohawks might be dead.

Native people have grievances at least as legitimate, in my view, as the grievances of the Palestinians. What's more, their demands do not pose even a fraction of the threat to our existence that Palestinian demands pose to the existence of Israel. Yet if our Indians acted (or were incited to act) in a manner similar to the Palestinians, I think we'd respond with no more forebearance than Israel has, and very possibly less.

All of which is not to condone what happened in Jerusalem last week. I just can't think of a nation that would be entitled to cast the first stone, so to speak, at Israel.

1990

6.

LITTLE

PINK LIES

Notes on Apologists

THE TRUTH ABOUT ETHIOPIA

Once again, there's famine in Ethiopia. Adults and children are dying by the thousands. Every night on television we see pictures of unspeakable horror. Our first response to this must be immediate and generous relief. No civilized nation can do anything else when faced with an emergency of this nature and magnitude. Our human duty is to give help first and ask questions later.

But eventually some questions must be asked. They must be asked—and answered—otherwise all our assistance will have been in vain. Once this famine is over, it will only be followed by another a few years down the road. Adults and children will be suffering and dying by the thousands again. Why is there famine in Ethiopa?

The first and most important reason is probably climatic and geographical. Ethiopia is a harsh and arid land. For one half of the year the average precipitation is under five inches. The soil is mostly reddish prairie (a little better than red desert) with great stony patches on the Plateau of Abyssinia. Not a hospitable region by any means. It is not flowing with milk and honey.

But there are regions equally or more inhospitable whose people have nevertheless come to terms with the land they inhabit. Deserts have been irrigated as in the Negev; lowlands have been guarded by dykes from the annual invasion of the sea as in Holland; and, as in Lapland, even Arctic regions have been harnessed to regularly support life. In many countries such accommodation with nature had been achieved in pre-industrial societies, without the aid of high technology. It is, therefore, likely that the second reason for the recurring famines in Ethiopia is cultural. Though no group of people would find life easy under such geographic conditions, some other groups might well be able to make a better go of it.

There is little doubt that the third and final reason is political. Ethiopia has an oppressive Marxist regime. Its leaders, only a short while ago, celebrated the tenth anniversary of their revolution with a banquet that reportedly cost over $2 million. This would be a considerable extravagance in a country as wealthy as Canada. It can only be called criminal in a country whose citizens were being reduced to skeletons even while the government was celebrating itself. But Marxists in power *are* criminals, whatever individual Marxists may be, for they govern by tyranny and tyranny is always a crime.

To avoid misunderstanding, I'm not blaming Marxists for the weather. They do not create droughts: they only make it impossible to do anything about them. They prattle on about western imperialism, build military bases for the Soviet Union, ruin what little economy there is in their country through corruption and red tape, then go on celebrating themselves while their people starve.

Famine certainly existed in Ethiopia before the Marxists—indeed, they came to power in the aftermath of an earlier famine and, in part, as a result of it—but while they cannot be faulted for the culture or the climate they inherited, their system makes it likely that things will forever go from bad to worse in their region. After all, the country which they try to emulate, which has become the patron saint of their petty dictatorship and supplies them with billions of dollars' worth of arms (though hardly any food), is the Soviet Union, whose own inefficient, brutal, and corrupt gulag economy has reduced it from a net exporter to a net importer of grain.

Ethiopians have little to hope for from a system that has at one time brought famine even to the bread basket of Europe, the unbelievably fertile Ukraine, through a combination of cruel purpose and mismanaged economy. The rocky highlands of Northeast Africa will hardly profit from imitating a regime that turned a great land, able to sell its wheat abroad even in the days when it was cultivated by teams of oxen, to one that today, in the age of fertilizers and tractor-combines, must buy it from Canada and the United States. An arid, backward, poverty-stricken country turning to such a system to improve its economy is a little like a man turning to drink to improve his driving.

The media in Canada have devoted much ink and many hours of broadcast time to the tragedy of Ethiopia, but hardly a whisper about the Marxist regime which is its contributing cause. A reader or viewer might not know from looking at the news stories or telecasts that Ethiopia is Marxist or that it has been a client state of the Soviet Union for about a decade.

On the contrary, the tone of the stories and newscasts frequently implies that the Ethiopian famine is somehow the fault of the West or, at the very least, we are negligent for not having done enough to forestall it by earlier and more generous foreign aid. In one recent newscast a relief worker, a liberation priest, was interviewed at length about his "anger" at the West for not heeding warnings about the impending disaster sooner and stockpiling food to prevent it.

This won't do. Not for the sake of the truth; not for the sake of the starving Ethiopian men, women, and children. Putting the blame where it does not belong, as a matter of reflexive western guilt, as a matter of superficial left-lib media fashion, will do nothing to prevent the recurrence of the Ethiopian tragedy. Only facing facts might do that.

At the risk of repeating myself, in the sort run there is no substitute for quick, generous relief. This is the only possible humane, civilized, Christian response while children are starving. But then the hard questions must come. The mushy liberal cant about north and south, so beloved of our former prime minister (Pierre Elliott Trudeau) and our current ambassador to the United Nations (Stephen Lewis), must give way to common sense. In the long run, truth is the best foreign aid.

1984

THE HITLER LEGACY

I know a person, the daughter of a camp survivor, who is a peace activist. In the past few years she has marched in two or three antinuclear demonstrations. She has seen and taken seriously every B-movie that deals with nuclear annihilation from *Threads* to *The Day After*, and she thinks that the Supreme Court of Canada should ban the cruise missile.

She also happens to be a virulent anti-Nazi. I suppose everybody is, with the exception of the handful of nuts who gather around Ernst Zundel, but most people can get through a day without giving the matter too much thought. After all, it's coming up to forty years since Hitler blew out what passed for his brains in a Berlin bunker.

Perhaps it's not surprising that this young lady can't get the Nazis out of her mind, though she wasn't even born until ten years after the collapse of the Third Reich. Her mother, whom she loves, is crippled. She has developed a crippling medical condition as a direct result of what she went through as a child of fifteen in the Nazi camp of Bergen-Belsen. You don't forget Hitler so easily when you live with a daily reminder of his handiwork.

One day, when the young peace activist lady was holding forth on how the Russians, too, are human beings and how only antediluvian cold-warriors, bent on blowing up the world, think that we can't peacefully coexist with them, I couldn't resist asking her a question. "Granted," I said, "that the Russians are human beings, which they certainly are. But the Germans were also human beings, even while they were ruled by Hitler. Should we have tried to peacefully coexist with them?"

"Oh, come now," the young lady replied. "For one thing, Hitler did not have the bomb."

"Suppose he'd had it?" said I. "What then? Should we have opted for detente? Should we have coexisted with Nazism, watched it spread from country to country, and scrapped our weapons in the hope that somehow it wouldn't spread to North America? Even if it didn't, your mother in Bergen-Belsen would certainly have been tortured to death and you—you'd never have been born."

The young lady considered this for a second, then said: "That would have been a terrible dilemma. Thank God, we don't have to worry about it today. The communists may be bad, but they're not like the Nazis."

I could have kissed her. I offered the entire line of argument just to hear her say this, and she did. Most people do, eventually, when they're backed into this particular corner, because there's nothing else for them to say.

The horrors of Nazism are known. Few people are consistent enough in their ideas of pacifism—or even in their fears—to say that they don't care about them. To say this would be to say they don't care what happened in Nazi-occupied countries, they don't care how many Jews, gypsies, socialists, or homosexuals were murdered, how many Slavs,

Latins, or members of other "lesser" races perished in labour camps, they only care about peace. Few people can bring themselves to say this. It would be to say that they'd sooner see their neighbours dragged into gas chambers than to lift a finger in their defence and risk "blowing up the world." And if they don't dare to say this about the Nazis, or even think it, because it would be an admission of insupportable callousness or cowardice, there's only one thing left for them to say. It is that the communists are different.

The argument that "communism is different" is advanced in many forms and in varying degrees of sophistication. It may come as a suggestion that we must distinguish between "Stalinism" and the post-Stalinist era. It may be the assertion that whatever the Kremlin's communism is like, communism in China (or Euro-communism or Cuban communism) cannot be judged by the same measure. It may be offered just as a superior snicker at Ronald Reagan's crass description of the Soviet Union as an "evil empire."

The truth, of course, is that the communists are in no way different from the Nazis in practice. Many people would argue, myself among them, that they are not different in theory either, but never mind that: they are certainly not different in what they actually do when they come to power. They establish tyrannies. They jail, torture, and murder their opponents, their perceived opponents, and often even their friends. They expand and colonize their neighbours—even if the neighbours themselves are communists. The Soviet Union invaded Hungary, Czechoslovakia, Afghanistan—all communist countries— and China tried to invade Vietnam even as Vietnam was invading Cambodia. They not only try to organize military coups or revolutions in non-communist countries, they try to destabilize each other, as Cuba tried in Grenada a short while ago by murdering the incumbent communist president. When was the last time one western democracy invaded another? How would it serve the cause of peace to allow communist regimes to spread all over the world?

This is the problem that the young lady and her friends are unwilling to face. The myth of "reform-communism" won't help, just as benign, non-Russian forms of communism are only myths. Stalin has been dead for more than a quarter of a century and God alone knows what happened to the Gang of Four, but only a few years ago Pol Pot murdered millions of people in Cambodia and the other day even the left-wing *Village Voice* was moved to describe the slaughter of one hundred and five unarmed Afghan men and boys hiding in an irrigation ditch. That's the problem. It's not just "Stalinism" or "Maoism" or "the Russians." The problem is communism, in any shape or form.

We can't say, "Thank God, we don't have to worry about what we would have done if Hitler had had the bomb." In this sense, Hitler is alive and he has the bomb. Come May 1, we'll see it being paraded through Red Square on TV.

1985

An Instrument of Dissension

Common sense tells us a number of things, simply because they stand to reason. We call them fair assumptions. For such fair assumptions, we don't have to know any particulars. We can assume that they are true, unless someone proves the contrary. This applies to everything in life, including Chief Justice Jules Deschênes' Commission of Inquiry on War Criminals in Canada.

We know that there were Nazis in Europe during World War II. We know that, in addition to Germans, they included sympathizers and collaborators in many other countries. We know that in Nazi Germany, as well as in countries allied to or occupied by the Nazis, grave crimes were committed against humanity. We know that these crimes were committed on such a scale that their commission had to involve many people. We also know that after the war masses of people emigrated to Canada from the very countries in which these crimes were committed. We know finally that, for reasons both good and bad, little or no effort was made to screen criminals from victims at the time of their immigration.

Knowing all this, it stands to reason that some people who partici-
pated in Nazi crimes did manage to slip into Canada thirty-five to forty
years ago. This much is a statistical certainty. It is a statistical proba-
bility that some of these people are still alive. It seems, then, that
simply relying on known facts and common sense one question facing
the Deschênes Commission can be answered in the affirmative. It can
be answered without spending a minute or a penny of the commission's time and resources. Yes, there are some former Nazi war
criminals in Canada.

A different and far more difficult series of questions are the following: can we identify any of these people? If so, can we provide
admissible evidence to indicate their complicity in war crimes? If yes,
can they be tried under Canadian law?

Although the last question may be the most important, I will not
spend much time on it. Personally, I find the legal arguments of those
who feel that existing Canadian law is not equipped to deal with Nazi
war crimes convincing. I agree with those who feel that our law cannot
be safely restructured in this regard, and who believe that bending the
law only to catch ex-Nazis would do lasting damage to our legal
system. I note that the people who believe this include eminent lawyers
and legal scholars, some of whom are Jewish, and all of whom abhor
Nazi war crimes as much as I do.

However, let's assume that we are wrong. Let's assume that the law
in Canada can deal, or can be made to deal, with war crimes without
any injury to our legal system. Let's assume that our only problem is
how to identify individual war criminals and how to prove their crimes
in court. No responsible person, no matter how much he wishes to see
Nazi murderers brought to justice, has ever suggested that accused
persons should be tried on the basis of anything but admissible evidence under our ordinary rules of criminal procedure. It is a safe
assumption that the Deschênes Commission, whatever its eventual recommendations, will not depart from this principle.

The problem is that the Nazis committed a great many, perhaps
most, of their war crimes in places that are currently under Soviet rule.
In many, perhaps most, instances we would have to rely on evidence

provided by the Soviet authorities to prosecute anyone. In my opinion, this would be unreliable evidence.

I could use stronger words to describe the potentially tainted nature of any evidence that may come to us from the land of the Gulag Archipelago. I could—as others have—point out that the Soviets, while they may in individual instances tell the truth, have an unenviable record of falsifying and manufacturing accusations and evidence for political purposes. I could point out that, at one time or another, they have committed almost every crime that the Nazis have committed. I could point out that, today, the Soviet Union is one of the few countries in which Jews face various degrees of persecution only because they are Jews. I could point out that, today, it is the Soviets who support most adamantly the enemies of Israel.

However, for the purposes of the Deschênes Commission it is unnecessary to say more than that Soviet evidence is unreliable. This much, at least, is generally acknowledged. There is almost no chance that evidence acquired through Soviet channels could survive in a Canadian court. This being so, collecting evidence through the Soviets can serve no useful purpose. It can only provoke and embitter a number of ethnic communities in Canada: communities which have good reason to believe that false or unprovable accusations may be levelled against their members by the communists for their own purposes.

The Deschênes Commission should not be the instrument in creating such pointless dissension in this country. In my view, the Jewish community in Canada should join other communities in dissuading Chief Justice Deschênes from pursuing this course.

1985

TRUTH—FIRST STEP TO PEACE

An editorial in the English-language Japanese *Times* plaintively asks the various peace groups that make up the Hiroshima-Nagasaki Peace Conference to please stop calling each other names. Peace is very much on people's minds in these islands in August 1985. It was in this country that the age of nuclear terror began exactly forty years ago.

The conference in remembrance of the first human victims began in Hiroshima, then moved to Nagasaki a few days later. The participants, as usual, ranged from people who simply wish for peace to people who want to use the opportunity to further the foreign policy interests of the Soviet Union. It is less than surprising that there is little peace between these two factions.

People who want peace are not necessarily idiots. They are not even always wide-eyed innocents, incapable of understanding when they are being cynically used for a purpose which is the very opposite of what they want to achieve. They know when they are being manipulated. They resent it.

At the risk of repeating the self-evident, various peace groups and campaigns for peace have been used, in the time-honored fashion of all fifth columns, to serve as instruments of Soviet policy. The only lull, in fact, came during those years of the East-West detente when the western powers slowed down or stopped their development and deployment of nuclear weapons. During those years the Soviets gave the peace movements a rest. They naturally wanted to be unhindered in the development and deployment of their own nuclear arsenal.

Once Moscow's own SS-20s were in place—and the West began showing signs of waking up to this fact—the peace movements came into being once again. Some paid a little lip service to their equal opposition to Soviet weaponry, but the majority of peace groups spoke and acted at all times as though western policies and western nuclear power represented the only threat to peace.

Western peace groups have been useful for two purposes from the Soviet point of view. First, for the creation of a public climate in which the research, development, and deployment of western nuclear and other military defences might be slowed down or stopped. Second, for the creation of a public climate in which any act of Soviet expansion or aggression might go unopposed because resisting it "might lead to war."

None of this is news. What is far more interesting, at least to my mind, is the fact that the majority of activists in the various western peace movements never consciously embraced these aims. Some simply failed to recognize them. Some may have recognized them but felt that they took second place to the all-important cause of universal peace. Many hoped that all hidden agendas of Soviet interest—though they could see them quite clearly—would eventually be swept aside in a world-wide tide of human desire for peace and goodwill on earth.

It is this hope that is wearing thin in August 1985, at the Hiroshima-Nagasaki Peace Conference. An increasing number of activists for peace, precisely because they are not conscious agents of Moscow, are refusing to be utilized for an ulterior purpose. They desire peace, not unchecked Soviet expansion. They want a world free of nuclear weapons, not a world held to ransom by Soviet nuclear might. This is the reason for the name-calling as the peace conference begins. I doubt if any number of plaintive pleas can stop it. I'm not persuaded, in fact, that it should stop. Sometimes name-calling can lead to the truth, and truth may be a necessary first step toward peace.

1985

RECONCILABLE DIFFERENCES

How times change. I'm old enough to remember the days when the entire political left—all manner of Marxists, communists, or socialists—hated the churches. They called religion "the opiate of the masses." They despised priests, ministers, and rabbis. They ridiculed their attitudes, customs, institutions, and beliefs, moral or temporal. The churches returned the sentiment in kind, and treated even the mildest manifestation of tolerance for "godless" communism as tolerance for Satan.

I'm speaking of "days" but that's just a figure of speech. A whole epoch was characterized by this antagonism. I personally recall only the tail end of it. Whether they worshipped dialectical materialism or some unfathomable deity, the two sides viewed each other's positions as irreconcilable. But all this is a thing of the past. Today only the so-called fundamentalist churches look at their creeds as irreconcilable with Marxism. Their adherents may number millions still, but they are apart from the mainstream.

The mainstream churches, of whatever denomination, are reconciling themselves to even the worst, most totalitarian manifestation of Marxism with alacrity. Not only in the captive countries of Soviet or other communist domination, which would be understandable. There the hierarchy of the churches has largely been replaced—or at least deeply infiltrated—by agents of the State. They may wear the habits, beards, or crucifixes of their faith but in reality they're communist civil servants. In those countries believers and their leaders are forced to accommodate the totalitarians.

It is far more puzzling that increasing tolerance for, or even fascination with, totalitarianism has characterized the free mainstream churches of the West in the last twenty to thirty years. Last week in Canada, for instance, seventeen senior church leaders urged Prime Minister Brian Mulroney to "confront" U.S. President Ronald Reagan over the latter's attempts to aid the Contra forces in Nicaragua. The signatories included such high Catholic and Protestant dignitaries as United Church Moderator the Very Reverend Robert Smith or the redoubtable Bishop of Victoria, the Most Reverend Remi DeRoo.

Of course, many people urge Reagan to refrain from involving Americans in the armed resistance against the Soviet-backed beachhead of communist totalitarianism in Nicaragua, which is what the Sandinista government is. Some say, for instance, that American public opinion is not yet ready. It may make a lot of military sense to resist at an early stage, but a free society cannot be successfully mobilized to resistance until it awakens to the danger. You have to let the boil ripen—so the argument runs—before you can lance it. While resisting communist expansion at a later date may call for much more sacrifice and pain, it is better to do it when the entire country is united behind the effort.

I don't necessarily agree with this argument, but I see how it can be legitimately advanced. It may be wrong, but it's perfectly honourable. I can even see (though I certainly don't share) the point of those who wouldn't resist the Sandinistas because they *like* totalitarianism. They are at least consistent.

The same is true of arch-conservative mystics who have no illusions about the Sandinistas but believe that suffering is good for the human soul and it leads to spiritual rejuvenation. They point to the Baptist believers in the Gulag or the Catholic Church's revival in Eastern Europe as proof. That, too, is a consistent position, even if it's not remotely to my taste, or to the taste of the most ordinary people who wish to live in peace and liberty without aspiring to sainthood.

But I'm certain (at least I think I'm certain) that the Very Reverend Robert Smith or the Most Reverend Remi DeRoo don't like totalitarianism. I doubt if they are mystics who wish to spiritually rejuvenate South or North Americans through suffering. I don't believe that they are Soviet infiltrators or agents. Nor do I believe that they wish to stop Reagan from aiding the Contras because they abhor interference in sovereign Nicaragua's domestic affairs. These churchmen have never opposed any interference in Asia, Latin America, or Africa, if it was on the side they favoured. They collected monies for all kinds of Marxist guerrillas. No. The simple truth is, they're blind. They like the Sandinistas. They don't recognize them for what they are.

These churchmen look to the communists for social justice. They don't realize that looking to communists for social justice is rather like looking to a crocodile for good table manners. They shifted their irrational faith from God to Marx, in a search for social relevance for which they have much ambition but little talent.

1986

SUBTLE SOVIET APOLOGISTS

Korean Airlines flight 007 deviated from its normal flight path between Anchorage and Seoul on the night of August 30, 1983. Instead of flying on a southwest heading along Kamchatka and the Kuril Islands, the 747 jumbo jet veered nearly three hundred miles further to the right. KAL 007 penetrated Soviet airspace north of Kamchatka. It overflew the peninsula, emerged briefly into international airspace over the Sea of Okhotsk, then re-entered Soviet airspace again. It was hit by a missile fired by a Soviet interceptor over the southern tip of Sakhalin Island. About eight minutes later the airliner crashed into the Sea of Japan, killing 269 men, women, and children.

None of this is in dispute. The Soviet Union first denied shooting down the plane—early Soviet communiqués simply said KAL 007 flew in and out of Soviet airspace and they had no idea what happened to it—but within a few days the Kremlin changed its mind. It said, in essence: "Yes, we did shoot down that 747. So what? We signalled it to land but it wouldn't. It tried to get away. Obviously it had been sent by the Americans to spy on us. Let them send another one, and we'll shoot it down too." Officially, the Soviet Union has never departed from this position. Unofficially, it may have. Within a short time, Soviet apologists and sympathizers in the West were coming up with a different version, whether inspired by Moscow or not.

Actually two different versions: one crude and one subtle. The crude version only consisted of attempts to prove the Soviet assertion—for which the Kremlin offered no evidence whatever—that the Korean jet was spying for the United States. Books like Oliver Clubb's *KAL Flight 007: The Hidden Story*; R.W. Johnson's *Shootdown: Flight 007 and the American Connection*, as well as the more scholarly *Black Box: KAL 007 and the Superpowers* by Alexander Dallin belonged in this group.

Subtle left-wingers were a bit embarrassed by these efforts. First, even to sympathetic eyes the evidence they offered seemed thin to the point of non-existence. More importantly, the argument was not comfortable. What if President Ronald Reagan put spy cameras into a passenger plane with his own hands, telling the pilots to fly over the Sea of Okhotsk and count the Soviet nuclear submarines? It was still a poor excuse to blast a planeload of civilians out of the sky.

Over the years there have been at least a dozen known incidents of Soviet airliners overflying western military installations. The consequences were, at most, brief cancellations of Aeroflot's landing rights. It has never occurred to any civilized nation in peacetime to put a missile through the passenger cabin of an airliner. The Soviets have now done it twice in one region alone—in 1978 they also fired at a Korean passenger plane, causing some loss of life. On both occasions, as they claimed, they did it on purpose.

Ah, yes, said the subtle apologists. But what if the Soviets lied? What if they did not do it on purpose? What if the Soviets mistook KAL 007 for an American reconnaissance plane—there was one such plane somewhere in the vicinity earlier that night—and shot it down thinking it was a military aircraft? What if they only learned about all those women and children the next day?

Now that would only be an accident. From a mistake like that no one could conclude that the communists are brutal maniacs. On the contrary, the lesson we might learn is that we should trust the Soviets instead of counting their submarines all the time. If we only stopped those reconnaissance fights so close to the Soviet border the Russians wouldn't panic and shoot at passenger planes.

Well for heaven's sake—you might ask—if that's what happened why didn't the Soviets say so? Why didn't they say it anyway, whatever happened? For a regime that wishes to appear civilized, one that wishes to inspire confidence in its humanity, it would be the only possible excuse.

Asking this—subtle apologists reply—only shows that you do not understand the Soviet Union. That poor country feels insecure. It has been traumatized by western support for White Russians seventy years ago. It has been hurt by our continual harping on the Gulag or on the invasion of Afghanistan. It has been offended by Ronald Reagan. Being insecure, the Soviets can't risk looking incompetent. They would rather look evil.

I have taken the last two phrases almost verbatim from *The Nation*, where I first encountered the subtle apologists' theory early in 1985. I wrote about it at the time. *The Nation*'s thesis, I thought, was worth framing as an example of the western left's delusional approach to reality.

Recently a book appeared by the Pulitzer Prize–winning American journalist Seymour M. Hersh. Entitled *The Target Is Destroyed*, it is a carefully researched attempt to justify the left's delusion. The book merits discussion in some detail.

Hersh, a top journalist, is a committed man of the left. (A former press secretary for Democratic presidential candidate Senator Eugene H. McCarthy, he won a Pulitzer Prize for breaking the story of the My Lai massacre in Vietnam.) Hersh may have been impatient and uncomfortable with the official Soviet position that they shot down the Korean airliner on the night of August 30, 1983, because the 747 jumbo jet with 269 souls aboard was spying for the United States.

Hersh may have been impatient with the spying charges because there never seemed to be any evidence for it. But he may have been equally uncomfortable because, as a civilized human being, he has understood that even irrefutable proof of spying would not exonerate the Soviets if they deliberately destroyed a scheduled airliner carrying 269 men, women, and children.

And Hersh has wanted to exonerate the Soviet Union. Short of saying it in so many words, he makes no effort to hide it. If we didn't think of the Soviets as ogres, it would reduce tensions and help the cause of peace. However, Moscow's position being of no assistance, Hersh had to embark upon the task of helping the cause of peace on his own.

The thesis of Hersh's book is that the Soviets made a mistake. They thought they were downing an American reconnaissance plane. U.S. officials knew, or at least ought to have known, that the Soviets only made a tragic error. However, in a mixture of Cold War gut reaction and cynical political gamesmanship, they chose to exploit the tragedy. Shooting from the hip, President Ronald Reagan called the Soviets ogres and murderers. Wounded and humiliated, the Kremlin hardened its position. Instead of admitting an innocent mistake, it hurled spying charges at the Americans.

Others have offered the same theory, but Hersh is a skilled advocate. He not only asserts his case, he tries to make it out. The main building blocks of his argument are an analysis of signals intelligence; an analysis of political personalities in Washington; an analysis of conflicts within the American intelligence community; a theory of how the Korean 747 jumbo jet might have gone astray over Soviet airspace; and a further theory of how the Soviets could have confused it with an American RC-135 plane on a "Cobra Ball" reconnaissance mission. The facts are intricate and interesting. It takes a little while to realize that, even piled one upon the other, they do not advance Hersh's argument.

It is a fact that there was an RC-135 in the area earlier, but it hardly follows that Soviet radar must have confused it with the Korean airliner. (As Hersh acknowledges, the two planes never flew parallel to each other. In any case, radar operators routinely identify dozens of planes flying in the same airspace, even in Russia.) It may also be true that signals experts have conflicting opinions and career interests. Most experts do. This, however, hardly proves that the opinions Hersh prefers must be better. Anyway, even Hersh's experts say little more than that the Soviets may not have been sure what they were shooting at.

It may be a fact that, in spite of inaccurate early reports, we never knew what Soviet ground controllers said to the interceptor pilot, but it hardly alters the fact that he shot down the plane or the likelihood that he was acting on orders. It may be a fact that even "flying abeam" a pilot is not necessarily in a position to identify a plane as a Boeing 747, but then he can't identify it as a RC-135 either. This only begs the question of why he was permitted not to identify whatever he was ordered to shoot down.

The Soviets knew about Cobra Ball, but they also knew about Korean airliners. They shot one down only five years earlier. And while it may be a fact that President Reagan would like to assume the worst of the Soviets, it's no more relevant than the fact that Hersh would like to assume the best.

Was it necessary for Soviet commanders in the area to have phoned Premier Andropov, saying: "Chief, we have positively identified an intruder aircraft as a Korean jumbo jet; should we shoot it down?" and for Andropov to have answered: "Please do," before President Reagan was justified in calling the Soviet action brutal murder? Hersh seems to think so. I do not.

Putting his evidence at its highest, all Hersh proves is that the Soviets shot first and asked questions later. That's not incompetence. That's usually defined as recklessness: an intentional disregard for the consequences of one's acts. Our criminal law does equate reckless homicide with murder.

It is easy to be persuaded by Hersh that it would help the cause of peace if we stopped thinking of the Soviets as ogres. It would help even more if the Soviets could be persuaded to stop behaving in a manner that invites the definition.

1986

SELLING OUT AFGHANISTAN

Now that the Soviet Union has begun its vaunted withdrawal from Afghanistan, it's time for my annual column on why Afghanistan is not exactly (or even remotely) the Soviet Union's Vietnam.

Over the last number of years, I've written several pieces outlining my reasons for believing that the parallel is false. It's false no matter how often—or how matter-of-factly—it's being reiterated in academic and media circles. But instead of listing my arguments (interested readers may look for them in my 1986 book *Crocodiles in the Bathtub*), what I'd like to do here is to explore the question from a different angle.

In the Vietnam War, the communists tried to extend their influence, and eventually their control, over Southeast Asia. Between 1959 and 1975, the Americans tried to stop them. When it appeared to the U.S. that it couldn't stop communist expansion at an acceptable price, the Americans withdrew. In Afghanistan, the Soviet Union attempted to gain full control over a region which was already under its influence by the time its tanks crossed the Afghan border in 1979. Nine years later, when it appeared to the Soviets that they had succeeded, they started to withdraw as well.

So the Americans withdrew in evident failure. They withdrew on their enemy's terms. The U.S. knew that Vietnam would not be safe for democracy after the last American helicopter took off from Saigon. The Soviets, however, are pulling back in apparent success. They're withdrawing on their own terms. The Soviet Union believes (maybe wrongly, but that's a different question) that Afghanistan will be safe for communism after the last Russian tank goes home.

The difference is awesome. It's a difference between getting out in the hope that one's objective has been achieved, or getting out in the firm knowledge that it hasn't. It's the difference between victory and defeat.

Which brings me to my central subject. It isn't the official policies of either the Soviet Union or the western democracies, but the attitude of the western left.

It seems that our political left—that is, our socialists or "liberals" as they're called in the U.S.—actually wish to secure Afghanistan for communism. They want to make sure that the region, like many other regions in the world, will be lost to the ideals of democracy or national self-determination. Regarding Afghanistan, this is manifested in the following way: now that the Soviets are going, our left-libbers say, let us make sure that they get what they came for. Let's immediately stop aiding the Afghan "rebels." Let's make certain they are crushed by Moscow's puppet regime in Kabul.

In other words, let us make the Kremlin a free gift of whatever it may not have secured by its own military efforts. The Soviets wanted control over Afghanistan? Fine, if the Soviets pull out, let's make sure they get it.

Imagine the Americans agreeing to the 1973 Paris peace accords on condition that Moscow abandon the Viet Cong and guarantee a democratic government in Saigon with friendly ties to the West. That would have been some "peace with honour." (In fact, it would have meant achieving our war objectives.) Of course, our American friends signed the Vietnam peace treaty in the full knowledge that, with Moscow's continued support to Hanoi, Saigon would eventually fall to the communists—as it did about two years later. We lost our war. God forbid that we should expose the Soviets to a similar risk.

Why is our political left uncomfortable with even a chance, a remote chance, that Afghan's freedom fighters may triumph on their own after a Soviet withdrawal? It can't be because they *like* communism (at least, they always say that they don't). It can't be because they oppose Islamic resurgence: they usually support it (at least against western,

Israeli, or just plain democratic interests). It can't be because they're against national self-determination as such; they're usually for it (maybe not for Poles or Sikhs or Ukrainians but whenever it takes some anti-American or anti-western form). So what is it? Is it self-hatred? Is it simply cowardice?

In 1938, the West delivered Czechoslovakia to Hitler on a silver platter. If today we have few friends left, it's because of a habit we developed around that time. Bluntly put, it's the habit of selling out our allies. It's the habit of trying to buy peace from our enemies, offering them in exchange the dead bodies of our friends.

1988

CHINESE SHOCK TREATMENT

Did anything good come out of the recent massacre in Tiananmen Square? This was the question somebody asked me the other day, and I wasn't sure how to answer. Obviously nothing came out of it that would be worth the lives of God knows how many idealistic young students who asked for nothing except those freedoms that would be every person's birthright in a normal country. Still, the communist tanks in Beijing may turn out to save the lives of some idealistic young people elsewhere by teaching us all a few lessons. Is it still necessary in 1989 for such lessons to be taught, especially at such a price? Well, let readers judge for themselves.

Ambassador Earl Drake, Canada's envoy to China and described by the *Globe and Mail* as one of Ottawa's most respected Asian policy-makers, was quoted as follows on June 14:

"We were all so terribly naïve....We've never been objective about China. People have closed their eyes to things they wouldn't have ignored anywhere else. They wanted so much to love this place. Because of all this emotional involvement, we feel betrayed."

I usually read statements like this with mixed emotions. On the one hand, I appreciate the sincerity of an honourable man admitting his mistake. I also feel gratified when the things I have been writing for years—to wit, that our policy-makers are naïve, that they're not objective about China, and they're closing their eyes to things they'd never ignore anywhere else—are now confirmed by one of the most respected mandarins in Ottawa.

I feel personally vindicated. After all (along with other journalists such as Peter Worthington, Lubor J. Zink, William Stevenson, Eric Margolis, or Barbara Amiel, to name only a few) I have been cold-shouldered or bad-mouthed by my peers in the media for suggesting precisely what our ambassador to China is now admitting. It would take a saint to be above all this, and lately I haven't been bucking for sainthood.

On the other hand, I feel a little irked. Just *why* would some of our people in Ottawa "want so much to love" communist China? It's one thing for young students to be "terribly naïve" when confronted by the complex phenomena of modern totalitarianism, whose twists and turns or high-sounding slogans might mask its murderous nature. It's quite another for learned academics, experienced journalists, or respected Ottawa diplomats to make the same error. The innocence with which a brave youth may sail into a storm is not nearly so fetching when exhibited by a ship's captain. In a professional seaman, entrusted with his passengers' lives, naïveté about storms at sea may amount to criminal negligence.

I won't accuse our opinion- and policy-makers of criminal negligence, but I will say that in recent years many of them have lacked the proficiency and discernment which would have entitled them to their positions. I will say that many of them have drawn their salary without deserving it. As proof, I'm content to rely on the statement of Ambassador Drake, one of Ottawa's most respected Asian experts.

As to the good that might come from the massacre in Beijing—well, for one thing, it has finally let our news media actually witness an example of totalitarian repression. This luxury is not normally available to journalists, except in old-fashioned "right-wing" dictatorships, such as Chile or South Africa. It's one of the reasons why South Korea has always had a worse press in the West than North Korea. Totalitarianism provides few photo opportunities.

It may be good for people who want "so much to love" communist China to have their illusions shattered once in a while. I doubt if it will cure them forever, because left-wing illusions have remarkable regenerative powers.

In the postwar years the opportunity for a permanent cure has presented itself on many occasions. For instance, chances for such a cure ranged from Nikita Khrushchev's speech to the 20th Party Congress exposing Stalin's crimes to Mikhail Gorbachev's latest statements exposing the crimes of Stalin's successors. You may note that I'm referring only to statements from the horse's mouth—in other words, the Kremlin's own confessions. Anybody who isn't cured of his illusions by those isn't likely to be cured by anything I might say.

They may be cured, though, by things they witness with their own eyes, which is why Tiananmen Square may not have been in vain. "Must then a Christ perish in torment in every age to save those who have no imagination?" asks a character in G. B. Shaw's play *Saint Joan*. The answer, alas, is probably yes.

1989

A TALE OF TWO SYSTEMS

Trying to compare two different countries is risky. So is an attempt to draw a parallel between two different political systems. No parallel will ever be exact. Comparisons, at best, can only serve as an illustration. Nevertheless, for the sole purpose of illustrating so-called progressive (and specifically Canadian) attitudes, I will risk drawing a modest parallel between the U.S.S.R. and South Africa. Despite many obvious differences, both countries and systems have arrived at similar crossroads in 1989.

Simply put, the similarity is this: the leadership of both countries has recognized during the 1980s that their fundamental ideas are untenable. To put it even more simply, both regimes realize that their systems stink. They're unacceptable to the majority of their own populations and unacceptable to the world. They're both morally bankrupt (also economically bankrupt, in the case of the Soviet Union). They must be completely overhauled. Critics have known this for a long time, of course. The point is that now the leaders themselves appear to realize it.

When not just the opponents of a political system, but its own ruling circles, its own beneficiaries, realize that the old edifice is crumbling—and maybe also that it richly deserves to crumble and *will* crumble unless they do something about it—a new and dangerous situation arises. It's a bit like a curve in the road. If you disregard it and keep going straight you'll end up in a ditch. But if you try to negotiate it at too great a speed, you'll flip and end up in the ditch anyway. This is why both Mikhail Gorbachev and F.W. de Klerk are trying to go slowly.

The equivalents of inertia, gravity, and centrifugal force exist on a political or cultural plane as much as they do in the world of physics. A sharp change of direction can result in an upset. In turns, safety lies in taking it easy.

De Klerk, who seems to be South Africa's Gorbachev in some ways, is attempting to take it easy. Still, both leaders may be genuinely trying to turn a corner. Both make near-identical pronouncements on the need for basic change. In de Klerk's language *perestroika* and *glasnost* are termed "reform" and "renewal." South Africa's new president takes pains to exclude the idea of "domination" in his proposed constitutional model, and to assure "participation for everyone."

Gorbachev and de Klerk also seem to try to gradually suit action to words. The Soviet leader is farther ahead than the South African in this regard, but he has had years at the helm. De Klerk has only had a few weeks. Still, he's now reportedly considering the release of some political prisoners, including Nelson Mandela.

Too little, too late? You bet—but the same thing could be said of Gorbachev's reforms. That's precisely what is being said about it by opponents in his own country. Gorbachev doesn't get many kudos for his attempts at changing the Soviet system. There are only new riots and demonstrations demanding more changes at a quicker pace. The same thing is happening in South Africa. Riots, bombings, protests, and demonstrations outstrip government concessions by a rate of ten to one. The more Gorbachev and de Klerk concede, the more their critics and opponents demand.

To avoid any misunderstanding, I don't blame the impatient critics—victims, really—of either apartheid or communism. My sole point is that riots, demands, bombings, and the rest are examples of political momentum at work. The quicker the pace around the turn, the stronger the centrifugal force. The more reforms, the more riots. It's as simple as that.

When it comes to Gorbachev's predicament, our "progressives" have no trouble recognizing this. They don't need any convincing that Gorbachev must proceed slowly, or that the victims of communism must learn to be patient. On the contrary, all left-libbers counsel patience. They urge full co-operation with the new (we hope) Kremlin: full co-operation and close economic ties.

But when it comes to de Klerk, left-libbers insist it ought to be business as usual. That is, no business at all, only continued ostracism, condemnation, and economic sanctions. Canada's policy should be to encourage the bloodthirstiest factions of the communist-dominated African National Congress, instead of the forces for possible renewal, reconciliation, and peace.

Someone could object that de Klerk's "reforms" are attempts to save a system that shouldn't be saved. This may be true, but it's equally true of Gorbachev's *perestroika*. In any event, what are the alternatives in South Africa? Back to square one? Or forward to a blood bath? Are they the progressive preference?

1989

WE SHOULD HAVE SAID NO

The young lady who looks after my teeth (no easy task) also sends me newspaper clippings once in a while—to make sure, I guess, that no idiocy in the Western world escapes my attention. She must figure that as long as may teeth are okay it doesn't matter what happens to my blood pressure.

The old gore certainly hit the ceiling when, as a result of one of her clippings, I learned of our government's position on Canada's collaboration with late Romanian dictator Nicolae Ceausescu. As I must have written at least half a dozen times, Atomic Energy of Canada Ltd. not only sold Candu nuclear reactors to the communist tyrant, but persisted in collaborating with him even after it became evident that Ceausescu was using conscripted labour to build his plant at Cernavodă, one hundred miles east of Bucharest.

Conscripted labour means slave labour. The term may be emotional, but it's perfectly accurate. Conscripts and prisoners—not to mention plain citizens ordered from their homes to do forced labour at designated sites—are slaves. Canada's nuclear reactor wasn't Ceausescu's only project that was being built by slave labour, but it was certainly one of them.

Nor was Romania the only communist country to use prisoners and conscripts on its industrial and construction projects. Czechoslovakia did it as well. (China, and maybe even the Soviet Union, are doing it even today.) However, in recent years Romania has probably been the only country in Europe to actually uproot ordinary citizens from their towns and villages and impress them into labour gangs.

This was common knowledge. As common as the knowledge that blacks in South Africa lacked fundamental civil liberties. True, the media didn't spend as much energy on slavery in Romania as they did on apartheid in South Africa, but it was occasionally mentioned even in the Canadian press. Now it appears the only people who had no inkling about it were Atomic Energy of Canada Ltd. and, of course, Canada's External Affairs Department. The very people who never wasted an opportunity to wax indignant about South Africa.

Candu's president Donald Lawson reportedly said that he had no evidence of slave labour being used at Cernavodă. External Affairs spokesman Mark Entwistle offered that our government didn't protest to Ceausescu because it couldn't verify these things to its satisfaction. "We've never had independent confirmation," Entwistle was quoted as saying.

Gee whiz. They must have tried real hard. I wonder what kind of confirmation Entwistle—or his boss, Joe Clark—would have needed to satisfy them on the nature of Ceausescu's regime? Eyewitness accounts? There were reams of it. Escaped Romanians have been talking about what was going on in their country for years. Even Candu's president acknowledges now that his Canadian employees have been aware of "conscripts" working on the Cernavodă project.

Canada has always had diplomats in Romania. Whether or not they could actually meet slave labourers, the nature of the system couldn't be a secret to anybody who as much as walked along the streets of Bucharest. Even communist Hungary has been protesting the treatment of Romania's ethnic minorities, at least since 1988. (Many slave-labourers were ethnic Hungarians.) Lieutenant-General Ion Mihai Pacepa, Ceausecu's former spy chief, wrote a book about the regime after his defection in 1978. Of course, even before this book appeared Pacepa had been debriefed. The essence of his hair-raising information had to be available to Canada's intelligence community.

Other ex-agents who defected in the early 1980s described particulars of Ceausescu's efforts to have people assassinated in the West and to steal classified nuclear technology under the guise of purchasing reactors from Canada. Is this news? Are we to believe, for instance, that no one in External Affairs has ever seen a copy of M.P. Haiducu's *J'ai refusé de tuer*?

It's too ridiculous to continue. Brian Mulroney, Joe Clark, and others at External or AECL knew everything. Why did they choose to keep silent? You tell me. Perhaps because they thought that silence was good for business. Perhaps because communist atrocities, as opposed to South African ones, did not offend their sensibilities.

With Ceausescu gone, there's suddenly plenty of "independent confirmation." Until three weeks ago our government could see, hear, and speak no evil. And now that it has found its voice, it's using it to insult our intelligence.

1990

THE PROBLEM WITH PEACENIKS

From the beginning of the Gulf crisis, and especially from the moment President George Bush drew a line in the sand at the border of Saudi Arabia for Saddam Hussein, peaceniks have been crawling out of the woodwork with renewed vigour. Few peace activists have professed any liking for Saddam. Few, if any, disputed the fact he was a bloody tyrant. Few, if any, endorsed his invasion of Kuwait. Most peaceniks simply declared that we mustn't employ force to stop Saddam's efforts to rape the Middle East.

At first, this included even the defence of Saudi Arabia and the enforcement of economic sanctions against Iraq, since both meant deploying soldiers in the region with an attendant risk of war. (Later, of course, peaceniks argued we should have given sanctions "a chance," conveniently forgetting that they started out by opposing sanctions, or at least opposing the military presence that sanctions require.)

Peacemongers have long fascinated me. They wouldn't have, if I had thought of them as communist sympathizers or agents. *That* would have explained everything about them—but I've always rejected the notion (taken as an article of faith by many critics of western peace movements) that peaceniks were simply Moscow's dupes or supporters.

A few Kremlin agents had no doubt infiltrated the peace movement occasionally. After all, agents of the Kremlin had infiltrated most western institutions at one time or another, including even our defence and intelligence establishments. But I can confidently say that at least half the peace activists I've ever known were agents of no one. They didn't even have any illusions about communism.

Over the years my own friends have included dozens of writers, artists, housewives, clerics, academics, or students of the type who make up the bulk of the peace movement to this day. As far as I could tell, they hadn't been duped by Moscow. Even the other fifty per cent, the pinko peaceniks, seemed to have relatively few illusions about the Kremlin itself (though they often had all kinds of vague Marxist or anti-capitalist illusions).

However, my greatest fascination has always been with the first fifty per cent—in other words, with my peacenik friends who were not only not Moscow's dupes, but had virtually no "new-left" illusions of any kind. It was their motives and thought-processes that puzzled me the most.

I'm not qualified to psychoanalyze anyone. Anyway, I happen to think it's presumptuous to psychoanalyze others just because they have different social or political views, so I'll leave this distasteful practice to my left-wing acquaintances. Rather than trying to dissect the emotional makeup of peace activists, I'll restrict myself to pointing out what, to me, seems like the greatest irony in their position.

I repeat, I'm not talking about the handful of peaceniks who may abhor, consciously or unconsciously, freedom and other western liberal values. I'm not talking about fanatical supporters of Islamic fundamentalism, Marxism, or the PLO, or about those who have a *belle de jour* complex about terrorists and tyrants. There's no irony in *their* position: it is perfectly logical and consistent. Who else would they try to shield but Saddam?

I'm talking solely about those who genuinely dislike war and violence, who truly oppose slavery and torture. I'm talking about people whose real, heartfelt political creed embraces parliamentary democracy, liberty, peace, and other good things listed in the United Nations' charter. In short, I'm talking about my own friends. People who share most of my own values and who, I firmly believe, amount to at least half of all peace activists.

Here's the irony: the very values they have been so anxious to protect have consistently prompted my peacenik friends to shield those forces that are the most dangerous to those values. Over the last twenty-five years their love of peace prompted peace activists to stand up for some of the nastiest warmongers in Asia, Europe, the Middle East, and Latin America. Their love of peace prompted them to make it harder for us to stop those tyrants and assassins who were the greatest danger to peace.

In the last few months, their love of peace would have prompted them to give Saddam—about whom they had no illusions—time in which to acquire nuclear weapons. Their horror of bloodshed would have prompted them to help a man, whose ambitions had by then caused the death of nearly a million people, to shed more blood than anyone before in the Middle East.

1991

7.

BEATING

CADDIES

Notes on Amusing Things

How Daddy Founded Feminism

When I was growing up, I'd often see my father cooking up a storm in the kitchen. I use the word "storm" advisedly. Whenever Daddy had a bout of the culinaries, the kitchen looked as if a tornado had hit it. Afterwards, the cook and the maid would spend hours sorting through the wreckage. The meal, however, was delicious. Daddy's fried chicken blood with onions was the marvel of Eastern Europe.

The reason my father preferred to do the cooking, as he often pointed out, was that good cooking required "soul," a quality of which women were in notoriously short supply. This was why the chefs in all great restaurants were men. "It's not the recipes," my father would say. "The recipes are in a book. The ingredients are available at the market. But the verve, the *élan*, the soul! That's why you can't leave cooking to women."

My mother never argued the point. Though secretly she believed that she was a better cook than my father, she was perfectly happy to be excluded from the kitchen. She drew, read books, listened to music, and worked as an executive assistant to a publisher. The latter was an occupation which, as she agreed with my father, required little soul.

It was only to placate the maid and the cook, the other two women in the household, that my mother would plot to keep father away from slaving over a hot stove too often. "Plot" may be too subtle a word. "Rosie will quit if you set foot in the kitchen," my mother would say, "and if Rosie quits, I'll leave you. So, what do you want for dinner tonight?"

"Venison at the Hotel Ritz," my father would reply with conviction. "I won't eat Rosie's slop."

Under these circumstances it is not surprising that I grew up believing:

a) A man's place is in the kitchen,
b) Restaurants serve the best food,
c) Women have no soul, and
d) Women should work in publishing.

I was twenty-one when I arrived in Canada and, of course, immediately contracted a case of acute culture shock. Other immigrants may get the same disease because of language problems or, if they come from Europe, on discovering that normal windows, opening horizontally as all windows should, are called "French doors" in Canada and are rarely used. The windows Canadians prefer slide vertically up and down, at least in theory, because in practice they're usually stuck.

This didn't bother me. I wasn't surprised that people who prefer silly windows should also prefer English or French, two notoriously difficult languages, instead of German or Hungarian, languages even a child could speak where I came from. No, my culture shock sprang from the discovery that Canadians think:

a) Cooking is woman's work, and
b) Home cooking is the best.

I didn't even realize at first that in Canada—this was back in the mid-'50s, remember—very few women worked in publishing above the level of filing clerks. That would really have put the lid on it for me. Imagine a country in which they put women in the kitchen, where they are only in the way, while they're forcing men to do the soulless work of publishing. Crazy.

Even more astounding was the insistence with which restaurants were recommending their services those days: "As Good As Home Cooking." Even big manufacturers of food products suggested that their canned macaroni was "Like Grandma Used To Make." Well, really. In my family Grandma wouldn't ever have seen a macaroni in its natural state, and had she encountered one by accident she would have slapped at it with her parasol, then asked the gardener to remove it. Never mind canning food, a truly complex undertaking. If you had asked my father, he would have said that Grandma couldn't do anything, except maybe publish.

This was why, when women's liberation eventually came to Canada, I greeted it with a sigh of relief. There, finally was a group of people suggesting some sensible things. First, they wanted to remove women from the kitchen where they had been doing incalculable damage for centuries. Excellent. Then, since they wanted women to work in real jobs, they would force more and more families to eat in restaurants where they might be served professionally prepared food and acquire some sophistication in their tastes. In time, I thought, this may even lead to the demise of peanut butter. It may improve the culinary and nutritional habits of an entire nation.

Then, as the woman's movement started gathering strength, it began putting forward some very specific recommendations about the role of women in publishing. Essentially, they wanted more women in key positions to spread the word in books, newspapers, and magazines that women should get out of the kitchen and into publishing where they belong. Exactly as my father had recommended many years ago. Who would have guessed? Daddy was one of the founders of modern feminism and he didn't even know it. One day they should erect a statue to him.

Now, fifteen years after feminism has acquired the status of state religion, my father would still agree with most of its recommendations. He would certainly agree with the proposition that, on the whole, women should run things. In our family they always have. He might balk at the suggestion that women have souls—which, though seldom stated specifically, kind of underlies the entire women's movement— but since he has never had strong views on souls anyway he'd probably let it pass.

I think my father would only draw the line at the idea that women can back up cars in a straight line as well as anybody else. He would definitely veto that notion. It would offend his common sense.

1985

A Tale of Two Sisters

I am going to tell about the girl from British Guiana. You can tell how old this story is by the fact that I'm calling her country British Guiana, which it hasn't been called since, I think, about 1966. It was then or thereabouts that the People's Progressive Party stopped shooting at the People's National Congress, and vice versa, long enough for Britain to quickly declare the little colony politically mature and independent.

Since that time it's been called Guyana, and has a flag that looks like a pyramid in the process of tipping over on its right side. This, presumably, is to distinguish it from nearby Saint Lucia whose flag has an upright pyramid, or Grenada which has two pyramids embarked on a head-on collision. (I'm not trying to put down Guyana's flag. As a design idea, you can only do so much with pyramids.)

In any event, by the time I met the girl from British Guiana, she was no longer from British Guiana or even Guyana, but from Canada. She was a rather splendid-looking girl, with auburn hair and large green eyes, complete with a shapely figure and a very white skin with just a hint of freckles. She was of Scottish ancestry, her people having settled in British Guiana's capital, Georgetown, somewhere in the middle of the last century. I thought it showed excellent sense on the part of Air Canada to hire her as a stewardess.

I met Sarah, which is not remotely her real name, in a restaurant. She was passing by the table where I was sitting with an acquaintance who knew her. "This is Sarah," he said to me, noting my appreciative glance.

"Hello," I said to Sarah. "Will you join us for a cup of coffee?"

"Okay," she replied, sitting down. She said it unhesitatingly, but without any enthusiasm.

This attitude, as I discovered in the coming months, was fundamental to Sarah's mental make-up. She was unfailingly well-spoken, polite, and agreeable, but she seemed to be devoid of the slightest preference or animation. Her invariable reply to any suggestion was "okay," accompanied by a barely perceptible shrug. How about a movie? Okay. How about dinner? Okay. How about coming up to my place for a drink? Okay. How about going to bed? Okay.

This was the way Sarah responded not only to all suggestions, but also to all inquiries. How do you like your job? It's okay. Was it fun going to school in Georgetown? It was okay. Shall we take the car, Sarah? It's okay with me. Or shall we walk? Walking's okay.

It was exasperating, but it also made me curious. Surely no human being can be completely indifferent to life. Everyone must have some preferences. There must be something—an activity, a thought, a person, a memory—that would make the eyes of Sarah sparkle or bring a smile to her lips.

But there seemed to be nothing. I have the patience of a saint, but after two weeks I was ready to throttle her. Except, of course, you can't throttle a perfectly nice and agreeable girl. Even throttling the other kind is viewed as a misdemeanour these days. "Methinks it's like a camel," I said to her once, recalling Hamlet's famous exchange with old Polonius, after Sarah said "it's okay" in response to two completely different suggestions. If my remark puzzled her, she didn't show it.

"Well, do you like *Hamlet*?"

"It's okay."

All right. As a writer (I said to myself) my job is not to throttle people, but to find out what makes them tick. People are interesting. All people love or hate something; they must. "Listen, Sarah," I said, ever so slightly gritting my teeth, "it's my task to find out about you. I have to discover what moves and excites you. I will see a flicker of enthusiasm on your features one day, or a flicker of annoyance: I don't care which. And if you now say *that's okay* to my proposition, I'll shoot you right between the eyes."

"Okay," she replied, as we both knew she would.

I spent the next few months researching Sarah. I took her flying and motorbiking; I took her to the opera and to the ballet. I talked to her and I invited her to talk. I introduced her to other people and tried observing her behaviour. She behaved with them as she behaved with me. Arousing her acquiescence was a breeze; arousing her enthusiasm, impossible.

We were sitting on the verandah of a friend one day, a seafood fanatic who was preparing a radical meal consisting of steamer clams, limpets, holothurians, and some other echinoderms. While he was in the kitchen, Sarah, on my invitation, was telling me about her child-hood in Georgetown. Her parents, she related, had a fairly big house there, situated in a garden surrounded by a spiked iron fence. It was in that garden that she had spent most of her time as a child in the company of her younger sister. Sarah answered my questions about her childhood as she answered everything else: unsmiling, and without a trace of animation. I was beginning to lose all hope. "What about your parents' garden?" I asked her. "Is there a memorable incident that stands out in your mind?"

"Not really," she replied, then hesitated. "Well, once my sister...." She stopped for a second, then continued. "We had this big tree growing right next to the fence, you see, and my sister wanted to climb it. She did get to the top, but then a limb broke and she fell out of the tree. Onto the fence. The way she fell, one of the iron spikes went right through her leg."

Sarah stopped and looked at me. It was amazing. The transfiguration was sudden and complete. Her features were no longer immobile. There was spirit and animation in her green eyes. Her face flushed, as if suffused with the one pleasant memory of her life: the memory of a younger sister impaled on an iron fence. For the first time ever, her lips parted in a warm, human, delicious smile.

1987

WHY I LOVE OPERA, & FIND IT IRRESISTIBLY FUNNY

My fascination with opera goes back to a Turkish lady called Fatime. More precisely, it goes back to a contest between my uncle's sense of balance and Fatime's abdominal muscle.

I should warn readers who expect a salacious story that they will be disappointed. No lady's abdominal muscle held much interest for me at the time, perhaps because I was six years old. My parents had asked me to join them at a dinner party for Fatime, a retired diva, who was visiting us with her husband. We often had operatic visitors, because my father (who had been a baritone at the Viennese Opera before giving himself up to the world of business) seemed to enjoy them, but Fatime's party was the first I was invited to attend.

As I remember it (later my mother and father were to dispute some details), the party began with Fatime standing against the wall in the blue salon. As a rule, my parents entertained only cultural guests in the blue salon. Business guests were usually herded into the dining hall, underneath Beethoven's deathmask, where the seating arrangements were more formal. But that night it was only Fatime with her husband, along with my uncle and aunt, and maybe two or three other people. This was probably why I was allowed to take my meal with the guests, though of course I was served at a separate table.

Fatime spoke German fearlessly, albeit with an intriguing Turkish flavour. Her rich alto was booming across the room. "Belly is rock, rock is belly," she declared, as if she were quoting Keats. "The voice is all belly. You say to me, 'A singer has the voice by the throat?' I reply: 'Ha-ha! I show you.'" Her glance fell on my unfortunate uncle. "I want that you push me!" she commanded. "Not where you sit like mushroom, but standing on legs like real man."

I looked up from my plate. Clearly, the conversation was taking an interesting turn. Fatime, her splendid abdominal muscle wrapped in a minimum of silk, was resting her back against the wall. "In belly," she instructed my uncle. "Not poke-poke-poke like chicken, but push! Make a ball with your, how you call them, fingers."

"With your fist, you know, there's a good man," suggested the Freiherr von X., whose name I no longer recall, but who had the rare fortune to be married to Fatime. "I often do it at home. You won't get any peace until you push her."

"You push like chicken," Fatime said to her husband, not without tenderness. "Maybe he push like man."

My uncle certainly had the bulk; what he may have lacked was the heart. He was a manufacturer of red as well as yellow bricks, born as Geza Stiglitz, but by then the possessor of a much more melodious name. My father, a man with some capacity for mental cruelty, had nicknamed him "Stiglitz the Nimrod" many years earlier, soon after learning that Uncle had joined a rather exclusive hunting club. This was not because my father objected to people shooting—or even to people named Stiglitz—but only because he objected to people named Stiglitz shooting for social reasons.

My uncle, who was strictly a social shooter, hesitated for a second, then essayed a tentative push against the undulating silk. "Ha!" said

Fatime derisively. "My nanny-goat push more, when little girl in Anatolia. Push like you give birth to locomotive."

A suggestible man, my uncle paled. "Please, dear lady," he whispered, "I'm quite heavy, I could hurt you by accident."

"Push!"

My uncle closed his eyes and began to push. He was pushing, still cautiously at first, then in earnest. Finally, he was driving his fist into Fatime's abdomen hard enough for the carpet to begin sliding under his feet.

"Good, just hold table with free hand," Fatime advised him contemptuously. "Now I will sing you."

My father, who must have known what was coming, had already seated himself at the piano. The black Bechstein roared to life, and so did Fatime's abdominal muscle. "*Stride la vampa!*" she began ominously, in the accents of Verdi's gypsy lady, her famous role in Vienna and Milan. Frightened and hopelessly off balance, with the rug slowly slipping out from under his feet, my uncle was no longer in a position to withdraw his fist. "*Sinistra splende sui volti orribili,*" Fatime insisted, staring into the middle distance. "*La tetra fiamma che s'alza al ciel!*"

Picture, if you will, the situation from my point of view. I was not particularly backward for my age, but until then I had led a rather sheltered life. It was my first operatic dinner party, and I was anxious to make a good impression, but it was a challenging spectacle for a six-year-old. There was Stiglitz the Nimrod, as red in the face as any of his bricks, balancing his entire bulk upon the belly of a well-dressed Turkish lady, who by then was screaming "*Grido feroce di morte levasi!*" at the top of her lungs.

Any healthy boy could see that it was to be a race between the aria and the heavy Persian rug, which was sliding slowly but as inexorably as a glacier from under my uncle's feet. Fatime, unperturbed, looked quite ready to go the distance. My father would eventually explain that Uncle did have an outside chance, because Azucena's tale was not a long one by Verdi's standards. But my uncle, who had never been exposed to *Il Trovatore*, had no way of knowing that. His expression soon began showing that abandonment of all hope that the Italian travel writer Dante Alighieri remarked upon in connection with one of his trips.

A brick manufacturer leaning at a forty-five-degree angle is not a dignified sight, and it doesn't help matters when he appears to be coaxing dark and powerful musical notes from the belly of a fat lady in silk. My behaviour didn't help, either. The fact is, I pointed my finger at them and began turning purple.

Later my father called me an annoying child. It was not a supportive comment, but it was not inaccurate. To say that I laughed would not begin to describe my reaction at the end of Azucena's lament. I howled. I hooted. I'm afraid I actually stomped my feet, while my poor Uncle slid slowly to the floor, still hinged, as it were, to Fatime's belly by one fist.

My musical education had commenced some years before this incident. My father believed that any civilized child should be able to play Clementi's *Sonatina* by the age of four, but my disgraceful behaviour at the dinner party convinced both of my parents that Herr Miller's piano lessons were insufficient. Opera especially, my father felt, had to be approached in a different light. "For example," he said to me, "ignorant people look at *Lohengrin*, and they say that you can't rely on German swans running exactly on schedule.

"Well, of course, any fool knows that you can't rely on German swans. The great Schlezak discovered that at the Metropolitan in New York when they dragged his own swan offstage before he could mount it, causing him to step into the river. But it made no difference. Schlezak, a tenor of great dignity drunk or sober, simply asked *"Wann kommt der nächste Schwann?"* as if he were at a train station in Berlin, and everybody knew that he was still Parsifal's son, damn it! You don't measure opera by puny standards."

Perhaps it should be noted that this phase in my life occurred in the spring of 1941. Though Hitler was already preparing for Operation Barbarossa, the Molotov-Ribbentrop pact still held. Initially, the pact had deeply disturbed everyone in our liberal circles, except my father, who thought that it was a perfect treaty between two identical systems. "Isn't it logical for the Nazis to be allied with the Communists?" he kept consoling his suicidal friends. "Isn't it natural? The unnatural thing would be for the great democracies to be allied with either one of them."

As it turned out, my operatic education continued against the backdrop of just such an unnatural development. "So Stalin is now a friend of Roosevelt's," my father offered, "yet some people find it incredible that Azucena should throw her own baby into the fire instead of the old Count di Luna's. Well, Azucena was a simple gypsy, while Roosevelt, for instance, is a man of education. He is Felix Frankfurter's buddy. Yet, if you ask me, if Roosevelt doesn't watch out, he could end up throwing his baby into the fire by mistake, as easily as Azucena."

Opera does arouse a certain kind of enthusiasm in people, my father explained. He gave the example of an incident that had happened at the Budapest Opera, when Anna Medek performed there shortly after the turn of the century. The orchestra was conducted by the famous Toccani, and at the end of the first act a gentleman set up a rhythmic chant, shouting "Medek! Toccani!" over and over again. He obviously liked the performance, and he may have forgotten that in Hungarian the words he kept yelling amounted to a statement of his intention to defecate without delay. "Go, by all means," someone said to him at last. "But why must you announce it?"

My father likened the incident to the Nuremberg rallies. "You shouldn't stretch the parallel too far, of course," he cautioned, "but it's a fact that many people don't know what they are shouting when they get carried away."

Operas were absurd, but they were majestic; it was silly for people to criticize them in the name of reality, my father suggested, when reality was just as absurd and often devoid of any majesty. "I've known some modern realists," he mused, "who walked out of *Tosca* because of Scarpia's behaviour in the second act. Well, perhaps Scarpia does act a little melodramatically—but then I've watched the selfsame realists sitting glued to the radio, listening to Mussolini speak."

Some years later—this is an aside—my father and I were watching a newsreel showing the bodies of Mussolini and his mistress hanging by the heels from a pole outside a gas station. "Scarpia?" I asked him.

Sotto voce, but with the wicked smile of someone proved correct by history itself, my father sang his reply: "*E avanti a lui tremava tutta Roma!*" One could sympathize with Madame Tosca's curtain line: by 1945, indeed, it was hard to imagine all of Rome trembling before a charred side of beef, in trousers, hanging from a pole. However, in 1941 the curtain was still a long way from falling.

I continued my operatic education while the fall of Moscow seemed imminent to many realists who considered operas absurd. My father was virtually alone in the view that Hitler would have had second thoughts about invading Russia if he had known, in addition to his favourite composer Wagner, the operas of Borodin. The German high command should have especially listened to Prince Igor's great baritone air, "*Oh dahtye, dahtye mnye svobodu,*" which gave some indication of how Russians might react to the idea of foreign, as opposed to domestic, servitude. My father immediately sang Igor's aria for me, in a comic version, of course. He accompanied himself on the black Bechstein, roaring with laughter, until my mother bade him stop.

Soon after our musical soirée, my socially ambitious uncle Nimrod was taken to a labour camp called Bor, quite famous in its time, in Nazi-occupied Serbia. Fatime and the Freiherr von X. began holding seances as the best means of communicating with their only son, Martin, who had disappeared at the Russian front. Except for the *Götterdämmerung*, I don't remember hearing any operas. The music on the radio was mainly brass in those years. The Gestapo had discovered other uses for piano wire.

1988

HAND ME MY BEATING IRON

London Times columnist Barbara Amiel sends me true stories once in a while from the British publication *Private Eye*. This magazine, as its name implies, features tales of alleged veracity. (I certainly hope the stories are true for the sake of the mental health of British journalists. It would take a very sick imagination to invent them.)

Amiel sends me these stories just for a chuckle, though she feels one or two may inspire me to comment. Until now this hasn't happened. Commenting on *Private Eye*'s "true stories" would be, in the immortal phrase of the bard, painting the lily or gilding the gold. However, one item in *Private Eye* is an exception. It is a story which I feel does call for comment.

In June 1988, Sudhar Varma, honorary secretary of the Chandigarh Golf Club, was moved to write a strong memo to members warning them about what he considered the ill-advised practice of beating caddies during play. "This is an extremely bad habit," Varma wrote, "especially on the part of players who are losing. If there are any further reports of caddy beating, strict disciplinary action will be taken against the member." Well, I do have something to say about this. I think Varma is well-intentioned, but he is taking too broad a position on the matter.

First, I think that to flatly say, as Varma does, that caddies should not be beaten is a rather sweeping statement. I'd certainly agree that caddies should not be beaten as a rule, but surely we all know of exceptions. For instance, Varma doesn't distinguish between caddies being beaten in cold blood and caddies being beaten in the heat of the moment. I think the difference is enormous.

Second, why would Varma say caddies should not be beaten *during play*? When exactly would Varma prefer caddies to be beaten? After play caddies often disperse, and finding them might pose significant difficulties for members. Also, in my experience, the impulse to beat caddies diminishes after play. In addition, beating caddies after play would be rather vengeful and should be discouraged on that account alone.

Finally, why does Varma single out *losing* players for his censure? Surely it is when players are losing that the desire to beat caddies arises most acutely. Does Varma seriously suggest it would be better for winning players to engage in such acts? But that would be quite senseless. Does he really want members to exchange sensible expressions of irritation for wanton, senseless acts of violence?

I hesitate to use so strong a word, but I find Varma's suggestion barbaric. On the contrary, it is only losing players, and strictly during play, who should engage in the act of beating caddies. Only when angered or upset, of course, and even then in line with all usual requirements of sportsmanship.

However, I would add one caveat that Varma omits—possibly because it's common sense and he may assume everybody knows it. I think, however, it's better to spell these things out. Members should carefully commit their own weight to memory, then compare it with the weight of their caddies. They should do so before commencing the beating, not later. They should never begrudge the few seconds this takes, no matter how irritated or upset they may be.

I recall meeting a sportsman once who forgot this simple precaution. He started beating a caddy who was nearly two stones heavier than himself. I bumped into this gentleman several months after the event and I must say he was still a dismal sight.

1989

THE BIRD AND THE BIKERS

I like birds, but I don't know much about them. The only ones I can reliably recognize are pigeons. When a bird screamed at me the other day, all I could tell about it was that it wasn't a pigeon. Pigeons rarely scream at me when I approach them.

This bird went off like a beeper—in fact, that's how I noticed it as it was sitting in my path, flapping its wings. My team and I were at the Shannonville racetrack, on a small grassy hill just outside Corner 7. It was the first day of the 1990 motorcycle racing season.

"What's up, birdie!" I asked, not really expecting a reply.

"Beep!" went the bird furiously, looking straight at me. Then it lowered a wing and hopped straight up and down. It ran about ten yards, put on the brakes, pivoted, and looked back at me. The challenge was just like a puppy's when it invites you to chase it.

"Sorry, birdie," I said. "Maybe later. It's too early in the morning for me."

I continued up the hill, with the bird hopping and beeping at me quite hysterically. I glanced down at the spot where it had been sitting. It was a good thing I did, because there were three small mottled eggs in a depression on the ground. Another step, and I could have crushed them.

So that's what the foolish bird had done. It had built a nest on what is a quiet grassy mound in early spring, but becomes part of the paddock on the last weekend of April when the Eastern Canada Challenge gets under way. Once racing begins, scores of competitors walk up and down that little hill. It's a good spot from which to check out the last corner before the start/finish line.

"Birdie, it looks like you have a problem," I said, "and I'm not sure how to solve it for you. There'll be a lot of traffic on this hill during the next couple of days."

Luckily for the bird, motorcycle racers are a sentimental bunch. When top Pro Twins competitor Terry Spiegelberg became aware of the young parent's predicament, he immediately proceeded to build a little fortress of rocks around the eggs. Someone else made a sign out of an empty cigarette package and stuck it in front of the rocks. The sign said: "Nesting bird. Step on my eggs and say goodbye to your new paint job."

Now comes the interesting part. Birds nest in pairs, at least Shannonville racetrack birds do, and pretty soon the second bird arrived to spell the first one. I took him to be the male, because he spent a lot more time beeping and hopping about and a lot less time sitting on the three mottled eggs. (If this is a sexist observation, make the most of it.)

In any event, the first bird, the one I took to be the female, got used to her new fortress-nest in no time. By noon she would hardly look up when someone approached the grassy mound. She'd still follow potential intruders with her eyes, but wouldn't get off the eggs to lure them away from the nest. She wouldn't even bother beeping, unless someone came really close.

But the male bird seemed incapable of learning. When it was his turn to guard the eggs, he would beep, run, and flop about at the slightest provocation. He'd continue putting on the amazing act that nesting birds display for predators: "Hey, come and get me! I'm a wounded bird. Easy pickings. Look, I can hardly flap my wings."

It was a self-fulfilling prophecy. By early afternoon the male bird was exhausted. He would still run and flop, but in shorter and shorter circles. His beeping was becoming hoarse and feeble. The female bird, meanwhile, when it was her turn, would sit on her eggs serenely. By the end of the day she'd even fall asleep, closing her eyes. She had learned that motorcycle racers are harmless to nesting birds.

So there they were, two creatures, presumably with the same bird-brains, possessed of the same instincts and faced with an identical situation. In the beginning they both reacted the same way. Then, within the space of a few hours, one adjusted to the new circumstances flawlessly, while the other became a nervous wreck. Whoever said that birds were equal?

Smart birds learn and adjust, while dumb ones run in circles and beep until they fall down. I hope when the eggs hatch at least one of the nestlings will take after its mother.

1990

8.

MASKS IN THE MIRROR

Notes on Books,

Movies, and the Press

IT IS HARD NOT TO BE AFFECTED BY HIS SPELL

The surface values of Raymond Souster's poetry are easily discernible and have been pointed out many times. He is gentle and humane. He frequently writes about small events and common people. He observes with affection the streets and characters of his native Toronto. He seems to like cats, baseball players, and newspaper vendors. His poems are simple and direct.

The Years, his new collection, supports and reinforces this view of Souster, perhaps with something of a vengeance. There is Bay Street Charlie. There is Max the adagio cat leaping two ways at once. There is Old Grey Cat Grigio with his ancient bladder. There are the Christmas lights of Yonge Street. Kew Beach and Humber Valley are revisited, along with the Grey Cup and the fruit-seller at Adelaide and Bay. But most of all there is The Problem, expressing that hard-core Souster dilemma that remains after all the milk of human kindness has been split:

> *How to share the aching feet*
> *of the already limping*
> *deliverer of handbills.*

How indeed. Little birds bump into big skyscrapers, and there is not a thing the gentlest of poets can do about it. Social evil may be identified, condemned, or even corrected by legislation or direct action, but what about boys with club feet, sick cats, or healthy ones that kill butterflies? What should the sensitive poet do in a world of cancer and Biafra, when he feels guilty as it is about the death of a field mouse or about not experiencing personally the pain of someone else's rheumatism? If one has the capacity, even compulsion, to pity a tractor because it has to pull a heavy trailer, this can be a very tough world.

Souster has this capacity, and it could make his poetry grotesquely sentimental and ultimately very bad. It is hard to say why it doesn't, but it is probably for two reasons. First, he means it. Second, he is a poet and not a pretender.

Genuine poets have a way of saying things, and genuine sentiments have a power of their own. The reader may disagree, may even feel a desire to dismiss, but it is hard not to be affected by the spell. In a way this is the true magic of art, this ability to draw the reader into the circle of its own logic, to make the death of a field mouse matter even to someone who would ordinarily take the death of a human being in his stride. Herein also lies its danger, or at least the explanation of why commandants of concentration camps could sit and cry while listening to Mozart or Beethoven. It is unfortunate, although certainly not Souster's fault, that someone could weep over his old men, sick cats, and crippled boys, and still go out later to put a bomb in somebody else's mailbox.

Some poems in *The Years* represent Souster at his epigrammatic best. There is "If I Were the Devil," "Max," "Big Al at the Kicking Horse," "It's Not That Easy," and the unusual "Small Boy in Church":

Could it be that what's puzzling him
as he stands there in the pew
with both fingers in his mouth
and looks at the people behind him
with his three-year-old untroubled
eyes,

is that on this so blessed
day of the Risen Lord,
they sit here with long long faces
having got no further than His Death?

Many poems show Souster as a lyricist capable of handling fragile atmospheres or fine images. "Little Boy Lost," "Waiting for the Rain to End," and "Caterpillar" are good examples but they should be read in their entirety. "Five Nighthawks" also belongs to this group and it is short enough to be quoted here: *Five nighthawks down a late August sky/ like all things earthly given wings to fly,/ soared, checked, dived, hung as though suspended/ between the night unborn and a day not ended.*

Souster is equally good, perhaps even better, when it comes to images that are dramatic rather than lyrical. His poem "The Beautiful Deception" would work even as a zoom back in a movie:

He could be an air force jet ace
breathing deeply through his face mask
as he takes his silver Shooting star
higher, higher into outer space...

Only he's in a hospital ward
only he's in an oxygen tent
only he's old and his heart no good
only he's got about a day to live.

The Years includes a well-known poem which, to my mind, represents Souster at his didactic worst. It was first read at the Central Library Theatre in 1968 and it is called "Death Chant for Mr. Johnson's America." One's main quarrel with the poem is not based on the disagreement with the political views it expresses. First-rate people, from Ezra Pound and D'Annunzio to Silone, Ehrenburg, and Gide may be temporarily or permanently mistaken in their politics without detracting from their value as artists; and it doesn't much matter whether in this instance Souster is wrong or right. But while he may be a master of the simple-minded love song, the simple-minded hate song is not Souster's speed. He is capable of making the sickliest sentiments about blind newspaper vendors ring true, but his curse on Imperial America sounds forced, faddish, and phoney. This is bad, because Souster's main asset as a poet is not inventiveness of form or profundity of thought, but emotional honesty and integrity. Normally he is not trying to be clever, current, or fashionable; he means what he says and makes the reader believe him. "Death Chant for Mr. Johnson's America" is the only poem where he has to resort to bombast and empty rhetoric of the "red-hot gun barrel flesh of brother turned against brother" kind instead of the quiet and direct minor-key effects that characterize his other work. In this one poem I can't believe him at all.

When it comes to convincing emotions the two poems "On the Way to the Store" and "The Cage" show the effects Souster can achieve, without even raising his voice, when he is completely sincere. Both poems are perfect, and I think anyone would recognize them as Souster's who has ever read any of his books. They are short poems; "The Cage" opens with a reference to the security room where presumably Souster works himself in a bank, which someone jokingly likens to a cage where the clerks are locked up as though they were animals. However, the real animals, the real monsters of this world are never locked up; they are called "sir" in clubs; live in large houses on quiet streets; have obedient, loving wives, ...*and often, just to show the weakness in the breed,/ have at least one untamed, very beautiful daughter.* In his poem "On the Way to the Store" an old woman

> *...stops on the sidewalk*
> *because some of the bottles*
> *have worked lose and fallen*
> *from her bundle-buggy.*

The poet sees her fumbling with shaky hands, wishes he could help her, but he is on a streetcar going by,

> *...can't do*
> *a single thing for her,*
> *can only hope she gets*
> *to the beer store and back*
> *without one cracked bottle.*

> *That's about all the luck*
> *I can safely wish her.*

Those who like to view poetry as a Freudian game may be interested in noting that while Souster's kindness and concern embraces cats, old women, blind beggars, GIs, the inhabitants of Dresden, and just about all other animate and inanimate objects, he speaks much less lovingly of younger poets, and in fact wishes on them abortion, pestilence, and other assorted ills in several of his poems. One should immediately add that these are only abstract sentiments; in real life there haven't been many poets who would have done so much for apprentice practitioners of their own craft as Souster. Having helped, promoted, and published a whole generation of young Canadian poets, he may be forgiven if he doesn't feel obliged to include all of them in his universal love.

Souster is neither a pedant nor a performer, and his word is not of the classroom or the circus. No don or demon, he doesn't lecture *ex cathedra* or strum his guitar from beyond the grave. His world, in fact, is the world of most men and women who work for a living in ordinary jobs, ride the subway, watch television, and kill a few bottles of beer in the evening. Souster shares their lifestyle and, on a different level of awareness, their inner lives: if they were in the habit of writing poetry it is Souster's kind of poetry that they would write. They are the people, and they certainly outnumber, possibly outweigh, and frequently survive professors and clowns.

1971

PEGGY IS A THING APART

Again and again Margaret Atwood told us that we didn't have to take the bad with the good. "The accuracies and fine points in this book," she said in her prefatory note to *Survival*, "were for the most part contributed by others: the sloppy generalizations are my own." Addressing the Empire Club in Toronto recently, she called her book "… a rather modest literary endeavour…. Published ten years ago, no one would have noticed it."

But as it happened *Survival* was published in 1972 and everybody noticed it. Nationalists greeted its appearance with joy. *Globe and Mail* critic William French called it the In book of the year. Others who like In things, the young and the old-enough-to-know-better alike, seemed ecstatic. There were dissenters such as poet Peter Stevens writing in the *Windsor Star*. In Toronto, novelist Morley Callaghan permitted himself a few words of irony. Margaret Atwood herself appeared pleasantly amused. "I have become a Thing," she told her audience at the Empire Club.

What actually happened was that Margaret Atwood, 33, poet, novelist, winner of the Governor General's Award for poetry in 1966, an editor of the small Canadian publishing house Anansi, decided to write a thematic guide to Canadian literature. She advanced the thesis that writers, especially novelists, are somewhat influenced by the country and cultural environment in which they work, and that their works in turn tend to reflect this influence. We all accept the proposition that certain works of art are Very English or Very Russian. The Canadianness of Canadian art, according to Ms. Atwood, consists of Victims being concerned with Survival. Our enemies may be nature or colonialism, but we are all victims trying to survive. This is the key pattern.

So far, so good. It may not be true, but surely this has never been a main criterion in literary criticism. Irving Layton has recently advanced the theory that all poets in Canada can be more or less put into one of the following four groups: the Loyalists, the disciples of critic Northrop Frye, the Indians, and the Jews. As far as can be detected by the casual reader, he was being quite serious. (Why not? I myself have long held that there are five groups of Canadian writers: the Tall, the Short, the Corpulent, the Lean, and the Ones with Dandruff. I am quite serious too.) According to Commissar Zhdanov (Stalin's pet literary theoretician), all prerevolutionary writers could be classified as either "formalists" or "critical realists," establishing a stronger bond between Dickens and Dostoevski than either would have presumably hoped for. Why should Margaret Atwood's theory excite such hue and cry?

Survival is in tune with the times. This is hardly a discovery: indeed, Ms. Atwood goes to some lengths to point it out herself. Every nation has a theory of its own literature: some of the biggest nations have several. (These nations also have many war-planes and advanced systems of nuclear striking power.) The times say that if there are American, French, Russian, and for all we know Danish, Armenian, and Ostyak theories of national literature, there ought to be a Canadian theory as well. Now, thanks to *Survival*, we have one.

The first group, then, that greeted the appearance of the book with cries of orgasmic joy were those for whom "Canadian" is a term of value judgment rather than description. They were closely followed by those who can recognize a bandwagon when they see one, and though they may require much instruction in literature, need none in the trends and fashions of the day. *Survival* was clearly the In book of the season, and they could be trusted to cherish whatever was In. This group noted that, apart from literary theories, Ms. Atwood seemed to be talking about many other In things, from colonialism to women's lib, and even allowed the odd word of In jargon—such as "overview"—to slip into her otherwise lean and muscular prose. They concluded that she talked their language and was therefore both Safe and Good.

The next group much taken with *Survival* were those who actually found merit in its argument. As is often the case, this group turned out to be the least important for the notoriety of the book. In a small and admittedly unscientific survey I talked to ten people about *Survival*. Seven admired the book, three hated it. Actually only two of the ten had read it. These two, incidentally, were among the admirers.

Those who hated the book seemed to fall in two categories: the ones who are simply Out of It (as opposed to With It) and the ones who, on reflection, found it sadly wanting. These people noted that Ms. Atwood's system seemed dogmatic and artificial, full of unforgivable omissions even for a frankly subjective study. Those given to dark and classical metaphors said it was bloodied by the torn limbs and dead bodies of Canadian writers who couldn't fit Ms. Atwood's Procrustean bed. They called the most conspicuous victim of *Survival* Robertson Davies, whose name did not even appear in a work containing eleven references to Roch Carrier and sixteen to Graeme Gibson. (This is a fascinating game: Marian Engel makes it five times, Sheila Watson six, Mordecai Richler six, and Malcolm Lowry once, by the skin of his teeth.)

Immaterial, cry the admirers: Margaret Atwood is concerned with her particular pattern and naturally writes about those who fit it, omitting those who do not. She does not suggest that they ought, for that reason, to be omitted from the existing body of Canadian literature. "Please do not take any of my oversimplifications, etc.," she says. (For my part I can promise that easily.)

The practical reader will now ask me to express an Opinion, not so much about the book as the controversy. Opinions have to do with Values withstanding the Test of Time. Now as Somerset Maugham pointed out (not a fashionable name, these days), posterity is maddeningly unfair in that it generally extends its grace to those who were already appreciated in their lifetime. It may not be enough to be known, but it is useful because the unknown seldom survive. And if survival is what it's all about, for a Victim to become a Thing may be a step in the right direction.

1973

Enlightening Thunderer

Irving Layton's collection *Taking Sides* is aptly titled: he is taking sides. If he also doubts, researches, investigates, and analyses before putting his pen against the blank sheets of paper, by the time the paper is covered with words that process has become invisible. Layton is a seamless thinker. His doubts are resolved, and his only concern is to resolve the reader's.

There is something attractive about such a clean, hard, uncompromising, polemical style, especially in contrast with cautious, qualified, all-ifs-and-buts, conditional, fuzzy academic prose. After all, much of the latter proceeds not from thoughtfulness, but from fear. Raw courage is more engaging than sophisticated cowardice. A sheet of glass compares well, esthetically speaking, with a bale of cotton.

But the soft, contemptible cotton is flexible; the hard, admirable glass is fragile. Layton advances, somewhat like Patton, conquering Sicily in a day, but then he burns his bridges behind him. He exposes his flanks, he stretches his supply lines beyond any reasonable limit.

The sympathetic reader, one who believes that Layton's cause is just, watches his progress with alarm. Why must he take such needless, foolish risks?

Why must he predict in 1967 (to use a very obvious example) that "It is only a matter of time before the pestiferous Viet Cong are cleared out from South Vietnam, and the South Vietnamese are able to determine their future under leaders and institutions of their own choosing?" The desirability of liberal democracy as a political institution is not predicated on its success in South Vietnam, nor is the pestiferousness of the Viet Cong predicated on their failure. Fascism is rotten, and it would be no less rotten if it triumphed all over the globe. Putting the two propositions in the same bed can only result in one catching the other one's flu: if Layton was wrong about the Viet Cong losing out— some will be tempted to say—he must also be wrong about the Viet Cong being pestiferous.

Yet this is Layton's style and, if the style is the man, this is what Layton is like. It clearly isn't a matter of not thinking: people who don't think don't change their minds and Layton has changed his mind considerably between 1935 and 1977, the period covered in this book. But whenever he glimpses what, in a given moment, seems to him the truth, he pulls out all the stops and thunders it like an Old Testament prophet. Though he may thunder the virtual opposite of what he thundered ten years earlier, he will thunder it with the same elemental force. He is right, he is right in every detail, and if you don't see it you are a spineless, corrupt, unmanly, cretinous shmuck.

It is possible to become so irritated by this as to lose sight of the fact that Layton *is* right, perhaps not invariably and not in every detail, but in things that really matter. A careful look also reveals that though he may change his mind entirely about the instruments of deliverance, in essentials he doesn't change his mind at all. He hurls philippics against whatever threatens the freedom and dignity of man: the right if it's the right, and the left if it's the left. If Layton's wrath is directed at different targets in 1935 and 1977 it is because the enemy has shifted grounds. It is logical to oppose Hitler and Mao for the same reason, and it is logical to point out that the most acute and imminent threat to the world's liberty in the 1960s and 1970s doesn't come from Bonn,

Washington, or even Johannesburg, but from Moscow and Peking. What is illogical is to embrace today's dragon in mortal fear of yesterday's. Layton, wisely, fights the beast, not the ghost.

There are many other subjects touched upon in this collection of articles and letters spanning forty years: Israel, Germany, Quebec, the writer in Canada. There is a particularly fine sketch about a woman in a Tel Aviv bookstore. In his 1946 M.A. thesis (on Harold Laski) Layton shows a shrewd understanding of the incompatibility of Marxism and liberalism, though his own sympathies seem to be with Marxism at the time. Only his criticism of film critics is disappointing: he appears to regard films as collections of symbols, somewhat like crossword puzzles, which the winning critic solves by coming up with the hidden meanings. This peculiar view enables Layton to mention in the same breath Fellini's admirable *Amarcord* with Cavani's ridiculous *The Night Porter*. It might have been a regrettable lapse of taste on the part of critic Martin Knelman to dislike the first if he did, but an equal lapse on Layton's part to admire the second.

What is most likeable about Layton in this collection is that he is a *militant* democrat—one is tempted to say a militant moderate. There aren't many of his kind left in this Yeatsian age where the best lack all conviction and the worst seem to have a monopoly on passionate intensity, and Layton will survive his critics for this reason alone. Still, what is least likeable is his demand for unconditional homage. It would, in fact, be easier to accord it to him if he did not seem to demand it so insistently. Some reticence in this respect is not necessarily a sign of anaemic gentility.

1978

THE MYSTERY OF MULTIPLE MURDER

Why did Boston strangler Albert DeSalvo or serial murderers Theodore Bundy and Edmund Kemper kill dozens of women? Why do mass murderers like Mark Essex (who went on a rampage through a New Orleans hotel in 1975) annihilate God knows how many complete strangers in one murderous outburst? What can possibly motivate human beings to commit such seemingly senseless crimes?

This is the question Memorial University of Newfoundland anthropologist Elliott Leyton raises in his new book, *Hunting Humans*. It is without doubt a worthwhile question. It is also one to which, so far, we have received insufficient answers from psychology, psychiatry, and criminology. Some of the answers have not only been insufficient but demonstrably wrong.

Can anthropology or "historical sociology"—Dr. Leyton's area of expertise—provide better answers? Readers of his thesis will have to make up their minds about this. For my part, I remain unconvinced.

I think, though, that *Hunting Humans* will be rewarding reading for anyone with a serious interest in the problem, as well as for those whose interest is merely prurient. Leyton writes for the lay reader, indulging in the special language of his discipline just enough not to risk losing his licence as a social scientist. His detailed and somewhat gory descriptions of the deeds of DeSalvo, Bundy, Kemper, Essex, as well as mass-murderer Charles Starkweather or serial-killer David (Son of Sam) Berkowitz make for shudderingly good bedside reading, at least for those whose tastes run in this direction.

But bringing a smile to his publisher's lips is clearly not Leyton's primary aim. His aim is to explain a type of behavior that to many people appears merely insane. Also, to demonstrate why certain other explanations are mistaken.

I think he makes a better job of his second quest than of the first. Admittedly, my opinion is coloured by the fact that I share Leyton's views concerning the inadequacy of most traditional answers. I'm very easily persuaded that Freudian psychology, extra chromosomes, or insufficient parental affection, whether coupled with grinding poverty or not, fail to provide an explanation for the acts of those who kill, torture, and sometimes cannibalize total strangers.

As Leyton points out, no consistent physical abnormalities have ever been found in the brains or chromosomal make-up of multiple murderers. Relatively few have been diagnosed—at least, unanimously diagnosed—as psychotic. Often, except for the acts they committed, doctors had no reason to call them anything but normal. Such neuroses, sexual appetites, or psychopathic traits as these killers may have, they share with any number of people who do not become multiple murderers. The same is true of their social backgrounds. Though they often come from unstable or poor families, they are no different from others who also come from unloving or otherwise deprived origins. In fact, in their life stories they resemble each other less than they resemble millions who do not become criminals at all.

To quote the novelist Petru Dumitriu (who is worth quoting on these matters before most social scientists): "What was peculiar to Caesar will never be found in the things Caesar had in common with a million other men." Or, as any philosopher might point out, poverty, overactive libidos, suffocating mothers, or abusive fathers are much too common to provide a cause for the acts of a Bundy or a Kemper. Certainly not a sufficient cause, and perhaps not even a necessary one.

Leyton makes mincemeat of many traditional answers, which is refreshing even if (in my view) no harder than shooting fish in a barrel. But what about his own answers? There the going gets much rougher for him, I believe.

In essence, Leyton theorizes that the multiple murderer arises at the greatest points of a stress in a given society. At such points he erupts like a volcano, and his reasons are social rather than pathological. For instance, the social position of his class—or his own position within his class—may be jeopardized, and he feels powerless to do anything about it. As a social reaction, he begins killing those who, in his view, represent the forces hemming him in.

So, according to the author, in the fifteenth century, when the rise of the lower orders began to put a special stress on the position of the aristocracy, the typical multiple murderer was someone like Baron Gilles de Rais, who sodomized, tortured, and killed hundreds of peasant boys in his castle. This, presumably, he did as an act of class warfare to teach the peasants their place. At the dawn of the industrial era, the typical murderers were petit bourgeois doctors and schoolteachers. They killed housemaids or prostitutes in an effort to discipline social inferiors who somehow threatened the murderers' own precarious foothold in the new social order. A "minor theme" also emerged: a few proletarians went on the rampage as a form of "sub-political rebellion that expressed their rage at their exclusion...."

In the modern era, says Leyton, the murderers are drawn from the upper-working or lower-middle classes. Their victims tend to be members of the class above—university students, aspiring models, pedestrians in middle-class shopping malls—who represent the nearest group that, in the murderers' minds, blocks and excludes them from their aspirations in the social hierarchy. The author's main point is that "unthreatened classes do not produce" multiple murderers.

The evidence Leyton offers is not too impressive even by the flabby standards of the social sciences. For aristocratic murderers, it rests on the sole example of the Baron Gilles de Rais. More importantly, it does not answer the objection Leyton outlines so clearly in relation to competing theories. If their backgrounds, neuroses, etc., do not adequately explain multiple murderers because they share these traits with so many people, how could membership in a "threatened" class explain them? They share this trait, too, with millions who have never hurt a fly.

Leyton recognizes that there must be other factors, but feels that there are "no data that would allow us to address the problem in any scientific fashion...." The trouble is no other problem is worth addressing half as much. Assuming Leyton is right and all senseless murderers come from threatened classes, why does only the tiniest fraction of the threatened classes become senseless murderers? Until we have answered this, we have answered very little. Besides, there are no "unthreatened classes" in any society. Multiple murderers probably suffer from social *angst*; most people do. But what makes a handful of them kill?

Leyton does offer some interesting insights. He emphasizes, for instance, the disparity between the ambitions and abilities of multiple murderers. This trait may indeed be more relevant to their personality disorders than any number of Freudian problems. Social impotence may well be as great a burden as sexual impotence. It is also true—though often overlooked—that crazy people are not necessarily original. They go over the deep end, but the deep end is still in the swimming pool of the times. Insanity has a social component just as sanity does. People may take leave of their senses without leaving the

Zeitgeist behind. For instance, a case could be made for the guiding spirit of our times being envy. If so, this motive force of sane and law-abiding citizens may become a mainspring for the acts of insane citizens as well.

Still, this does not prove that multiple killers are "normal." Individual pathology is likely to play a greater role in their acts than Leyton would allow. A malfunctioning radio picks up signals broadcast by "society," but then it garbles them in its own way. Though Leyton has no maudlin sympathies for multiple murderers, he comes perilously close to suggesting that, for a garbageman like Starkweather, killing strangers is a rational and all but legitimate path to his own identity. The author appears almost surprised that all garbagemen do not turn into mass murderers.

The role of sex, while probably overrated by most psychiatrists, seems somewhat underrated by Leyton. Multiple murderers do show a marked preference for killing sex-objects: women, if they are heterosexual males; men, if they are homosexuals; and men also, if (rarely) they are female serial killers. Common sense suggests that sex is of some significance in their acts.

In the end, are Leyton's answers better than previous answers? I doubt it. But I do believe that he raises better questions.

1986

CROSSING THE BARRIER

Dian Fossey was an American naturalist, reported to have been killed in Rwanda, Africa, in the last days of 1985. I knew Fossey only as a reader of her 1983 book, *Gorillas in the Mist*. In her mid-thirties she started a detailed observation of the last known groups of mountain gorillas who range in the Virunga mountains between Zaire, Uganda, and Rwanda. For the past eighteen years Fossey lived among the gorillas. She made her home in a hut within walking distance of their foraging grounds on the slopes of Mount Visoke in Rwanda. Clearly, she was unlike most people.

Most people live exclusively, even narrowly, within the group into which they happen to be born. Not necessarily physically, for such people may also travel or even emigrate, but mentally and spiritually: in their interests, habits, language, culture, and custom. No matter how much benign attention they may pay to other groups, people generally identify mainly with their own.

There are some exceptions, of course. A few individuals may make a conscious decision to break with their own group and join another. For any number of reasons, ranging from the psychological to the situational, they choose to assimilate into a foreign tribe, religion, culture, or class.

Often they do it with a vengeance, becoming, as the expression goes, more Catholic than the pope. They earnestly mimic the new group in gesture and inflection; they adopt their manners and dress; they try to copy not only their virtues, but also their vices, and sometimes champion their causes with a fanaticism that is truly blind.

To avoid misunderstanding, I'm not talking about people who simply exhibit a friendly interest in other tribes, etc., who learn about their customs or see the point of their causes and demand justice for them. No: I'm talking about people who try to cross the formidable barriers that exist between groups, not out of intellectual curiosity or even a liberal wish to diminish the significance of such barriers, but because they prefer the other side. Fossey appears to have been such a person. In a way, she may have carried it further than most. She did not merely try to cross the line that exists between tribes or cultures. She tried to cross the line between species.

It is not doing her an injustice to say that when it came to choosing between people and gorillas she chose gorillas, because she said so herself. Gorillas, in her view, had a dignity that people generally lacked. They were brave without being aggressive; they were intelligent, affectionate, and peaceful. They were also virtually extinct, with the two to three hundred living in the Virungas being the last of their kind. Fossey wanted to save them.

Gorillas, like many other animals, are threatened by people in two ways. One, people hunt them. Though more spectacular, this is a pressure animals find relatively easier to withstand. It is the second pressure that truly threatens wild species: the encroachment on their natural environment by human farming and technology.

Many zoologists who love animals feel that preserving them in the wild is probably a losing battle. As human populations grow, farmers want to graze their cattle to feed their children, then build factories or look for oil to improve their lives. They won't let a bunch of gorillas stop them. It's unreasonable to expect people to remain in some picturesque Paleolithic stage of development so that they can peacefully coexist with creatures in the wilderness. To preserve species, the solution is to learn to keep and breed them in zoos.

Dian Fossey had a different view. She felt that her gorillas were entitled to their mountain, which was supposed to be a protected national park anyway. She did not want hunters to kill two adult gorillas in order to capture one baby gorilla for a zoo. She did not want cattle in the Virungas. So Fossey fought a lonely battle against hunters, farmers, and fellow scientists. She spray-painted obscene words on stray cows, offered rewards for poachers, and was once said to have held the child of a native woman as a hostage against a captured baby gorilla.

In her book Fossey offered some of the most memorable descriptions and photographs of animals that I have ever seen. The scientific value of her work may have been considerable. But in trying to cross a species-barrier, she invited turning herself from a naturalist into a crank. A noble and sympathetic crank, but a crank nevertheless. Her death, probably at the hand of a local farmer, hunter, or other antagonist, was as tragic as it was inevitable.

1986

LEFT-HANDED APOLOGY

Against All Hope is the memoir of the Catholic poet Armando Valladares, who spent twenty years in Fidel Castro's prisons. The book is a powerful document. It describes the seldom-discussed Cuban link in the chain of Gulags that run through the entire communist world.

In an earlier review, I wondered if Valladares' account about Castro's palm-treed Siberia—the political prisons, executions, tortures—would receive any attention from the same journalists, politicians, and church-men who are usually vocal in objecting to infringements of human rights. I wondered if they would write about Valladares' book. I asked if they would organize protest meetings or urge trade sanctions against Cuba. I expressed curiosity if the book might generate a moral outrage to be mentioned in the same breath with the outrage generated—right-ly—by the practices of South Africa's government. And if not, I won-dered why not.

My questions received an answer on September 20, 1986, when the *Globe and Mail* ran a review of *Against All Hope*, written by the essay-ist, editor, and biographer George Woodcock.

Woodcock is one of Canada's great men of letters. He has been a friend of George Orwell, and is himself a noted figure in western polit-ical thought. Like Orwell's, his work represents the most honest and humanitarian ideals of the left. As a man of the left Woodcock allows the reflexive hope flit through his mind that Valladares' account may be untrue, but as an honest man he dismisses it. "I wish I did not believe Valladares' narrative...[but] the book is entirely authentic in tone, and enough in keeping with other evidence that has come to us to form a terrible indictment of the self-styled revolutionary regime of Cuba and of Castro personally."

Good enough; only note the adjective "self-styled." When you have a left-winger's attachment to the word "revolutionary" any regime that proves unworthy of your romantic ideal can be distanced from it by calling it "self-styled." But we must be fair to poor Fidel. Whatever he is guilty of, he did not bestow the title on himself. From day one his regime was styled revolutionary by the entire progressive left.

This isn't a mere semantic quibble. It is one important way in which Marxists or apologists have managed to separate their ideas from their consequences for the last sixty years. When the truth about Stalin's crimes finally had to be acknowledged, the great revolutionary figure would quickly become "self-styled." The faith would be transferred intact to the next leader and the next regime. All right, Castro is self-styled—but what about Ortega in Nicaragua? He must be the real article.

Hold it; that's not Woodcock, apart from one slip of the tongue. For the rest he points out, in the finest Orwellian tradition, that: "Reading such a book, and believing it, brings us face to face with the glaring hypocrisies of our time and our society. We condemn South Africa for its atrocities...[but] for years we have known that Cuba is governed by a regime just as harsh as that of South Africa...."

He also points out that "...cruelty has no colour. If a man is tortured or murdered it doesn't matter whether it happens for racist reasons or not. The Gulag is no less atrocious than the Holocaust, and what happens in Cuba is just as bad as what happens in South Africa.

"Stalin and Hitler were brethren under the skin," Woodcock continues, "and so, *Against All Hope* tells me, are Fidel Castro and P.W. Botha."

Great. Lines of this nature could have been written (and frequently were) by "right-wing" journalists alphabetically from Barbara Amiel to Lubor Zink. What, then, is the difference? "It is time we recognized," writes Woodcock, "there there are two kinds of left, the Tommy Douglas left and the Fidel Castro left, just as there are two kinds of right...."

Yes—except the right has always recognized this. Only the left was, and is still, having some trouble. No neo-conservative or classical liberal journalist has ever attempted to apologize for the Nazis. None suggests, not even through a slip of the tongue, that Mussolini or Franco were merely "self-styled" fascists as opposed to some worthier, abstract ideals of fascism. The respectable right has no reflexive sympathies for the extreme right whatever. Unlike the left, the "Tommy Douglas left," the respectable left. They have long suffered from reflexive sympathies to the extreme left: the Maoists, the Castroites, the Soviets. They still do today. The exceptions, such as Woodcock himself, are rare.

"Our sentimentality consists in believing that the left is never guilty of the same sins as the right," Woodcock writes. Indeed. Which is why Cuba never had to worry about aroused liberation theologians calling for trade sanctions to protest the torture of a fellow Catholic, and why a Liberal prime minister of Canada could cheerfully shout "Viva Castro!" outside the walls of Armando Valladares' prison.

1986

THE NORMAN MYSTERY

Nearly thirty years ago Canada's ambassador to Egypt, Egerton Herbert Norman, committed suicide by jumping off the top of a Cairo apartment building. Last week the solicitor general was asked two questions in Parliament about the late scholar and diplomat. A Calgary MP wanted to know if the government had been aware of certain evidence tending to show that Ambassador Norman might have been an agent for the Soviet Union.

It is unusual that a question of this nature should be raised after the passage of more than a generation, but the case of Herbert Norman is unusual in many ways. What he may or may not have done is still a mystery. But Canada's official attitude about the mystery of Herbert Norman has itself been mysterious.

Questions that have been bubbling under the surface for three decades are rising to the top again. The main reason is a recent book by James Barros, an American historian who teaches political science at the University of Toronto. Entitled *No Sense of Evil*, the book examines the evidence against Norman. It does so in a meticulous, scholarly manner, as even critics hostile to the book's conclusion concede. Professor Barros' conclusion, simply put, is that there is a valid case against Norman which has not been answered to this day. He believes that it should be answered, no matter where the answers might take us.

Why should anyone be hostile to such a conclusion? (Anyone other than fellow Soviet agents, that is, or those who now worry that they may have negligently assisted Soviet agents over the years. Obviously such people would be hostile to the idea of seeking answers that might implicate them.) Still, such people would not exist in great numbers.

Why is there a general reluctance to discover—or perhaps only to reveal—the truth?

That there has been such a reluctance is, to my mind, beyond doubt. The evidence shows that, minimally, Norman had lied about his background which included being or having been a communist. Minimally, he had moved in circles that were recruitment grounds for spies, then denied—and allowed then-External Affairs Minister Lester B. Pearson to deny on his behalf—having done so. And, minimally, he was named by other confessed agents as being one of them.

When so much is undisputed—and it is—silence is not enough. Allowing the myth to stand that Norman was a victim of some American uglies of the McCarthy era who hounded him to his death over youthful associations—or over the errors of an inquiring mind and a sensitive social conscience, which in the climate of the times he could not bring himself to admit—is simply insufficient. It is also inaccurate.

I hold no brief for the person or methods of the American Senator Joe McCarthy who gave an era his name. However, by the time Norman killed himself (for reasons best known to him) the McCarthy period was over. In 1957, the Americans raising questions about the Canadian diplomat were not grandstanding witch-hunters but ordinary investigators. As it turned out, the questions they raised were valid, and Norman's only reply was jumping off a roof.

In criminal law, of course, all persons are presumed innocent unless proven guilty beyond a reasonable doubt. The proof against the late ambassador, as outlined in Barros' book, would not meet that test, but it is not being offered with a view to a criminal conviction, posthumous or otherwise. (Arguably, being a Soviet agent of influence may not even amount to a crime in Canada.) Barros offers the evidence simply to set the record straight and to point out the need for further inquiries.

Essentially, the Americans said to us in 1957: "Look, you have a fellow in a high and sensitive place who untruthfully denies having been, or maybe being, a communist." And essentially we replied: "Oh you crude Yankee meddlers!"

But, as we now know, the Yankee meddlers were right. Did we know it at the time? Did we have any information that ought to have enabled us to know it? If so, who, specifically, had this information in government? Whose decision was it to put our heads in the sand and pretend, to the people of Canada and to the world at large, that the Americans were hurling baseless accusations at an irreproachable civil servant?

Our Conservative government is in no way heir to the errors or sins of Liberals in power thirty years ago, whatever they may have been. But even a Liberal government would owe Parliament an honest answer. What did we know about Herbert Norman and when? Did we knowingly perpetuate the myth that the Americans raising questions about him were only paranoid? And if so, why?

Those who dislike the U.S. should remember George Orwell's remark that something may be true even if Lord Beaverbrook says it's true. Those who think that the Soviets use no agents in the West should spend a few weeks in a library. And those who think that there is nothing wrong with assisting the Kremlin, provided one doesn't actually sell them material under the Official Secrets Act, should examine their conscience. Curiously, this may have been what Herbert Norman did in the end.

1986

OLD BOOK, FRESH IDEAS

In addition to newspaper items, confidential memos, and leaked government documents, sometimes I receive entire books from my phantom clippers. This is how I've come to be reading John Steinbeck's *The Log from the Sea of Cortez* for the last week or so. The late Nobel Prize–winning American novelist muses about a great many things in that personal account of a 1940 expedition of marine biologists to the Gulf of California, whose likable participants may have been pickled in alcohol almost as much as the cute little invertebrates they collected.

I can control my fascination with the commensal fish that carves out its ecological niche in the anus of a sea cucumber but, as my inner circle of phantom clippers knows, I enjoy whimsical musings. Especially by writers like Steinbeck, who look at the world as it is rather than as they think it ought to be, and who let the chips fall where they may.

Of the many things Steinbeck mused about in the Gulf on that long-ago trip (relaxing with a lukewarm beer, having pickled his daily quota of snails, flatworms, and limpets) was the law. He wrote: "It is often considered, particularly by reformers and legislators, that law is a stimulation to action or an inhibitor of action, when actually the reverse is true. Successful law is simply the publication of the practice of the majority of units of a society...."

I found this an interesting remark, echoing something that the great American jurist Oliver Wendell Holmes wrote in 1934: "While there is still doubt, while opposite convictions still keep a battlefront against each other, the time for law has not come...." Really? Tell it to any of our modern day pressure groups. Tell it to the feminist lobby. Tell it to the Human Rights Commission.

I don't disagree with Steinbeck or Holmes at all, except I'd have to substitute the word "desirable" for "successful." I share their way of looking at the law, but I can't share their illusion that it is the only way to look at it.

The great American author and the great American jurist, writing nearly half a century ago, looked at the law from the point of view of free human beings living in a free society. For them "successful" law was the codification of voluntary practices (or at least ideals) that had evolved freely and were shared by the community as a whole. It was not rules designed by one segment of society to coerce all other segments to share their ideals and practices. It was not the expression of one group's despotic will to further its own philosophy and interest.

However, other types of human societies—say, in feudal, theocratic, fascist, or communist periods of history—simply regarded the law as an instrument of coercion. "Successful" law was whatever set of rules enabled the dominant class, religion, oligarchy, or power-elite to make other people toe the line. In modern times, the party-line.

What happens when the Ayatollah Khomeini dislikes a certain practice in his society? Does he say with Justice Holmes that "the time for law has not come" just because many people see nothing wrong with that practice? Hardly. The Ayatollah first laughs, then passes a law forbidding the practice, then laughs some more at Steinbeck for saying that the law prohibiting such a practice cannot be successful. How can it not be successful, when fewer people engage in the practice now that they have had their hands chopped off for doing it?

The Ayatollah's amusement in this regard would be shared by most NDPers in our own country, and even by some Liberals and Conservatives. It would be shared by Human Rights Commissioner Gordon Fairweather and by all Status of Women types. They may not wish to chop off any hands, but they would pass laws precisely where there is much doubt, where opposite convictions still keep a battlefront against each other—in other words, where their own views must be legislated to prevail.

In our neo-feudal age we look at the law as an instrument of social engineering. We regard the law as a gun that whichever group captures the government's arsenal can point at the heads of all others. Steinbeck is right when he says that, in spite of the illusions of legal reformers, they can neither inhibit nor stimulate social action, merely record in their law books a consensus that has already been reached. Except Steinbeck talks about a *free* society, the only society he knows. What the fine, progressive author—born in 1902, the tail end of the classical liberal era—leaves out of his calculation is that not all societies are free.

1987

FATALLY FLAWED REACTIONS

A movie called *Fatal Attraction* is packing them in at the box office these days. It is also making some critics hopping mad. I'm no longer an avid movie-goer, but when opinion-makers start calling a film "wretched and evil" (as one critic did recently in the *Toronto Star*) I become curious. Last week I bought a ticket to see what the fuss was all about.

Coming out of the theatre I was a little puzzled. *Fatal Attraction*, though nicely done, is only a routine bit of diversion. It is crafted according to an old formula, often used to great effect by such masters as Alfred Hitchcock: take an everyday situation, then carry it gradually to some far-fetched, horrifying extreme. This recipe—ordinary premise leading to extraordinary conclusion—can often keep you at the edge of your seat. Naturally, like all recipes, it must be well-prepared and attractively served. Hitchcock could serve it up memorably, and so can writer James Dearden and director Adrian Lyne, the creators of *Fatal Attraction*.

The ordinary premise in the movie is that a handsome young lawyer and family man (played by Michael Douglas) is lured into a weekend romance by a sensuous and sophisticated career woman (played by Glenn Close). This, to put it mildly, happens in real life often enough. What's extraordinary is that the Glenn Close character feels that this brief encounter has entitled her to a permanent place in the Michael Douglas character's life, and goes to horrifying extremes to achieve it.

Edgar Allan Poe may have originated this type of Gothic formula with his story about a cat that hates and kills the old man who owns it. As Poe knew, the formula works only if it is convincingly developed. Unless the reader can be made to believe that an ordinary house cat can come to hate and kill its owner, there's no suspense.

Realizing this, the creators of *Fatal Attraction* take care to develop their story convincingly. The main characters are drawn as highly recognizable types. The initial situation is quite realistic. Douglas and Close, in their roles as a couple of big-town yuppies, say and do things many people of their ilk tend to say and do.

As a result, much to some critics' dismay, the movie becomes a pretty accurate portrayal of human beings. It presents some real patterns of emotions and motivations, and not just those that students of modern myths would like to see attributed to men and women.

For instance, to begin with a minor point, there's a certain male vulnerability to a sexual challenge which some women are not above using and exploiting. This is hardly a new discovery, but the mere acknowledgment of it is enough to infuriate a few people these days. It breaches the convention according to which all women are victims, and men ought to be portrayed only as aggressive, manipulative beasts.

Some feminists have an even greater problem with what they take to be the film's message, namely that a "cheap" one-night stand can wreck a "valuable" marriage. They consider this an evil suggestion, saying that it not only exalts the patriarchal institution of marriage, but may cause people to fear liberated sex, the cornerstone of female equality.

As it happens, this isn't even the film's message. The plot simply requires a husband to prefer his wife to a lady barracuda who likes sex in freight elevators. If he didn't, he'd just push the "up" button and ride off with her into the sunset. Men don't invariably prefer their wives, but unless the Michael Douglas character does, we don't have a story. Few affairs pose such Gothic threats to families as the one in this movie does, but affairs can still be fatal to a marriage. That's what makes the premise somewhat realistic.

True, in the end the story becomes far-fetched, but I suspect some critics find its initial realism more upsetting. The character played by Glenn Close seems so poised, so attractive—yet in a way so near to the insane harpy at the film's end. Her character progresses so easily from "We're adults, aren't we?" to the accusation: "You're responsible!" The hideous Medusa that she becomes, with the almost snake-like curls in her hair, emerges so naturally from the cool, assertive career woman, the modern lady who believes that she is entitled to everything she desires.

Fatal Attraction is just a horror-thriller; I'd be surprised if its creators wanted to convey any message at all. Like all clever craftsmen, they observed a contemporary phenomenon with some accuracy, then pushed it to (or just beyond) its logical extreme. In doing so, they cut a bit too close to the bone, which explains the fury of some critics and the happiness of most movie-goers.

1987

SUBTLE SUBVERSION

This is not going to be a review of *Spycatcher*, the best-selling autobiography of former British counterintelligence officer Peter Wright. It is only a review of a single sentence in his book. The sentence occurs on page 350, where Wright describes the efforts he and his friends had to make to secure the appointment of Michael (later Sir Michael) Hanley to the top job of MI-5, Great Britain's security and counterintelligence service. Though Wright and his friends considered Hanley, a career officer, the best man for the job, apparently some top-ranking civil servants in Whitehall had different ideas.

To make sure of Hanley's appointment, strings had to be pulled. Insiders were going to put some pressure on then-Prime Minister Edward Heath. Hanley was asked to co-operate, at least to the extent of having a meeting with one of Wright's friends in high places. But Hanley bridled at the idea. As Wright puts it: "There was just a trace of socialism about Hanley, which showed itself in utterances about achieving the job on his merits, not through the old-boy network."

The sentence struck me when I read it. I thought it was astounding—but perhaps revealing is a better word. Wright's use of the word "socialism" to describe someone's preference for merit over patronage illustrates beautifully our confusion of ideas.

It is important to note that Wright is not a left-winger. On the contrary, many people would call him an arch-conservative or even a zealot. He spent a lifetime observing evidence of Marxist penetration and subversion of western government circles and defence establishments. Yet even a man of such inclinations and experience uses the word "socialism" to contrast promotion on merit with promotion through contacts or status.

The truth, of course, is the exact opposite. It is under a centrally planned system of state enterprise—in other words, under socialism—that appointments and promotions are based mainly on contacts and status. Based on the old-boy network, if you will. Anyone who has ever worked for a crown corporation knows that merit or efficiency count for nothing compared to someone's standing with the senior bureaucracy. This is so even in a liberal democracy where government is relatively limited. Imagine what it is like in socialism, where government is the only game in town.

Inasmuch as it's also true of Whitehall, it's because every bureaucracy is "socialist" by nature. Not in the sense that they are politically left-leaning, but in the sense that they are infused with a civil service mentality. In fact, once a corporation is large enough, it's true even of private enterprise. Any big organization is likely to sprout a bureaucracy just as a big tree sprouts moss.

A bureaucracy is always parasitic. It cares about little except status. It produces nothing but office politics. Administration, once it grows powerful enough, turns into a living organism feeding on the body that acts as its host. Under socialism, it feeds on the entire body politic.

This tendency of a bureaucracy is somewhat limited under a free-enterprise system. It's limited by competition, whether of goods or ideas. It's limited by the bottom line on balance sheets. It's limited by the diversification of power. Consumers limit it in the marketplace and voters in the polling booths. It's limited to the extent that government itself is limited in free societies. Socialism stretches these limits by a big margin. *Totalitarian* socialism—communism—removes them altogether. The ultimate socialist state is bureaucracy unlimited. It's the old-boy network reigning supreme.

Try talking about merit or efficiency to the old boys (or girls) of socialism: the cadres, the apparatchiks, the nomenclature. Try explaining to them that they shouldn't make appointments on the basis of patronage within the party apparatus. Tell it to the Politburo. That's what Gorbachev is trying to do—allegedly—and without much success so far.

Oh, well, you might say. Peter Wright is an expert in scientific intelligence, not in political philosophy. He must have used the word "socialism" very loosely to describe a state of mind that rejects patronage. He just used it carelessly. It's probably not his considered opinion. No doubt—but it's still revealing.

Wright wouldn't have said, even carelessly, that Hanley bridled at the old boy network because "there was just a trace of fascism" in him. Yet it would have made no less sense. The way our own minds have become confused and subverted by the slogans of socialism—even the minds of our spycatchers—might, in the end, prove to be as dangerous to the West as any number of Soviet agents and traitors.

1987

Rewriting Nazi History

By coincidence, just as I was reading Sebastian Haffner's book *The Meaning of Hitler*, a friend remarked on the emergence of a whole body of revisionist literature about the Third Reich. He was not talking about the lunatic fringe. He didn't mean neo-Nazis or Holocaust-deniers like Robert Faurisson in France or Ernst Zundel in Canada. These people belong to the realm of pathology and aren't worth wasting one's breath on. The writers my friend had in mind were people of a different calibre and kind.

My friend wasn't talking about hate-mongers or historical illiterates, but decent, lucid, and sometimes quite brilliant people. Learned writers and essayists, such as Haffner himself, or German and British historians like Joachim C. Fest and David Irving. Far from denying or excusing Nazi crimes, these authors confirm and condemn them. They're only trying to re-evaluate old conclusions about Nazism. They analyze or criticize conventional wisdom, and attempt to throw some new light on the Hitler era.

They do not agree with each other on everything (and tend to agree on little with David Irving, who ascribes the Holocaust to Himmler rather than to Hitler). What they have in common is the desire to take nothing for granted—other than indisputable facts, of course—and to regard nothing as being above re-examination.

Needless to say, this is just fine, whether it's done in relation to Hitler or to any other historical figure. Such independent re-examination is a natural function of all gifted thinkers. However, much as I support honest and intelligent re-examination, it doesn't necessarily lead me to revise older ideas. Some notions put forth by revisionists may impress me; others may not. New opinions and insights, just like old ones, have to stand or fall on their merits.

Many things in Haffner's analysis impress me (as they did in Fest's when I read his Hitler biography some years ago). I agree, for instance, with Haffner's discussion of the Nuremberg trials. I won't try to summarize his points here; people who are interested can order the book from the U.K. I also agree with his warning against discrediting every notion just because Hitler may have held them. No doubt, the formula 2x2=4 can safely stand even if Hitler endorsed it.

However, I consider Haffner's main thesis flawed. He seems to view Hitler as a combination of three personalities. One, a brilliant political—and at times military—strategist with the uncanny instincts of a predator, or rather a vulture. He could sense and exploit his victims' and adversaries' weaknesses. Two, a totalitarian socialist's personality, with a vision of a community gathered around a supreme leader. Three, a mass murderer's personality, in the strictest criminological sense.

It was Hitler the mass murderer who took over in the end, Haffner suggests. By this he ruined his victims, obviously, but also himself. He ruined things for Germany, for Europe, perhaps even for the world. Implicit in Haffner's thesis, unless I misunderstand him, is that Hitler the brilliant totalitarian wasn't such a bad thing. His vision of Europe under the hegemony of a modern, highly organized, and disciplined Germany might have saved western civilization from other, more baneful influences.

A Hitler of the first and second personality, without the criminal lunacy of the third, would not only have been tolerable but probably successful. If not for his insane, murderous lusts, Hitler could have won the war. Better still, he could have won without a war. He could have turned Poles, Ukrainians, and even Russians into friends. He could have cut some deal with the West.

Totalitarian socialism is viable. It even has some pluses, Haffner says; after all, look at the pluses of communism. Most Germans, far from liking Hitler's homicidal anti-Semitism, only tolerated it for his other qualities. Hitlerism 1 and 2, minus Hitlerism 3, would have been capable of peaceful coexistence.

I'm paraphrasing and condensing Haffner, maybe unfairly. But if this is what he says, he's wrong. Totalitarian socialism, Nazi or Marxist, is in itself homicidal. That's precisely why a less murderous Hitler might have been viewed as a liberator in the Soviet Union—and that's why, as a totalitarian socialist, he couldn't be less murderous. He was what he was.

Hitler may well have been a mass murderer in the strictest criminological sense: a mass murderer of Jews, Poles, Germans, and whoever else caught his homicidal fancy. But it wasn't just part of his personality. It was its essence. All his other ideas and actions flowed naturally from it.

1988

9.

A

TOLERANCE

FOR SIN

Notes on our

Times and Temper

DEATH'S PLAYING FIELDS

Last week, more than one hundred people were killed or injured when English and Italian fans decided to have a go at each other during a soccer match in Belgium.

I suppose shocked disbelief is the immediate emotion with which most ordinary people respond to such news. The disbelief is tempered only by the knowledge that, while the Belgian incident may be one of the worst, it is certainly far from being the first one in the sad history of spectator violence. After the shock and the anger one naturally feels over such utter waste of human lives, the next impulse is to list the conclusions that can legitimately be drawn from a tragedy of this kind.

Sports events—international competition, in particular—have long been held to be a harmless way in which human aggression may be sublimated. The theory has been that competitive sports, like lightning rods, may serve to divert our violent energies into safe channels of civilized ritual. To some extent, this thinking was behind the revival of the Olympics around the turn of the century.

Such eminent scientists as the late Konrad Lorenz theorized that while human aggression may be deep-seated and instinctive—and as one tool in nature's survival kit it may be neither practical nor wise to suppress it—the idea of confining it within the boundaries of sporting ritual may be both practical and necessary.

Necessary yes, but practical no, it seems to me. All evidence points to organized competition having done nothing to sublimate whatever instincts for aggression we possess. Organized international sporting competition has never been more highly developed than in the last one hundred years or so, and it was during the same period that we have also seen the most cruel and destructive wars.

Sports have not caused them, of course; but they have done nothing to sublimate them. If anything, international competition has often only whipped up, in spectators and participants alike, the kind of adrenalin-euphoria that usually precedes actual violence. In this sense, competition has served more as a rehearsal than as a substitute for conflict. In some cases, such as the Belgian soccer stadium, a game has simply provided an additional excuse for people to bash each other over the head.

All of which is not to suggest that sporting events between nations should be curtailed, only that we should not ascribe a function to them that they clearly cannot and do not serve. At best, soccer matches or Olympic Games may not aggravate international tensions; they do nothing to relax them.

The second conclusion, for what it's worth, is that there seems to be no relationship between the violence or danger inherent in a sport and the amount of spectator violence it may engender. The relatively tame sport of soccer appears to be an all-time leader. Far more "violent" sports like ice hockey or football do not come close, nor do boxing or car racing, though they are often described as blood sports. If one includes spectators, my guess is that one year of soccer has resulted in more death and injury than a decade of Grand Prix racing and boxing combined.

The third conclusion, again for what it's worth, is that what happened in Belgium last week underlines how unrealistic it is to expect even civilized westerners to behave in a civilized manner. The rioters in Belgium were English and Italian, members of two of the most highly developed nations on earth, descendants of the creators of the Magna Carta and the Sistine Chapel. The issue over which they killed and maimed each other was a soccer game. If such people are capable of violence over such an issue, what possible expectations of restraint can we have of recent savages with no tradition of law and order? What can we expect of people who may be only one step removed from a Stone Age culture, and who may be facing issues fundamental to their survival? In proportion, it is a miracle that there isn't far more mayhem in the world. By the standards of the English and Italian soccer fans, entire nations should exterminate each other every year.

Which leads to my final conclusion: the danger inherent in groups. It is a fair guess that not one of the rioters, English or Italian, would have been individually prepared to kill a fellow spectator. But groups assembled for a purpose—any purpose—seem to have an innate capacity to become mobs. One person is generally harmless and reasonable, unless he happens to be wicked or sick. A hundred persons can run amok, even when they are individually sane and healthy. Not only when they're soccer fans, but when they assemble as political parties, labor unions, pressure groups, or anything else. They may not always be violent but they are always far shorter on temper, common sense, and equity than any individual.

Uniting people for a purpose, even to watch a concert, or even for a spiritual abstraction like religion or philosophy, may be the most dangerous of all human activities.

1985

THE POWER OF FASHION

The great German poet, Friedrich von Schiller, knew about fashion. Not in terms of the latest clothes or hairstyle, but in terms of the latest trends and ideas that may be in vogue from time to time. Schiller thought that fashion, in this sense, was a particularly powerful and merciless weapon. In his famous *Ode to Joy*, he likened it to a sword.

I believe Schiller was right. The edge of fashion is as sharp today as it was when he expressed this perception nearly two centuries ago. The sword of fashion is neither righteous nor wrongful, only mindless. Once in motion, it just goes snicker-snack, cutting through friend and foe alike. When a word becomes fashionable, people begin using it whether it fits or not. When an idea becomes fashionable, people begin acting on it whether it's right or wrong. When a concept becomes trendy, all other considerations go out the window. People just adopt it as if it were gospel.

Not at all fashionable ideas, words, concepts, or clothes are wrong, useless, or ugly. It's just that it doesn't matter whether they are or not. If they are in vogue, that's enough. Fashion is me-tooism run amok. That's easy enough to see when one looks at the fashion of other times or places. Yesterday's fashion is often the most ludicrous thing in the world, not only in clothes, but also in science, philosophy, politics, or religion. How could civilized twentieth-century westerners have believed in the curative powers of cold water, for instance? But they did, and not such a long time ago. The cold-water cure used to be bigger than acupuncture today.

The point is, it's almost impossible for most people to view the fashions of their own times and places as dispassionately and objectively as they can look at historical or foreign fashions. When it comes to the past, or to strange places, everyone can pick and choose, according to their tastes or to their considered judgment of what is true or false. They can say: this looks right, that looks wrong; this looks fine, that looks ugly. But the fashions of their own times usually render them speechless. They just follow and parrot them like automatons.

What fashion often does—especially in areas such as health, human relations, or lifestyle—is to get hold of a kernel of truth, then blow it all out of proportion. Fashion can take a bit of common sense—say, that it's not good to be grossly overweight or that one should not be unreasonably strict with one's children—and turn it into a taboo, a mania, or an obsession. When weight becomes a trend you'll see hordes of people trying to diet and exercise their bodies into unnatural shapes. In the '60s many youngsters from an entire generation lost their bearings, partly because their parents, frightened by Dr. Spock, had become so worried about "frustrating" their children that they had stopped raising them altogether.

A friend returning from a recent visit to California reports the story of a young man who felt constrained to break up an affair of long standing. "She was interfering with my exercise program," explained the young man, according to my friend. "I will only date casually from now on." The young man was quite serious, as Californians often are about whatever fad happens to catch their fancy. In that part of the world people are really earnest about fashion. Nowadays if you ask for a cup of coffee, for instance, a California restaurant is likely to serve you the decaffeinated kind—automatically. You have to specify, even insist sometimes, if you want the real stuff.

Few things illustrate the power of fashion as clearly as current attitudes to cigarette smoking. Medical science has been unanimous all over the world about the potential harm of smoking for quite some time. People know about the probable link between smoking and heart disease in France or Spain or Austria every bit as well as in North America. But the *fashion*—as opposed to the mere medical knowledge—has not caught on in most parts of Europe. People have not become hysterical about smoking. They simply note that it's potentially bad for you, like alcohol, greasy foods, or trying to cross the Champs Élysées against a red light. Then they go on smoking—or not—as they please. Not in California, boy! There, smoking is regarded as a moral failing, almost as bad as disliking granola.

When the late actor John Belushi and his friend Cathy Smith were ordering what turned out to be Belushi's last breakfast in Los Angeles, they specified that the toast should be whole wheat. It seems they didn't want to ruin their bodies by eating junk food. There they were, sitting in a hotel room, shot up to the eyeballs with cocaine, heroin, and God knows what else, but being careful not to break the codes of California's health-food trends. That's fashion.

1985

A LONE GHOST FROM THE '60s

The gentleman sitting on the sidewalk across from Tokyo's Shibuya Station is the owner of a little fat puppy. The puppy clearly thinks that it is very silly to sit there in the 90-degree heat, and is trying to get under the shade of the blanket which the gentleman has spread on the sidewalk. The Sunday crowds swirl in a little eddy of interest around the puppy and his master, perhaps because dogs are not a very common sight in Tokyo. It's not because the Japanese are not fond of dogs—in fact, a statue right outside Shibuya Station commemorates the legendary faithful dog Hachiko—but because in Tokyo it's hard enough to find room for fifteen million people and their cars.

The owner of the puppy is not Japanese. His pants and T-shirt are earth colored, and he wears his thinning hair and scraggly beard in the

Christ-like fashion of the 1960s. His possessions seem to consist of a small bundle of rags and a few crayons in a tin cup. He is not begging, though. He just sits on his blanket in deep contemplation. Around him, the high-tech materialism of the West, which he no doubt attempted to exchange fifteen or twenty years ago for what he thought were the spiritual gifts of the Orient, now blares and pulsates with a vengeance from the label-conscious electronic elegance of the Ginza to the frenzied liquid-crystal displays of the Akihabara. A veritable parody of the American century, pursed with Japanese single-mindedness, surrounds the aging flower child at the end of his quest.

While Western Europe may have started, and America may have perfected, everything that Chaplin caricatured in his film *Modern Times*, it is the Japanese who are bringing it to its ultimate conclusion: more and better business, more and better organization, more and better technology, more and better high fashion. For that matter, more and better personal hygiene. The values of the West are reaching the state of the art in the Far East.

Perhaps the reason is as simple as an innate gift for numbers. Most people in Japan seem to be able to add up a column of figures at a single glance. In a given building all units will begin with the number nine. A new marketing strategy will be referred to as the two S's for, say, safety and service. It is a mind-set tailor-made for the Computer Age.

Another reason may be illustrated by the evident amusement of a teenage girl in the subway at the sight of three Americans: one a huge brunette, the second a slight blonde, the third a medium-sized redhead. The fact is, occidentals are so haphazard. They grow every which way. They come in all kinds of colours. The girl simply can't help giggling— very politely, behind her hand—at the sight of such confusion and disorder.

In her natural world the Japanese girl would never be exposed to such a profusion of shapes and hues. People would be quite different from one another, of course, but within reason. A few inches maybe, or a few pounds or a few gentle shades. Nothing to compare with the chaotic anarchy Europeans exhibit by their very physical presence. Orderliness, ritual, and discipline are the key to modern times. They may be its very foundation. Software programmed to hardware in so many predictable bytes. Ultimately, ironically, homogeneous and ritualistic Japan may be intrinsically better suited to the twentieth century than America or Europe.

It seems so. In any case, at this moment in time, in front of the Shibuya Station the greying, decrepit American hippie sits on his blanket. He owns nothing but a tin cup of crayons and a puppy dog. He dropped out of his culture to explore the mysteries of Asia, which has now chosen to explode around him in a frenzy of electronically amplified rock music, video arcades, Givenchy originals, and fuel-injected Suzukis. Up-to-date Japan passes by the bewildered fakir, courteously amused.

1985

BEWARE THE UGLY TOURIST

My uncle came back from Europe the other day and said: "Drat! They swarm like bees. You can't drop a needle." He wasn't talking about the natives. He was talking about tourists. I knew what he was talking about because I remember a day, not long ago, on St. Mark's Square in Venice where large ladies in pant suits outnumbered the pigeons. I remember arriving in Salzburg, Austria, by car then driving another two hundred kilometres to Vienna because I couldn't find a parking place.

Before anyone assumes that this is going to be some kind of a philippic against travellers or travelling, let me make something clear. I have nothing against travelling. I'm a frequent traveller myself. What I'm talking about is ladies, with their husbands and often their children in tow, all dressed in a manner wholly appropriate for a visit to the zoo but somewhat out of place around the shopping districts or historical sites of Paris or Rome, who travel thousands of miles for only two discernible purposes: one, to search for a lavatory and two, to photograph each other searching for it.

I would also like to make it clear that I'm not talking about the Ugly American (or Canadian). I'm talking about the Ugly Tourist, who for the past quarter century could be a citizen of any of the industrialized nations: America, certainly, but also Germany, France, Australia, or Japan. The Ugly Tourist is not distinguished by nationality. He has several traits in common with others of his kind, but nationality is not one of them. Neither is religion nor race.

The main characteristic of the Ugly Tourist is his total spiritual unpreparedness for a journey abroad. Any journey. He is relentlessly ignorant of the countries he visits; he will know nothing about their history, customs, or language. Often, he will even know nothing about their geography, currency, climate, or cuisine. He will have no intention of ever conducting any business in them. It will be a complete, abiding mystery why he wants to visit those countries in the first place.

Not only will the Ugly Tourist have no knowledge, he will generally lack a sense of awe or even curiosity. The architecture will bore him. The gibberish of foreign languages will irritate him. The food will make him sick. As often as not, he will return from his trip abroad worn out and in a foul mood. If he has travelled with his spouse, he will be lucky if he returns with his marriage intact.

In addition to a penchant for photography and a weak bladder, what the Ugly Tourist will have in common with other ugly tourists is a disposable income sufficient for a return ticket, economy class, and a nature vengeful enough to be determined to bore his neighbors with slides of his journey at least as much as they have bored him with their slides the previous year. He will be the kind of person who is willing to ruin his own vacation, and deplete his pocketbook doing it, for an act of revenge.

The minor curse of the vulgar tourist is peculiar to modern times, and it came with the invention of the transoceanic jet. Until then, traveling was a fairly complex matter. At a minimum, it involved more time than the two-week period normally available to massed phalanxes of the polyester set. Until recently, people who travelled came in three categories. One, there were the people who had some business in the countries they travelled to, and were engaged in attending to it instead of spoiling the view in front of the Notre Dame. Two, there were dedicated travellers of modest means, for whom a trip was a sufficiently major matter to spend years preparing themselves for it, and consequently knew as much or more about the countries they were visiting than the people who lived in them. Three, there were the idle rich who, whatever their failings, were very few in number. Rolls-Royces were incapable of causing a traffic jam.

All this has changed through the mixed blessings of general affluence and modern technology. Any boor with ten days of leisure time and a few installment-plan dollars can clog up the arteries of Europe or the Orient, and is relentlessly doing so. This may be great for airlines, travel agents, and hotel chains. I'm not knocking it. I simply point out that it is not great for those who wish to see and savour the world.

If you do not wish to be an Ugly Tourist, here are some simple rules. Don't travel, unless (a) you have some business in the place you're going to, (b) can pass a high-school exam in the culture, or maybe conduct a simple conversation in the language of the place you're planning to visit, or (c) can afford to fly the Concorde. If you can meet one of these three conditions, your trip will not be a complete waste of fossil fuel and you may even enjoy it. More importantly, you won't spoil the enjoyment of others.

1985

FORTUNES OF WAR

Exactly thirty years ago the 25th of October fell on a Thursday. I remember being in a blue funk. Earlier that week an actress I had been hoping to date finally agreed to meet me for an espresso, the tiny bitter cup of coffee over which most people used to meet in Budapest (and probably still do).

It was to have been a heavy date, but it never came about. What prevented it was the Hungarian revolution that broke out in the evening of the 23rd, a Tuesday. It turned the cafe where I was supposed to meet Marika into a rebel stronghold by the next afternoon. The place was still under sporadic fire when I got there, making my way with the grim determination of a twenty-one-year-old in lust. Two marble tables, overturned for barricades at the entrance, had cracked from the impact of bullets, and the trays of pastries on the counter were sprinkled with powdered glass.

Marika didn't show, proving that girls have slightly more sense in these matters than boys. I left the country a month later, and nearly fourteen years were to pass before she and I could have our cup of coffee. By then both of us had married, divorced, and remarried. "History prevented us from making love," she declared when we finally met, sounding a trifle dramatic and pleased with herself. She was, after all, an actress by profession.

There is a sense in which all history is personal, whether one is an actress or not. A friend of my grandfather used to reply, when asked about the Great War: "For me, boy, the First World War was three yards wide and fifty yards long. That was the size of the trench in which I was squatting for two and a half years, keeping my head low."

My memories of the 1956 revolution in Hungary are grander. A missed date is part of what I remember, but only a small part. The truth is, I remember enough to have spent a lifetime trying to sort it out and I'm still not finished.

Sometimes I regret that I was only twenty-one when I lived through the revolution. History, like so many things, is wasted on the young. Sometimes, however, I'm glad. Experience in itself teaches you little. It's the time you have to think about it that teaches you—and only if you're lucky, because time has a way of running out.

For a friend of mine named Emil it ran out before the end of that week in October, thirty years ago. A short fellow, Emil had dropped out of school to become a jockey. That's how he came to be sitting with a group of other jockeys in the open loft of the stables at the racetrack, watching some Soviet tanks rumble across the field. The jockeys didn't make the slightest effort to hide their curiosity—which they would have, if they'd had any hostile designs on the tanks. When the turret of one of the T-34s started swinging toward the loft, Emil and his friends continued sitting there, smoking, with their feet propped up on the benches.

That was, at least, what a survivor said after the tank fired a single shell.

Emil himself didn't say much. The explosion tore off his shoulder and, trying to explain to rescuers what had happened, he only said: "In the stables...goddamn Russians...Mother, mother...." Young men often call for their mothers when dying of traumatic wounds. Funeral homes were closed in wartime, so we buried Emil in the garden behind our apartment building the next day.

I'm recounting the episode not because it proves much, but because it happened. Soldiers in tanks are also young and frightened men; that's why we shouldn't send them into other people's countries.

Recently I asked a different question of George Faludy, the Hungarian poet, after re-reading his poem to Imre Nagy, Hungary's prime minister in 1956, who was executed by the Soviets after the revolution.

The thing to know about Faludy, 76, poet, social democrat, and Nobel Prize nominee, who has been living in Toronto for the past eighteen years, is that in the 1950s he had spent years in a communist labour camp in Hungary. The thing to know about ex-prime minister Nagy is that while Faludy was being tortured and starved in the stone quarries, he was a very high-ranking official of the communist regime.

"Yet in your poem," I said to Faludy, "you set him on a pedestal. You describe Nagy as a hero. Aren't you being too saintly? Shouldn't people be held responsible for the consequences of their ideas, even if they too fall victims to them in the end?"

Imre Nagy certainly ended up as a victim. After 1956 he was hanged, which in that part of the world means being garroted, probably after having his arms broken before his execution in the Soviet fashion. Whatever his former comrades say today, they killed Nagy only for trying to save Hungary for communism; save it by reform, so that communism might have a human face. Because that was all that Nagy wanted—though, in fact, Hungary's political life might have changed far more fundamentally had the revolution succeeded.

Faludy shook his head. "Look at how Nagy behaved in the final period of his life," he replied. "A man has a right to be judged by his final acts." So does a country, Faludy added, or an ideology, even those with the bloodiest record of mistakes—if they do not run out of time.

1986

THE SMOKE DETECTORS

Transport Minister John Crosbie announced last week that the cabinet will consider banning smoking on all domestic flights of two hours duration or less. Enforcement will be the air carriers' responsibility, Crosbie said. They will be required to remove any passengers at the next available stop who continue puffing after being requested to desist.

I was impressed with the government's wise restraint. After all, our rulers could have requested air carriers to remove such passengers in mid-flight. (The half-measure of merely removing unrepentant smokers at the next available stop will probably leave anti-smoking lobbyists dissatisfied, especially as it dawns on them that by then most such passengers will have arrived at their destinations anyway.)

The government also showed its willingness to compromise by not extending the ban to cockpit crew members. As Crosbie put it, "We can't see them having withdrawal symptoms as they are attempting to fly the aircraft." Well, I don't know. Why sacrifice important principles to such minor matters of expediency? I'm sure that dedicated non-smokers' rights advocates would prefer a chancy landing to some nicotinist engaging in his unspeakable practices behind closed cockpit doors. (By now the ban *has* been extended to the cockpit.)

Instead of making such allowances to crass realism, the very use of the sexist word "cockpit" should be reconsidered, as Canada's government gets on with the vital task of purifying the unconscious linguistic prejudices of a smoke-free society for which it has been elected in the first place. (However, as a discussion of this might take us too far afield, I will tear myself away and return to my original point.)

Spokesmen for Air Canada as well as two private airlines were quoted in the papers reacting to Crosbie's announcement. Their reactions gave a perfect illustration of what I can only describe as the essence of both public and private enterprise's attitude. Forget about the issue of smoking. What their remarks illustrate has nothing to do with smoking as such: their attitude would be the same on any other subject.

Private enterprise, in the persons of Max Ward from Wardair and Donald Party from Canadian Pacific, welcomed the government's decision. Their reason, according to the papers, was that it allows industry to step back from something it has been loath to touch as it might alienate customers either way. What is a poor entrepreneur to do when some people smoke, some are bothered by second-hand smoke, and some don't give a hoot one way or the other?

The truth is—obviously—that a total smoking ban is not yet a market demand. If it were, it would be quite unnecessary for the government to legislate it. Customers would simply flock to the airline that does not permit smoking. But since it is not, whatever an airline decides, it might lose out to a competitor who makes a different decision. Even worse, a sharp competitor might come up with the devilish idea of creating two cabins with separate ventilation systems for smokers and non-smokers. In the space age it's technically feasible (to put it mildly) to devise such a system; it only costs some money. Or even simpler, he may schedule a smoking and a non-smoking flight. What if a competitor decides that it's worth it, and what if he's right? Then Ward or Party would have the headache of having to spend a few million dollars themselves on matching systems, or watch the competition gain an edge.

There may have been a time when private enterprise prided itself on giving the best service, and on trying to satisfy all tastes and demands. The idea was that the customer came first. Not anymore. Industry's great discovery in Ward's and Party's day is that the customer no longer has to be satisfied—as long as the government makes sure that no competitor can satisfy him more.

Please give us more regulation, say today's entrepreneurs, as long as it applies to all of us equally. Relieve us from having to use our heads as the demands of the market shift with the times. Don't let those of us who are smarter or bolder gain an advantage. Just tell us what to do. Should we stop providing any convenience—pillows, coffee, booze, anything—it's fine with us. Just as long as the competition is not permitted to provide them either. Protect us from each other, dear government. Then we will be good boys and never try to protect our customers from you.

As for the customer's standing with public enterprise, it was succinctly expressed by Air Canada's Vladimir Slivitzky: "I'm a smoker, and if I can go without a cigarette for two hours, so can others." A bit high-handed, you say? Even arrogant? Heaven forbid. It's just a standard test all state-owned enterprises apply to their customers: whatever Slivitzky can go without. We can thank our lucky stars that Slivitzky is not overly abstemious or continent, or else Air Canada would no longer feel obliged to provide galleys or heads on shorter domestic flights.

1986

What Men Really Want

A friend of mine, a highly accomplished man, is a confirmed bachelor. Though the expression has gone out of fashion the practice has not, and there are probably as many confirmed bachelors around today as there ever were.

However, I'm not going to talk about confirmed bachelors here but their nieces. Confirmed bachelors often have nieces. (They also have nephews, of course, but I'm narrowing the subject.) In any case, nieces or nephews, they tend to be fond of Uncle Billy, and sometimes prefer him to their own parents.

Uncle Billy is also fond of them, generally speaking, and he expresses his fondness by giving them presents and smoothing their paths in life in other material ways. It is only when they want guidance that Uncle Billy is often stymied. After all, one of the fundamental reasons he stayed a bachelor was not to be obliged to give guidance to the pitter-patter set.

I'm not a confirmed bachelor, but I sympathize with Uncle Billy. Juniors of either sex are notorious for craving guidance while bitterly resisting it at the same time. Some people find this charming. I find it something of a bore. As Uncle Billy's friend, however, I can't very well decline when he calls to send his nineteen-year-old niece around. As he puts it: "You are a writer, aren't you? You're very free with your advice to the Western world. So, give some advice to Sally."

"Sally and the Western world have one thing in common. Neither of them listens to me."

"Good, then you're not in for any surprises," is Billy's usual reply.

In the past Sally has wanted to know how to become a writer. I have tiptoed around the subject over the years, with Sally and with others, not having the heart to tell them the blunt truth. The blunt truth is that if you have to ask someone how to become a writer you're probably not cut out to be one.

This time Sally only wanted to know about the nature of man. Man as in "male" not as in "mankind." What she asked was: "What makes men tick?"

"You mean, what makes them tick for you?"

"Yeah," Sally replied. "That too. That mainly," she added with disarming candour.

"I can give you a long answer," I said, "but the short answer is smile and wash your hair."

"You mean, men are sexists and they like women to be accommodating and pretty?" asked Sally, frowning.

This has become a touchy subject these days, but I see no point in giving advice unless it is the best of my knowledge, which is that everybody prefers everybody else to be accommodating, and—except for kinky people who are turned on by acne scars—everybody likes everybody else to be pretty. (Of course, one person's "pretty" may not be exactly the same as another person's "pretty," but on the whole everybody knows what pretty means.)

Women prefer these qualities in men no less than men prefer them in women. The only difference is that women tend to use the word "kind" for accommodating, and the word "handsome" for pretty. Another difference is that while women find it natural that they prefer kind and handsome men, some women have come to resent that men prefer accommodating and pretty women.

"I smile when I feel like it," said Sally defiantly, "and when I feel like it, I wash my hair."

"That's sufficient," I said, "if you feel like it often enough. If you don't, the fellows may go for a girl who feels like it more often than you do, or who does it whether she feels like it or not."

"But isn't that unfair?"

"Not really. It's only unfortunate for sullen people with unkempt hair. You're not such a person, are you?"

Sally thought about this for a minute, for an amplitude of reasons. "Isn't it more important to be intelligent, concerned, and honest?" she asked finally.

"Yes, if you want to be some guy's executive secretary. Or his boss, for that matter. If you want to be his girlfriend, no."

This was a half-truth, I suppose. Intelligence and concern can make up for a lot, even a bad temper and a bad complexion. But if they are to be used as compensatory qualities, matters of the spirit or the mind have to exist in true abundance. A bachelor's degree from York University may not be enough.

"Don't you think that this is just a question of social conditioning?" Sally asked. "That if we educated them differently men would see what is of real value in a woman?"

"You mean that what's-his-name, Teddy, would have declared himself to you in a non-sexist society?"

"Well, yes," replied Sally, "if you must put it this way."

I'd like my readers to think of me as a man of moral courage. I'd like to be able to report that when Sally asked me this question, I looked her straight in the eye and said: "No way, baby!" But the truth is, I'm a coward. When I looked Sally in the eye all I could say was: "Gee, Sally, maybe. I really don't know."

1986

A BANDAIDS SOLUTION

Nothing is as "in" these days as pushing advertising for condoms in the battle against AIDS. Even the *Globe and Mail* may get into the act, not to mention mother CBC. Groups are already talking about promoting condoms to thirteen-year-olds in schools. Soon glossy pictures of the little rubber sheaths will be as common on the nation's TV screens as pictures of Florida oranges.

I don't particularly object to this; I only find it ludicrous. I think it's also very typical of our ostrich society, intent on sticking its collective head into the sand on this and most other important matters.

Ask any doctor, ask any research or clinical student of the deadly epidemic of AIDS. Oh, they'll probably agree that condoms provide some protection against the disease; they will probably say that they are better than nothing. They will also add that the protection condoms provide is *insufficient*. There isn't one medical person—certainly not one I have ever heard about—who would knowingly risk engaging in sexual intercourse with an actual or potential (that is, seropositive) AIDS patient relying on a condom for protection. Sexual intercourse? Many workers in the field won't even *touch* AIDS patients without rubber gloves.

The reason politicians, public health and educational bureaucrats, as well as media pundits are jumping on the condom-bandwagon with such alacrity is simple. It permits them to sidestep the real issue a little longer. Why do they wish to sidestep the real issue? Because it cuts too close to the bone.

AIDS is a contagious and, at this point in time, fatal disease, transmitted chiefly through sexual contact. Some people believe that it has been visited upon our generation in punishment for our sins. I certainly believe no such thing, but I do believe that, by sheer coincidence, AIDS has struck at the roots of the hedonistic, permissive society that ours has become since about the early 1960s.

The main reason that AIDS is the kind of threat it is, the main reason that it may become an epidemic to rival the Black Death in western societies, is because of our tolerance of sexual promiscuity in general, coupled with our fear of appearing to be intolerant of homosexuality in particular.

Without these factors, AIDS might have cropped up as a rare disease. It might have spread from central Africa to the rest of the world in the era of jet travel and popular tourism in any event, but it would never have threatened to reach epidemic proportions. There are other local or tropical illnesses, some equally deadly, some equally contagious, that pose no such threat. AIDS does, precisely because we are the kind of society we are. The cause of the disease is a virus—but the cause of the epidemic is a lifestyle. The use of condoms won't change that. They won't even serve as bandAIDS.

The only effective prophylactic measure against an epidemic such as AIDS is to refrain from casual or indiscriminate sexual contact with a variety of partners. Although this would not stamp out the disease, it would probably contain it until a cure can be found. It would prevent it from becoming a major hazard to public health.

But how can politicians or media pundits advocate this? The entire basis of our modern society in the last quarter of a century has been the promotion of a "liberated" lifestyle. Doing your own thing, indulging in your own sexual tastes, and having "non-judgmental" attitudes in matters of morality has become the only possible stance of so-called enlightened or progressive people. Actually the only *lawful* stance, since refusing a job or an apartment to, say, an unwed mother (or, lately, to a homosexual) for reasons of private moral disapproval has been pro-hibited by "human rights" codes.

We need not single out homosexuals. Today, if we withdrew social approval for casual sex with a variety of partners, we would have to re-think certain aspects of the entire women's movement. Our new "no-fault" divorce laws, which were introduced to encourage, or at least to protect, sexually promiscuous behavior, would have to be returned to the drawing board. How can we contemplate such a fun-damental turnaround?

It is simpler to push condoms on TV, or to thirteen-year-olds in school. It is simpler to pretend that it's a solution. It is simpler to pro-mote a sense of false security (which in the long run can only aggravate the problem) while we keep our fingers crossed that medical research will somehow get us out of the mess.

1987

A RIGHT TO BE INFECTIOUS?

A gentleman of my acquaintance, upon becoming a widower a few years ago, started leading a rather active romantic life with a variety of partners, in spite (or perhaps because) of his advanced age. Recently his daughter asked him if he wasn't afraid of AIDS.

"Let's see, my dear," replied the sturdy old fellow, "I'm now eighty-two. I understand AIDS has an incubation period of five or six years, and then it takes another two or three years before it kills you. No, I guess I'm not particularly afraid of AIDS."

I wouldn't vouch for Romeo Senior's mathematics because no one is quite certain about the incubation period of AIDS. The time it takes for the illness to run its fatal course varies from person to person. Still, once you reach the shady side of eighty, the calculation may make some (selfish) sense, especially when, like the oldster in question, you belong to a staunchly heterosexual, low-risk group.

Alas, I've heard much younger members of very high-risk groups talk about AIDS with similar nonchalance. Nonchalance may not be the right word, actually; aggressiveness is probably a better one. The fact is that, though some people have fundamentally changed their sexual habits (if not their orientation) because of AIDS, others have reacted with something very close to defiance.

I have no idea whether it's the chickens or the hawks who are in the majority in this regard, but it's evident that both attitudes exist. While the chickens tend to be quiet, some of the hawks are quite vocal. Their attitude is on display, among other places, in the letters-to-the-editor columns of the current issue of *Toronto Life*, which ran a cover story on AIDS three months ago. Some AIDS-hawks, having been angered by the article, wish to convey the following messages:

1) AIDS is barely infectious, so no one should fear or ostracize members of high-risk groups. E.g.: "Granted, there is much we don't know about AIDS; however, we *do* know the disease cannot be transmitted through casual contact."

2) AIDS does not require people to change their sexual habits, only their techniques. E.g.: "Sex doesn't kill, AIDS-related illnesses kill." Or: "You can be very safe without relying on condoms, and still have sex with thousands of different people, or even have sex regularly with someone who has AIDS."

3) People who list monogamy, not to mention celibacy, among the

possible ways of checking the epidemic are impractical, moraliz-
ing hate-mongers, who lack understanding and compassion for
AIDS-victims, homosexuals, and liberated men and women in
general. E.g.: "[Paul] Roberts [writer of the *Toronto Life* article]
has set compassion back centuries."

I hate to seem harsh, but it's precisely these attitudes that may force
society to take drastic measures to protect itself. In fact—unless
medical research solves the problem within the next few years—the
case for Draconian public hygiene laws may become overwhelming.
What else will subdue some people whose capacity for selfishness is
exceeded only by their incapacity for grasping plain facts—and possibly also by their sex-drive?

A few years ago someone could, perhaps, have expressed the
opinion in good faith that AIDS "cannot" be transmitted except
through intimate sexual contact. Today no one can honestly say this.
The only honest statement that can be made these days is that AIDS
does not seem to be highly infectious—as infectious diseases go—and
that the risk of catching it through casual contact is low.

As for catching it through somewhat less casual contact, such as
mutual masturbation—well, what can one say? The risk is no doubt
lower than through anal intercourse, but probably higher than through
a telephone call.

Saying that sex doesn't kill, only AIDS does, is quite true. It is also
quite meaningless. If we refrain from shaking hands with lepers it's not
because we think that handshakes kill, only because we fear that leprosy
might. We know that speeding doesn't kill either, only crashing does,
but having discovered some causal relationship between the two, we still
frown at people who drive at 160 km/h upon the public highway.

The AIDS-hawks insist on their absolute right to their own (sexual)
driving habits. They promise only to improve their driving techniques,
as far as practicable. Should we answer that this may not be enough,
they charge us with a lack of compassion. I don't know.

"Compassion" seems to be a curious word in the mouths of those
who view it as a human right to spread a fatal disease.

1987

WORLDLY-WISE RELIGIONS

Let me say a few words about liberation theology. Since I'm not a Catholic—or a believer of any kind—obviously my views will be those of an outsider. I offer no apologies for my breezy tone. It's the only way I can talk about the subject.

Traditionally, the greatest thing about religion used to be that it gave people a second kick at the cat. Virtually all faiths included the promise of an afterlife of some kind. What happened to someone in this life was not the whole ball game.

In addition, almost all religions included the concept of a judgment. This was also great. It not only prevented some nasty people from behaving as obnoxiously in this life as they otherwise might have, but it reassured the rest of us—the good guys—that our merits would eventually be rewarded. Somebody up there would notice how noble, useful, and self-sacrificing we had been. That was good news for many of us, because we always suspected that nobody noticed it down here.

However, in this century most religions have lost much of their transcendental nature. Put another way, religions retained only one of God's domains: the Earth. They lost the other two: heaven and hell. Not entirely, and not for all of the faithful, but enough to bring about a change of emphasis.

It was the transcendental part of religion that concerned itself with afterlife and judgment. Religion had many other concerns, such as custom, ritual, or morality, but these had to do with the here and now, not with the great beyond.

The here and now looms large even today. Custom, ritual, and morality, in changed forms maybe, are still very much with us. The churches still function splendidly as clubs, schools, pressure groups, or political parties, even in the computer age. It is only the great beyond, religion's transcendental concern, that got lost somewhere along the way. This, it seems to me, has been the origin of some theologians' preoccupation with "justice."

Until recently, the emphasis of religion has not been on justice, whether social or economic. Of course, wordly justice was always regarded as an ideal. The just or charitable man was always highly praised. Still, equity on Earth was not religion's main preoccupation. The faithful were urged to be just and charitable, but chiefly for the salvation of their own souls.

This was natural enough in God's triple domain, of which Earth was only one, and not even the most important, part. When Earth was just a practice run, so to speak, it didn't matter so much how well people did in it. In fact, compared to eternity, it was pretty insignificant. What mattered was that people should be well placed for the main bout.

Once heaven and hell started being de-emphasized, once even religious persons started suspecting that life on Earth may *be* the main bout, it followed that secular life became the most important thing. The only important thing, in fact. If religion could not offer justice on Earth, it had very little else to offer.

There was only one problem with this. It was that in many people's vocabulary "justice" simply meant having at least as much of the world's goods, power, or prestige as the next guy. Few people ever thought that if they (or their group or nation) had less than others it might be exactly what they deserved. On the contrary, people always tended to regard having less than others as the plainest proof of injustice.

Religion, in its transcendental days, never resisted this universal human tendency but it did not give into it either. "What do you expect?" the churches used to say to the faithful. "The world is supposed to be an unjust place. That's why you, personally, should strive to be charitable and just. Then you'll have something to be rewarded for in the next life."

Religion took this position in the understanding that social justice was separated from envy by only a very thin line. The job of separation had better be left to God. Bishops used to assume that they knew no more about worldly justice than economists or statesmen, and in many ways they knew even less.

The theologians of "liberation" seem to have lost this humility, along with their faith in heaven and hell. In fact, the only thing in which they have retained any faith has been their own moral authority.

However, such moral authority as theologians have ever had came from their transcendental beliefs. *With* this belief, of course, justice could safely be left to God. *Without* it, theologians or bishops are no more assured than the rest of us that they can separate the virtue of justice from the vice of envy.

1987

THE RIGHT TO BE CRAZY

The German philosopher Immanuel Kant believed that insanity could be cured by lessons in philosophy. Insanity, argued Kant, consists of faulty reasoning; ergo, if philosophers instructed madmen in the art of correct reasoning, the madmen would get well again.

Such a theory makes us chuckle these days. Reason with madmen? We look at faulty reasoning only as a symptom of madness, not as its cause. We rarely try to "talk sense" to people we consider to be insane. We don't use logic to prove to paranoiacs that a pop song is not a secret message, or that their stockbroker is not using gamma-rays to put bad thoughts into their heads. On the whole, we don't even consider insanity to be an "emotional" illness. We have gone far beyond not only the Kantian Age of Reason, but even the psychoanalytic age of Professor Freud. We still send harmless neurotics to a shrink, but are likely to regard full-blown madness as something physical. We look for a brain lesion or a chemical imbalance of some kind, and generally try to treat (or contain) it with drugs or surgery.

But what about insane *opinions*? What about social, political, or economic views held by a person (or a group of persons) that everyone else in a given society regards as utterly, demonstrably false? What about opinions that run counter to plain, easily observable facts? What about insane opinions when held by a country's government (even if by few citizens) or held by an entire nation (even if by no other nation on Earth)?

What about South African apartheid or theocratic Iran? What about China under the Gang of Four? What about the ideas of a Pol Pot or Idi Amin—to mention just a few recent examples?

What about far-left or far-right groups within a normal country, such as Canada? Are the views of a person like the pamphleteer Ernst Zundel anything less than mad? Can we use any other word but "insane" to describe his opinions?

I certainly can't. Zundel claims that something didn't happen—namely the Holocaust—that I witnessed with my own eyes as a child in Europe. What else can I call Zundel but a madman?

That's what I called the late Canadian poet Milton Acorn at the other end of the political spectrum. Acorn kept insisting that the Soviet Union sent tanks to Hungary in 1956 to defeat a fascist revolution. As an eyewitness, I knew that Acorn was as crazy as Zundel. (There was a difference. Zundel got criminally charged for his views, while Acorn received several Canada Council grants.)

But how do we deal with madness as a socio-political phenomenon? Do we start *reasoning* with the insane? Introduce them to philosophy? Do we oblige Idi Amin to read the collected works of Wittgenstein? (Even Immanuel Kant might chuckle at this idea.) Or do we send Zundel or Acorn to a psychiatrist? Do we subject them to electric shocks? Do we put people who hold insane socio-political views into an insane asylum?

God, no: that's what they do in the Soviet Union. Except in a communist system it is generally the *sanest* citizens, those who try to reason against the madness of their government, who end up in psychiatric wards. We cannot follow the example of such countries.

So how do we deal with socio-political insanity? Punish it? But we never punish people who think their stockbrokers bombard them with gamma rays. It isn't unlawful for a person to view himself as a Bengal tiger, or refuse to sit down because his posterior is made of bone china. Being crazy is an illness, not a crime.

Madness doesn't become a crime just because it happens to take a socio-political form. Whether he believes himself to be racially superior or a roast duck, the madman's delusion is not under his control. He's just as entitled to his madness as he is to his kidney stones. Being crazy is a fundamental human right.

If a nut thinks he's a windmill and starts flailing his arms at people, we can put him in a straitjacket. But the socio-politically insane rarely flail their arms. More often they just try to insist on their crazy ideas, from white supremacy to rent control, contrary to all facts and logic.

Yes, I did use the example of rent control. Yes, it can be mentioned in the same breath with white supremacy. So can "pay equity." If the test for madness is demonstrable falsehood, many of the current economic or political ideas of the "progressive" left are as crazy as Zundel's. Not nearly as evil or dangerous, but every bit as divorced from reality.

You can't reason with madmen—they're mad. You can't feed them Valium or put them in jail—they're entitled to be mad. What *can* you do? Well, wait for Santa Claus I guess. Hope for some peace and good will on Earth.

1987

THE VIEW FROM THE FENCE

There is often a superficial resemblance between saints and people who just don't give a damn. It's true that modern liberals wouldn't condemn a woman taken in adultery any more than Jesus did in The Gospel according to John, Chapter 8, but our urbane contemporaries would decline to cast stones for a different reason. Christ had a tolerance for sinners; modern liberals have a tolerance for sin.

I'm using the example only for illustration. It isn't current sexual mores in particular, but an overall tendency in western thought that disturbs me. It is more than just our taste for moral equivocation: it is our belief that such equivocation adds up to some higher form of morality.

It has often puzzled me why we have come to regard it as such a great achievement to take no position on anything. It may calm us, but it's easy to be calm about things that do not engage our passion. Detachment, taken in itself, is hardly a virtue. It is true that saints, too, look at human conflicts dispassionately (or rather compassionately) sometimes, but not by reason of being blind.

Someone asked me recently if I could express in a paragraph what irks me most about the mainstream of academic thought and media opinion in our society. I replied that perhaps it's the pride we take in no longer seeing any issues of right and wrong—coupled with the belief that we're somehow *above* what we cannot see.

Also, I singled out what I've called a peculiarly Canadian illusion: the illusion that moral leadership in the world requires strict neutrality, not just between East and West, or communism and capitalism, but between good and evil.

I call it Canadian, because today no country exemplifies this tendency more plainly than Canada. Not even Sweden. We have raised fence-sitting to the level of an Olympic sport. Soon we'll hand out medals not for human achievement or for valour, but for being sufficiently non-judgmental and value-free.

The syndrome is not restricted to Canada, of course. Liberals all over the world are basking in the belief that they are being charitable or judicious when they are merely sticking their heads in the sand. They remind me of my grandfather, who acquired an undeserved reputation for stoicism during the war.

Grandfather often gathered up his shaving kit in the middle of the worst air raids, heading from the shelter to his own bathroom upstairs. "For heaven's sake, Mr. Klug, aren't you afraid?" people would scream at him over the explosions. In fact, the old gentleman was extremely hard of hearing. "Why, bless me, it's quiet now," he'd reply, adding once: "It's just a little dusty," having no idea why the plaster was shaking loose all around him from the walls.

To my grandfather's credit, he was never under any illusion that his auditory ailments added up to courage. Despite the similarity of external symptoms, he knew he wasn't brave—only deaf. Today's liberals, however, have come to believe that there is something courageous, perhaps even saintly, about hearing, seeing, and speaking no evil.

For instance, they regard it as very crass and vulgar for President Ronald Reagan to refer to the Soviet Union as the "evil empire." Not that liberals deny the historic acts that merit the adjective—not even the Kremlin bothers denying them anymore—but that it's somehow crude and untutored to use the word. Why, it's a judgmental word; not a word to be used in the best circles.

Similarly, words like "freedom fighter" (or "terrorist") are gradually disappearing from the liberal press, to be replaced by neutral words like "insurgent" or "rebel." These days it's only "rebels" who are fighting the Soviet army in the Afghan mountains.

Frankly, even taking the wrong side of an issue seems better to me than this smug form of moral cowardice, especially when it's masquerading as superior enlightenment. Much as I abhor the views of the Ayatollah Khomeini, at least he's not trying to elevate a vacuum into a virtue. This is the specialty of today's middle-of-the-road liberals.

The poet W. B. Yeats' commented on our century: "The best lack all convictions, while the worst/ Are full of passionate intensity." Yeats only made a rueful observation, of course; he did not recommend discarding all convictions as a route to excellence. Maybe today's liberals have misunderstood him.

As they seem to have misunderstood the lesson of The Gospel according to John, Chapter 8. "He that is without sin among you, let him first cast a stone at her," said Jesus to the accusers of the adulterous woman. But after they withdrew, convicted by their consciences, Jesus did not explain to the woman that in an enlightened society adultery ought to be a human right. He said to her: "Go, and sin no more."

1988

BUTT 'EM IF YOU HAVE 'EM

The story may be apocryphal, but it seems a motorist stopped to pick up a hitchhiker on the highway recently. When the car got under way again, the motorist fished out a cigarette from his pocket.

"Would you mind not lighting up?" asked the hitchhiker. "Smoke really bothers me."

"Gee, sorry," said the driver. "It's, uh, you know, my car and…. Oh, never mind. Maybe I'll just open the window."

"You want me to catch a cold?" asked the hitchhiker indignantly.

"You're just taking me a few miles down the road. Can't you do without a cigarette for half an hour?"

The story, as I heard it, ends there. I can't tell you what the driver replied (though I could certainly tell you what I would have replied in his place). Anyway, I can describe the full dialogue in another story because it happened to me.

The scene is a restaurant. The cast of characters is my date, myself, and a couple at the next table.

My date lights a cigarette. Our neighbours look at each other, then the man turns to me.

"Would you ask her to put it out?" he says. His tone is quite self-assured. "Smoke bothers us."

"Well, I can try asking her on your behalf," I reply, "since you prefer an indirect approach. But before I do, let me ask *you* something. This place has a great non-smoking section. Why didn't you get a table there?"

"Well!" the man says. His confidence vanishes and he seems flabbergasted. "There were no other tables when we came."

"Have you tried the restaurant next door?"

His companion pipes up. "What is it to you?" she says. "We have a right to come here."

"You sure do," says my date, who is not as patient as I am. "You have a right to come here and you have a right to go to hell. You just don't have a right to try and bully *me*."

My date was mistaken. Militant anti-smokers believe they do have a right to bully everyone, regardless of situation or merit. It's quite interesting how a little social licence brings out the martinet in some people and the coward in others.

This piece is not about smoking, incidentally, but about human nature. Smoking is an unhealthy habit, except this fact is not nearly as important—or scary—as our propensity for witchhunts or unfairness. Many people, when the social climate lets them to get away with it, start mercilessly hounding others who belong to some despised group.

Not only that, but with a neat reversal of logic they convince themselves that they're the victims.

The Nazis believed they were the victims of the Jews. I kid you not. (I'm making the comparison for this limited purpose only: I'm not, repeat not, suggesting that the No Smoke Gestapo share all other Nazi impulses as well.)

Some anti-smokers, however, do suggest it about smokers. There was a fellow who haunted a little delicatessen on my street until the owner asked him not to come again. The delicatessen permitted smoking, but the fellow was going from table to table demanding that people stop. He was quite obnoxious about it, too.

Many restaurants in the neighbourhood are non-smoking or have separate facilities for smokers so I was curious why this chap would make his own life difficult. When I asked him once, this was his reply:

"I read you in the *Sun*. You're a fascist."

I still cherish this definition of fascism, so characteristic of our times. The group that has the social licence of the period—in our days anti-smokers, say, or feminists, just as formerly it might have been patricians or white supremacists—comes to believe that its habits, ambitions, or convenience is part of the moral order of things. Their views (or their bias or hysteria) take precedence over everyone else's habits, ambitions, or convenience.

They blithely equate their desires with justice. They progress from a (very reasonable) request for an equal chance—e.g., non-smoking facilities in public places—to a demand that you stop smoking wherever they decide turn up. Including your own car.

In the same vein the same types escalate "equal pay for the same job" to "equal pay for different jobs." Or escalate the plea that you respect them to the demand that you stop respecting yourself.

If you refuse, they call you rude, inconsiderate—or a fascist. The funny thing is, many people give in to the bullies. Not only under Hitler or Stalin (who had machine-guns), but even under such vocal anti-smokers as Liberal M.P. Sheila Copps. They start behaving like second-class citizens. They apologize for being smokers or males or WASPS or what have you.

My dentist, a perceptive lady, said to me the other day: "Many of my patients are smokers. However, they make excuses. They keep promising to stop. You don't."

"Baby," I replied. "I've come a long way."

1988

POLITICALLY INCORRECT 219

A Matter of Survival

A few days ago I was looking at an essay in the field of social science. It happened to be a perfectly sensible paper for a change.

Without going into details—it's not important for what I'm about to discuss here—the writer struck me as a rare bird: an academic who acquired special knowledge without losing touch with reality.

Perhaps I shouldn't use the word "rare." Common sense may not be so unusual as to make its possessor an exception among academics; it's only less than a rule. It seems to me that about half the people who manage to learn something about trees tend to lose sight of the woods. It's one of the reasons why I've never found higher education an unmixed blessing.

This is an aside. To get on with what I want to talk about, even in this very sensible paper there was a line that set my teeth on edge. It was just a passing remark, but it showed how some quasi-Marxist fallout has clouded the thinking of otherwise clear-sighted people in our times.

In noting a male preference for sexual exclusivity, the writer remarks that this phenomenon derives from our cultural notions of property. We own our bicycles, *ergo* we own our wives. Really? I wonder where the same phenomenon derives from in animal societies that have scant notions of property. Male sea lions rarely own bicycles, yet they spend most of their time guarding and herding their spouses.

Why this preference for sole mastery in the males of species that don't even worry about territory, never mind property? The bulls of some gazing species want to own nothing except wombs. As many wombs and as exclusively as they possibly can.

Living things like to ensure the survival of their personal genes. It's pretty basic stuff and it seems to make the world go round. Different species have chosen different reproductive strategies to achieve it, but a fairly common one is for males to impregnate as many females as they can while preventing said females from being impregnated by other males.

It's the old double standard. Not all species play it, but many do. It makes sense to them, regardless of how they feel about the ownership of bicycles.

Female estrus is cyclical; rutting season comes only so often. Impregnate as many females as you can, stop other males from tying up available wombs, and you'll have more chances for having your personal genes survive. Males may be crazy, but they're not stupid.

Females need a different strategy to achieve the same ends. Once impregnated, their genes are committed for the entire gestation period. It's possible to have sex with many males, but you can become pregnant only by one. As a female you have maybe a dozen chances in a lifetime to propagate your genes, so you look for quality impregnation. You look to it from the strongest, oldest bull.

A strong bull for obvious reasons; an old one because in nature bulls don't get old unless they're healthy. It's one way to assure good genes. In pair-bonding species an "alpha" male also represents an edge during the nurturing period: he can feed and protect you better. That's why your game must be quality if you're a female. You leave quantity to males.

This is only a hypothesis (or a guess, to use a shorter word) about sexual behavior, but as guesses go it's better than pseudo-Marxist babblings about property. It accounts for what animals do in a way that theories of property (or other cultural theories) do not. It explains a long observed (and fairly cross-cultural) tendency for greater promiscuity, coupled with a stronger drive for sexual jealousy, in human males than in females.

Needless to say, such "natural" origins for our tendencies oblige us to nothing. They need not be reflected in our current mores, customs, or institutions. Our primate ancestors do many things—sampling their own excrement is one that springs to mind—that we have no wish to perpetuate.

The point isn't that we must emulate gorillas or sea lions; only that it helps to be aware of the possible origins of some of our feelings. It helps to realize that our cultural constructs, though artificial in the sense of being man-made, are not always arbitrary. They don't necessarily cause human behavior, only recognize, ritualize, and build on it.

For instance, our notions of property may be derived from our instinct to "own" wombs rather than the other way around. Long before making sure that we own bicycles to pass on to our children (as the property-crowd would have it) we tried to make sure that it was our own children to whom we'd pass on our bicycles.

1988

My Father was Only a Realist

I was glancing at an article in a Canadian Jewish newspaper the other day. It outlined how living standards have improved for the Arab population in the occupied territories since 1967.

It was in 1967 that the West Bank and Gaza were captured by Israel during the Six Day War. They're not the only territories in which Israel's presence is disputed, of course. Many Arabs continue disputing the entire existence of what they call "the Zionist entity" in the Middle East, as they have from the beginning. Still, the current focus is on the West Bank and Gaza, and it's there that the *intifada*, the Arab uprising, erupted some eighteen months ago.

The article in *The Jewish Times* views the *intifada* as Arabs biting the hand that feeds them. As proof it lists the educational, medical, and economic improvements that twenty-two years of Israeli presence has brought to the Arab population of Judaea and Samaria (the West Bank) and of the Gaza Strip.

For instance, life expectancy has risen from an average of forty-eight years in 1967 to sixty-two years in 1986. Infant mortality has declined from 90 per 1,000 babies to 45 per 1,000 during the same period.

The Arabs had no university in the region under Jordanian rule; Israel has built five. The percentage of those with nine or more years of education has doubled from nineteen per cent to thirty-eight per cent. Before the Israeli presence in Gaza only eighteen per cent of homes had electricity and fourteen per cent had running water; by the mid-'80s these numbers have risen to eighty-eight per cent and fifty-one per cent, respectively. The percentage of homes with household appliances of any kind used to be a mere five per cent. Today it's thirty per cent for washing machines, sixty per cent for refrigerators, and eighty per cent for stoves.

These figures (*The Jewish Times* gives no source for them, but they sound accurate) seem to fill the writer of the article, Michael E. Kay, with pained bewilderment. Why, Israel has been as magnanimous with its enemies as any country could be. In twenty-two years it has doubled the living standards of people who "wanted little else than the destruction of the Jewish State."

And what has Israel received in return? Terrorist attacks, rioters, stone-throwers, and a bad press throughout the world.

In spite of my sympathy with Kay's feelings, I draw different conclusions from the same facts. To me they prove once again that politics, especially tribal, religious, or national politics, are entirely different from economics or welfare. The difference has probably been summed up best in the famous dictum: self-government is better than good government.

As a Jewish child in Nazi-occupied Europe I recall listening to endless debates between my Zionist uncle and non-Zionist father. The State of Israel was only a dream then, and the reality for Jews was impending death at the hands of the Nazis guarding the ghetto. Yet my uncle, a man already in his eighties, was talking about the bright future of a Jewish home in the Middle East after the war.

"And what about the Arabs?" my father asked.

"Well, what about them?" was my uncle's response. "We'll bring them enlightenment and prosperity. We want nothing but freedom and equality for everyone, Arab or Jew. Trust me: once the Arabs understand this, they'll support us."

"Trust *me*," my father replied, "the Arabs will hate you. They may desire prosperity and health, but only from their own hands, not from yours. The more you give them the more they'll hate you, so that you'll be forced to dispense your gifts with one hand and shoot them with the other."

My uncle, a passionate optimist, viewed my father as an embittered cynic for such remarks. I had no opinion of my own, but as most nine-year-olds I was an idealist. It seemed to me that my uncle *ought* to be right. If he wasn't, then human beings were not rational and there was little hope for the world.

Today I'd say that my father wasn't a cynic, only a realist. The fact that he turned out to be right doesn't mean that human beings are irrational or that there's no hope for the world.

It only means that people are motivated by a lot of things in addition to statistics on running water or infant mortality. It means that unless a state can reach a political—indeed, a spiritual—accord with all its inhabitants, the electrical appliances with which it provides them will only fuel their discontent.

I don't know whether such an accord can be reached between Israel and its Arab population (and neighbours) at this time, or perhaps ever. Without it, though, it'll make little difference whether Israel behaves cruelly or magnanimously. As long as Jews rely on having given schools or fridges to Arabs who think of them as having stolen their land, they can expect nothing but stones thrown at them in return.

1989

LIVE & LET DIE

I'm not necessarily opposed to abortion, but then I'm not necessarily opposed to killing. Doing away with children, in particular, can be a salutary act under a variety of circumstances, as anyone who has had experience with children can attest.

I could also be persuaded that the best arbiter of when to kill a child ought to be its mother. King Solomon certainly thought so; in fact, much of his reputation for wisdom rests upon this belief. True, Solomon grounded his opinion on a parallel belief that no mother would lightly kill her child. The good king had the fixed idea that an authentic mother would rather give up her child than kill it, in which he might have been a trifle too optimistic.

Be that as it may, giving parents full discretion in the matter rests on venerable historical precedents. For instance, parents in ancient Sparta used to pitch their substandard children off a cliff (if memory serves, on Mount Taygetos). Despite the sport offered by this exercise, I don't doubt that progressive parents would have preferred pre-natal vacuum suction, had the technology been available at the time.

Spartan authorities saw no reason to question a parent's own definition of "substandard." They must have figured it was a private matter of conscience. Considering the period, "substandard" probably meant physically deformed to Spartans (as it would to many people today).

I doubt if it's a huge leap to extend the meaning of "substandard" to a fetus that's simply inconvenient. After all, a deformed child is a great inconvenience. Once we depart from absolutes, whether in ancient Greece or in contemporary Canada, the remaining standards will be relative. What else could they be?

True, the Spartan model has had a mixed press. Some people have gone so far as to call it brutal. I'm not advocating it myself, but then I advocate nothing except perhaps an abstinence from fuzzy thinking.

I don't see why so many people go into a tailspin at the idea of killing. All societies permit killing under some circumstances. As for delegating this decision to the conscience of putative mothers—well, societies always delegate the decision of whom and when to kill, subject to some procedural strictures, to the conscience of designated groups ranging from judges to liege lords to commissars. Or, indeed, to fathers. Some societies, as recorded in Prosper Mérimée's fine story *Corsican Justice*, have entitled fathers to shoot their minor children if, in their view (which was not necessarily unfounded), they deserved to be shot.

I see no obvious difference between such precedents and "prochoice" demands that we should extend the seigneurial rights of life and death to women carrying unborn children. *Pourquoi pas?* as the feminists had it some years ago. Unbridled choices by Canadian mothers, like earlier unbridled choices by Corsican fathers, will either be compassionate or corrupt, selfless or selfish, thoughtful or capricious. That's the nature of all human choices. No bureaucrat or judge could choose on any other grounds—so why not, indeed?

Ergo, I don't particularly mind abortion on demand. I only dislike the arguments used to support it. My quarrel is with those who would, for instance, oppose abortion if they thought that it amounted to killing. *I* have no problem with abortion, but they do. They have a whacking big problem.

First, they must pretend not to know when life begins. They must pretend not to realize that life is an autonomous process, a continuum from zygote to old age pension, a self-elaborating force which begins when it begins and keeps growing unless it's vacuumed out first. They must pretend not to recognize something that a cat recognizes: the difference between things alive or dead, animate or inanimate. They must pretend not to see that if a fetus were not alive, it wouldn't have to be killed.

They must cling to the illusion that a court can actually choose for life to "begin" at some arbitrary point, whether at six weeks, six months, or six years. They must stifle their suspicion that someone could just as easily put in the law-books "at the age of majority" or "at the conclusion of military service." (In such matters no safety margin is too wide. I think legal fiction should adopt the notion that life begins at forty for the comfort of those who cherish their convenience, but have no stomach for killing.)

Then there are those who put the question in terms of women controlling their own bodies. It's a handsome point, and one that would certainly arise in the realm of plastic surgery. Alas, when it comes to abortion, the question seems to be centred on women wanting to control someone else's body. (I realize that as a man I have no authority to speak on the matter, but then I'm not speaking as a man. I rely solely on my authority as an ex-fetus.) At any rate, it would be interesting for a captain to abandon ship in mid-journey based on the argument that he has full control over his own body.

This goes to the heart of the issue in more ways than one. There are those who rely on the helplessness of a fetus, its total, abject dependence on its mother, to deny it the status of life. Lack of self-sufficiency, however, is common to many life-forms; suckling infants, for example, or passengers on a Concorde. Ditto, unconscious people or patients on life-support systems. If self-sufficiency were the test, only a tadpole could pass it.

I'm writing these lines just as the Supreme Court is pondering the issues. Maybe by the time you read them our justices will have overruled King Solomon. Maybe they'll have found for the claimant who'd cut the child in half. Or maybe they'll have granted Canada's women a

007 licence simply to remedy nature's inequality. After all, had God bothered to look at the Charter, he/she would scarcely have discriminated against women by placing the sole burden of pregnancy on them. Luckily, it's not too late to redress the balance and raise the Creator's consciousness.

1989

ON TAKING A CHANCE

Once in a while it's more interesting to muse about human nature than about human events. It may even be more rewarding, because it's human nature that causes human events, not the other way around.

The problem, though, is that human nature is fairly complex and difficult to figure out. It changes a little from culture to culture, age-group to age-group, gender to gender, historic epoch to historic epoch, and it especially changes from person to person.

Often when you think you're making an observation about "human nature," you're just making an observation about the nature of your friend Theodore or your Aunt Matilda. Politics are notoriously difficult to call, but sometimes it's still easier to predict how an entire party, nation, or sub-continent will react than an individual human being. You can't even be sure about yourself.

You may have doubts about your own motives; you may have no idea how you'll feel about something until you do it or until it happens to you. The only safe prediction is that if you generalize about people, yourself included, you're likely to be wrong.

With this in mind, I will now proceed to generalize about a subject that has puzzled me for some time.

I happen to like inquisitive, risk-taking people, and I'm fascinated by activities that take one close to the edge. This usually means "dangerous" activities, activities of some uncertainty, whether in a physical or intellectual sense.

People I admire include explorers, promoters, mavericks, investors of venture capital, investigators of crime, agents of intrigue, war-correspondents, experimental pilots, mountaineers, speed contestants, and sky-divers. They include, of course, unorthodox thinkers or artists. Some are my friends, and I think I know what makes them tick. I can see their fascination with their jobs or hobbies, their fascination with going to the edge, and once or twice I've even tried to follow them as closely as I dared.

This, of course, is purely a matter of taste. I fully appreciate people of a different type: people who prefer more mundane occupations or pastimes. There's nothing wrong with being prudent, going with the flow, accepting conventional wisdom, or taking a nine-to-five job with a decent pension plan.

Men and women who go for the safe or the predictable are the salt of the earth. Cumulatively they do the world much good, and individually they're not likely to cause it much harm. On the whole, they'll come to grief less often and they may even live longer.

What I've found puzzling, though, is that the type of person or activity that fascinates me, so often arouses resentment in others. Risk-takers and risk-taking usually invite scathing comments, ranging from the disdainful to the hostile.

Explorers, whether of the spirit or of the physical world, will be described as sick or suicidal. Often they'll be accused of greed for money or for publicity. These labels are stuck not only on people who try to go over Niagara Falls in a barrel (not that it would necessarily fit even stuntmen or daredevils), but even to such meticulously trained and highly disciplined explorers of the boundaries of human knowledge as test pilots or astronauts.

In this mean spirit, entrepreneurs are habitually called "greedy." Original artists or thinkers become "headline hunters." Similar labels will be attached to sky-divers or racing drivers, who are referred to as "crazy" even by people who have to visit their shrinks every day or "stupid" by people who can't tie their own shoelaces.

My theory—and I apologize for the generalization—is that people who view risk-takers in this fashion have a big problem themselves. In fact, they have two big problems. The first is that they're cowards. They're chickens, physically or intellectually. Their second problem is that they can't come to terms with it.

Understand me: I sympathize with chickens, being one myself, but I've learned to accept my limitations. Those who call racing drivers stupid have trouble accepting theirs. They can't come to terms with the idea that *they* may lack courage or curiosity. Since there can't be anything wrong with them, they work it out that there must be something wrong with other people. This way, they can elevate a fault or a shortcoming into a lofty moral position.

Mind you, I won't knock it because it's a useful method. It enables a narrow, petty mind to view itself as prudent. It permits the worst yellow-bellied coward to think of himself—unlike those greedy Neanderthal risk-takers out there—as highly civilized and responsible.

1989

FORGET ABOUT MR. BIG

It seems to me that in our celebrated war on drugs, in the United States as well as in this country, we're getting a trifle confused. For instance, it has long puzzled me why our American cousins have been so eager to extradite a few drug barons from Colombia.

Why import big-time criminals? Why go to great lengths to bring into one's own country the corruption and terrorism that the presence of such people inevitably engenders? The U.S. has enough major crooks. *Exporting* a few to Colombia would make much more sense.

Drug barons can't be extradited until they're captured, and once they're captured they can be dealt with in Colombia as easily (or uneasily) as in the U.S. If the Colombians don't have enough maximum security prisons, it would be simpler to lend them the money to build some. Simpler still, the U.S. could lend them a few electric chairs.

If the drug barons are rich and desperate enough to intimidate the Colombian authorities, they're rich and desperate enough to try the same thing in the U.S. Maybe they won't succeed, but they'll certainly try. They'll hire the best lawyers, and if the lawyers fail, they'll hire the best gunmen. True, the gunmen may also fail in America, but meanwhile they can hurt a lot of people.

Why do it? Especially why do it when no individual drug baron, not even the biggest, is essential to the trade. While he's fighting his legal or illegal battles in the U.S., back home his nephews, cousins, or competitors will carry on.

Which brings me to the central issue. In our war on drugs we have always concentrated on "Mr. Big." We've always figured that if we could only take Mr. Big out of action, the whole problem would somehow disappear. Alas, it's not true. In fact, Mr. Big is only a small part of the problem. The big part of the problem is Mr. Small.

Mr. Big is a supplier. He's in business because there's a demand for his services. True, like the manufacturer or distributor of any other product, he's also helping to create a demand, but he's still at the mercy of the market. If the demand dries up, he's out of business.

No doubt, fighting the demand is much tougher than fighting the supply. The demand-side involves many people; the supply-side involves only a few. There may be millions of drug users in North America, while dealers, importers, and manufacturers number only thousands. However, fighting the demand would help, while fighting solely the supply is pointless. It is a waste of effort.

As long as there's a demand, there will always be people to supply it. This is an economic law. It's inescapable. When it's made illegal to supply a demand, all that happens is that it's supplied more furtively and more expensively. It gives rise to secondary industries of corruption and crime. In fact, the social problems created by these secondary industries tend to outweigh the initial problem.

This is what has happened with mind-altering drugs in America. The damage that drugs do to addicts, great as it is, is by now dwarfed by the damage dealers and users do to all citizens as they steal, rob, and kill in order to buy the expensive drug (or to secure the profits from it) and to escape the law.

One solution, of course, is legalization. I'm not advocating it, but there's no question that it would solve all the secondary problems. If drugs were legal, a percentage of the population (no one can guess how large a percentage) would become hopelessly addicted. These people would have to be supported for the rest of their brief lives. However, there would be no more gunplay, stealing, and corruption. The drug barons would vanish.

Another solution is to reduce the demand. Unlike the first solution, it can't be done with a stroke of a pen. It requires a lot of social pressure and education, probably coupled with Draconian laws. Against Mr. Big by all means—but also against Mr. Small.

If a first conviction for simple possession of a mind-altering substance carried a mandatory penalty of seven years at hard labour, the drug market would shrink. It would shrink quickly and drastically. The drug barons would become much poorer.

The cost? Well, prison expenses would go up, but there would be a savings on burglary insurance rates and, eventually, on undercover policemen. Some people would be gainfully employed in building, guarding, supplying, and populating penal colonies in the frozen North. Meanwhile, mankind could get on with trying to solve a few more pressing and interesting problems.

1989

HITLER'S GHOST STILL HAUNTS EUROPE

The history of the twentieth century was marked by two great wars. Both were begun, largely if not solely, for the sake of the aggrandizement of the German state. Both resulted in grievous losses and social disintegration. In addition, World War II was characterized by the unprecedented inhumanity of the Nazi system, which held Germany in its sway. All this happened within living memory. It's hardly surprising that most European nations, and many individuals in all parts of the world, are uneasy by the prospect of a united Germany.

Even people who have nothing against nationalism, people who are nationalists themselves and take their right to their own nationalism for granted, look at German nationalism with suspicion. They even suspect ordinary patriotism when it comes from Germans, and equate it almost reflexively with proto-Nazi sentiments.

As a native European who has lived through the war (I was ten years old when it ended, but my memories of it are still quite vivid) I find such suspicions easy to understand. As a Jew, I understand them by instinct. At the same time, I consider them dangerous habits of mind.

Dangerous, because the best way to turn ordinary nationalism into a hostile, cancerous growth is to deny its legitimacy. The best way to make our suspicions a self-fulfilling prophecy is to hinder the re-unification of Germany. In a sense, we have done it before.

Today few historians dispute that following World War I hardly anything assisted the rise of Nazism in Germany more than western suspicions and vengefulness. Justified or not, they turned out to be a mistake.

Back then the question wasn't reunification as such—Germany hadn't been divided—but "punishing" Germany and preventing it from assuming the natural stature to which its industry, population, technology, and culture entitled it became a cornerstone of western, especially French and British, policy. Nazism, of course, was a complex phenomenon and our policies didn't create it, but they certainly helped Nazism along.

After World War II we were much more careful not to repeat the same mistake with respect to West Germany or, for that matter, with respect to Japan. As a result, both countries have become successful, stable, self-sufficient entities, and staunch allies of the West.

In two or three decades it became possible to say that, though Japan and Germany had lost the war, they had won the peace. Soon they were at least as well off as the victorious nations. Maybe this made Japanese or West Germans competition a bit irksome to the wartime Allies, but it eliminated fear and hostility on both sides.

Meanwhile, the "other" Germany was abandoned to its fate.

Today, of course, nearly everyone is welcoming the demise of the Berlin Wall and the emergence of East Germany from a nightmarish period of its history. Nearly everyone hopes it will not turn out to be a mirage. At the same time, we view with aversion a natural consequence of this happy development: German reunification.

Understandable as this may be, it shouldn't determine our policies. Reunification—perhaps not in the immediate future, but before very long—is a logical outcome of the events of the autumn of 1989. If we don't prevent it artificially, reunification is likely to be beneficial. If we try to prevent it, it's certain to cause future strife.

The best way to resurrect a hostile, aggressive form of German nationalism is to stifle the hopes and legitimate expectations of a people who have endured forty years of agony. Whether the agony was "deserved" or not is totally beside the point, and not for us to decide now.

Culturally, linguistically, and historically there's no more reason for two Germanys than there would be for two Frances or two Englands (and rather less than there would be for two Canadas). There may be political reasons for a division—which is why even Germans wish to proceed slowly and cautiously with reunification—but we should look for ways to resolve them. We should certainly not try to put up any new political obstacles.

Germany is a great nation. It's not defined by the worst moments or worst characters in its history, just as other nations aren't defined by their worst moments or characters. If we persist in trying to remember Germany, or even German nationalism, solely in terms of Hitler, we run a risk of conjuring up his ghost.

It's a needless risk, in my opinion. It's also an ungenerous and foolish risk that may come back to haunt us within another generation.

1989

THE AGE OF COMPROMISE

Shortly after F.W. de Klerk became president of South Africa, I referred to him as South Africa's Gorbachev. My colleagues in the media were slower to follow suit, but in the last few weeks, especially since Nelson Mandela's release, I've seen the comparison crop up in print now and again.

Other journalists weren't necessarily slower because they couldn't see a parallel, but because for them Gorbachev is a synonym for "good"— a term of high praise which they don't lightly bestow on South African politicians. Since I regard "Gorbachev" merely as a descriptive term (other than a proper name), I have no hesitation in applying it to anyone it may fit. I certainly think it fits F.W. de Klerk.

But why did de Klerk do what he did? Why did he release Mandela? Why did he legalize such organizations as the African National Congress and the South African Communist Party? Why is he trying to dismantle apartheid at this time?

De Klerk was asked these questions almost word for word by an ABC-TV reporter this week. His answers were skilful, if somewhat guarded. Since I can't read de Klerk's mind, let alone his subconscious, I can only guess at his real answers. To me they seem to be the following:

De Klerk may be, as Nelson Mandela put it, a man of integrity. He may be a man of goodwill and peace. But over and above that, the 1980s were a lousy decade for tyranny. The year 1989 was somewhat like the year 1848 had been a century earlier. Suddenly people all over the world decided, almost as if by osmosis, that they've had enough of being dominated by other people.

Once this *Zeitgeist* takes hold of people, its grip is almost irresistible. This doesn't mean, of course, that reactionaries don't try to resist it. Monarchists resisted it, with temporary success, one hundred and fifty years ago. The Chinese Communists resisted it last year at Tiananmen Square, also with some temporary success. But this same spirit often brings to the surface politicians like Gorbachev or de Klerk who attempt a genuine compromise.

They attempt it partly to salvage what they can, yes—but also to make the inevitable transition less devastating for everyone. Certainly they're motivated by self-interest: they hope they can hang on to more of their powers and privileges in a negotiated settlement than they could by fighting to the bitter end. But they also do it to avoid bloodshed.

When does compromise hold out any hope of avoiding bloodshed? Only when the time is right. To me it seems logical that a politician of de Klerk's brand would come to power in 1989 and not before. Even if he had come to power earlier, he couldn't have followed the same policies. Only a few years ago it would have been suicidal to legitimize the ANC or the Communists, or even to release Mandela.

This wasn't because the ANC's demands for racial equality or civil rights had only recently become justified. Those demands had been justified from the word go, but in the postwar period they came wrapped in a package with the threat of communist savagery. Until the middle of this decade, Marxism had been in its virulent expansionary phase.

During this phase a compromise might have invited genocide, quite literally, for white South Africans. Even at best a compromise could have resulted in South Africa being run into the ground, socially and economically. Many other African countries had been run into the ground following post-colonial Marxist takeovers.

Today this danger has been somewhat reduced. The Kremlin, far from seeking to export its influence, is just trying to survive. Communist rhetoric still persists within the ANC, with demands for nationalization, clenched fists, and the ritual greeting of "power," but there's a chance Mandela's comrades may follow their best rather than their worst impulses. There's a chance for a better exchange than just a black racist regime for a white racist regime, or a quasi-communist for a quasi-fascist chamber of horrors.

There's now hope for a society in which black and white South Africans may co-exist in harmony: a society of neither white nor black domination, as both Mandela and de Klerk put it in recent speeches. A country where a minority no longer excludes the majority, but where the majority respects the rights of a minority. In short, a society we in the West ought to regard as ideal.

It's a long road, with many twists and turns, but better than the available alternatives. We'll see if western liberals will help de Klerk on his difficult journey as assiduously as they've been helping Gorbachev to traverse a similar road.

1990

10.

FREE LUNCH, PLUS TAX

Notes on Economics

FUNNY YOU SHOULD ASK

The world being what it is, every day I read something or hear something that reminds me of an old Jewish joke. The other day, Tanzania's delightful President Julius Nyerere was quoted as saying something that reminded me of a very old joke I first heard from my father.

Nyerere, of course, is one of the Marxist enlighteners of what used to be called the Dark Continent. Since 1980 we have assisted his noble endeavor to bring scientific socialism to the tropics with some $100 million, give or take a million. I'm not talking about total western aid either: I'm talking about Canadian aid alone. But let me tell the joke first.

Mr. Cohen is upset. He can't sleep; he's tossing and turning. He wriggles so much that he finally wakes up Mrs. Cohen.

"What's wrong?"

"Eh, it's nothing, it's nothing.... You know Silberman, next door? Well, I've got to pay him back his $2,000 by noon tomorrow and I haven't got the money."

"Is that your problem?" asks Mrs. Cohen. She dials the telephone by the bed. "Mr. Silberman, listen," she says, "my husband's supposed to pay you $2,000 by noon tomorrow and he hasn't got the money." With that, Mrs. Cohen hangs up.

"Okay?" she asks her husband. "Now let *him* toss and turn."

I have no idea if Nyerere is a connoisseur of old Jewish jokes or not, but what he suggested a couple of months ago was that African states should default on their combined debt of $150 billion or so to make the West sit up and take notice. "We have this debt power and we simply do not use it," the Marxist sage of Africa observed. As did Mrs. Cohen before him, the president of Tanzania discovered that not paying debts was one way to make creditors have a few sleepless nights. Why should the borrowers have all the worry, when they can make the lenders toss and turn?

The great African statesman has a point. While everybody knows that he who pays the piper calls the tune, only a few leading economists like Mrs. Cohen and Nyerere have grasped that you can also call the tune by *not* paying the piper. Especially if you have not paid him a few times before. He'll just have to keep playing your tune, running after his money. Hope springs eternal in the human breast, even in the breasts of western bankers, and smart socialists can parlay yesterday's bad debts into tomorrow's good credit.

True, if a bank or trust company tried to put its depositors' money out into the domestic market on such financial principles, somebody like Consumer and Commercial Relations Minister Robert Elgie would legislate it out of business faster than you could say the word "default." But not when it comes to Third World or Soviet-bloc countries, of course. With them, throwing good money after bad is regarded simply as sound business practice.

People often quote V.I. Lenin's saying that "the capitalists will sell us the rope with which we'll hang them." However, not even old Vladimir Ilyich imagined that the capitalists would give him the rope on long-term credit. It's a pity he didn't live to meet Nyerere.

While on the subject of economic jokes, I heard a youthful and as yet untenured Canadian professor of the social sciences hold forth at a dinner party the other day. The young scholar had apparently discovered that in people's democracies like Czechoslovakia or Poland, rents are very low. "Imagine," he said to our hostess, "a worker there may pay as little as five per cent or eight per cent of his income on rent. In Canada, he's lucky if he gets away with thirty per cent."

This, of course, is not untrue, strictly speaking. Rents in such countries are often very low. The problem is it's next to impossible to find an apartment, not even in a grey concrete box or in an ancient ruin with battle scars inflicted in World War II. When young people marry, they usually look forward to sharing a one-bedroom with their in-laws for the next fifteen years, under a leaky ceiling and with the elevator permanently out of order. But it's cheap—and it enables the young socialist couple to spend the twenty-five per cent they save from their rent on meat, eggs, and vegetables, on which they will have to spend about seventy-five per cent of their income anyway. The joke of which this reminds me is about the farmer who goes to Mr. Cohen's general store in the village to buy a new leather strap for his harness.

"I've got one for you," says Mr. Cohen. "You've never seen such a leather strap. It's five dollars."

The farmer is outraged.

"Five dollars?" he says. "In the agricultural co-op across the street they sell them for three dollars."

"For three dollars they sell them?" responds Mr. Cohen. "So, why don't you buy in the co-op, then?"

"Well, they've been out of stock for the last little while," the farmer replies. "They've got them on back order."

Now it's Mr. Cohen's turn to be outraged.

"The thieves, they sell for three dollars?" he says, "Listen, whenever I'm out of stock on leather straps, I'll give you for a dollar."

Which is something to remember the next time you hear someone extolling the virtues of rent control.

1985

A Serving of Liberal Mush

A correspondent asks me to specify what I mean by the phrase "liberal mush" in our media and academic circles. I don't remember using the expression, but I'll adopt it. Here is a recent example, courtesy of my phantom clipper.

Earlier this month the *Globe and Mail* ran an article in which McGill Professor Arvind K. Jain explained why lending money to tyrannies is bad business. He pointed out, accurately, that what "these countries have in common is not petty political corruption, but a system in which decisions on public expenditures are made not on the basis of their value to the taxpayers but on the payoffs they can yield for the decision-makers."

Well—that's quite true. It's also true that such countries often over-borrow, default on debts, or divert funds from their own citizens' needs into their dictators' pockets. Such regimes actually hinder the development of their nations. It's foolish for western-style democracies to keep tyrannies afloat by lending them money. It may even be morally wrong.

However, looking at the list of tyrants the professor chose for illustration, one was struck by a curious omission. He mentioned Argentina's ex-President Leopoldo Galtieri and Chile's General Augusto Pinochet. He talked about Jean-Claude Duvalier of Haiti, Ferdinand Marcos of the Philippines and the late Anastasio Somoza of Nicaragua. He represented Africa by the example of Mobutu Sese Seko of Zaire—and no one else. Specifically, he breathed no word about any of the *communist* tyrants or tyrannies.

Could Professor Jain be unaware that western bankers and taxpayers have kept communist tyrannies afloat through loans and credits for God knows how many years? Or does he consider Ethiopia or Romania less a "personal fiefdom" of their left-wing rulers than Pinochet's Chile? Was the professor's selection purely accidental? Did he simply list the first few tyrannies that popped into his head?

Even if this were so, it would be revealing. Unless someone's head is filled with liberal mush, the first few tyrannies that pop into it would include the odd "people's democracy" and a Marxist tyrant or two—say, like Romania's comic-opera dictator Nicolae Ceausescu. Unlike ex-presidents Marcos, Duvalier, Somoza, and Galtieri, these scrupulously unmentioned Marxist tyrants would still be in power. Various Canadian government agencies or private institutions would still be giving them credits or loans.

Assuming that it wasn't just an oversight, why would a learned professor exempt Marxist tyrannies from his otherwise thoughtful and accurate analysis of why we should press dictatorial regimes to democratize, or get rid of their corrupt leaders, before extending them loans or credits? And if he had specific reasons for leaving out Marxist tyrannies, why would he not share his reasons with his readers?

As written, Professor Jain's piece leaves the impression that either there are no tyrants in the world except right-wing rulers friendly to the West, or that the West gives no economic support to unfriendly, i.e., left-wing, dictators. But why would the professor want to leave such an impression? He ought to know that both propositions are untrue.

Or does he? If he doesn't, perhaps that's what I mean by the expression "liberal mush" in our academic and media circles. Incidentally, "liberal" is not a dirty word for me. I consider myself a liberal. What, you might ask, is the difference between my kind of liberal and a mushy left-liberal?

Well, a classical liberal might say: "Don't lend money to tyrannies. Period. Have nothing to do with them, whether they are friendly or hostile to western-style democracies."

Mushy left-liberals say: "Don't lend money to friendly tyrannies. It will look as if you endorsed them. But lend as much as you want to hostile ones. Then they'll become friendly." Left-libbers generally stop here. If they continued, logic would compel them to say: "When they become friendly, stop lending to them, of course, or you'll seem to endorse them. When they become hostile again, give them another loan...." The mind boggles.

Some left-libbers prefer not to elaborate. They simply talk about how wasteful or wrong it is to support dictators, then pretend that no such animals exist on the left. They just never mention them. "What, Ethiopia? Well, there's a famine there," they'll say if you point out the omission. "Ceausescu? He's not such a bad fellow, is he? At least he's independent of Moscow." Then they go and print the whole hogwash in the *Globe and Mail*.

1988

It's Everybody's Business

Private business is much more efficient than public business. I'm claiming no credit for the discovery. Economists, business people, and other observers of the real world have been pointing it out for a long time. The fact is, it has not been seriously disputed by anyone in the last quarter of a century.

Even those who used to dispute it—armchair socialists, orthodox Marxists, NDP types, and the rest—have lately restricted themselves to the observation that efficiency is not the highest value in human society. Present-day socialists no longer argue that a state-run economy is efficient; they simply emphasize that efficiency isn't the only thing that matters.

In the abstract, this is true. Efficiency, productivity, and sensible management aren't the *only* important things. However, they are very important, and even more important is that their opposites—namely inefficiency, lack of productivity, and senseless management—will ruin a country. Socialist-type management has, in fact, come perilously close to ruining formerly wealthy countries like Britain (until rescued by Thatcherism). The same type of management has completely stopped poor countries in the Third World and in East-Central Europe from achieving their potential. They have also played havoc with their citizens' quality of life.

Senseless management breeds poverty and corruption. It retards a nation in every area of its development. No inefficient and unproductive country has ever achieved the very things socialists say they value most highly: justice, dignity, and equality, to say nothing of high standards of living, technology, health, and education.

All these good things go hand in hand with economic efficiency, which in turn is infinitely better provided by private than by public enterprise. This isn't just my opinion, or the opinion of a few classical liberal or neo-conservative economists, but these days it comes close to being the (unstated) opinion of the Kremlin. In a sense, that's what *perestroika* is all about.

Britain's Margaret Thatcher or former U.S. President Ronald Reagan aren't the only champions of "privatization" or "deregulation" anymore. In this regard they can number among their allies such life-long socialists as Communist Party chief Mikhail Gorbachev along with about half of the Soviet Union's (or China's or Hungary's) Politburo. The great reform movements sweeping the communist camp from Budapest to Beijing are, to a significant extent, about privatizing the economy. Considering the performance of privatized economies, as compared with socialist or nationalized economies, this is hardly surprising. It's the private economies of South Korea or Taiwan that we refer to as "economic miracles," while the state-managed economies of Africa and Asia continue to be economic nightmares.

The difference is most glaring when you compare the economic performance of two systems that share the same ethnic and cultural make-up, such as North and South Korea, Taiwan and mainland China, or East and West Germany. They are, in a sense, the purest experiments in the relative efficiency of private and public enterprise—

along, of course, with the relative merits of socialism and capitalism as repositories of human rights and civil liberties. (This is not to say that a place like South Korea is a model in this regard; only that compared to North Korea it's paradise.)

Closer to home, it's enough to glance at some recent statistics in London's *Sunday Express*. Ever since the government of Britain sold off its share in such companies as British Aerospace, British Telecom, Jaguar, Rolls-Royce, British Steel, British Gas, and others, the "privatization stocks" have gained anywhere from about thirty per cent to almost four hundred per cent. As measured by the market, these companies have improved their performance from 150p to 585p in eight years (British Aerospace), or from 60p to 84p in a single year (British Steel) after privatization.

Recently I had occasion to look at some CBC budgets. Simply put, I found that if something costs the CBC, say, six dollars to produce, a private producer can put it on the air for four dollars. Not only that, but he can make a profit—and without paying a penny less to craftsmen or artists than the CBC does. It wasn't an eye-opening discovery, but it was interesting just the same.

None of this is to suggest that certain enterprises should not be state-owned and managed. The army, the fire department, and maybe even the CBC could never exist as privatized entities. We should simply understand that public enterprise is like arsenic. In selected instances and in tiny doses it may be medicinal, but otherwise it's a deadly poison.

1989

THE WORST OF BOTH WORLDS

Last Wednesday, a Canadian financier told me he's about to invest $100 million in Hungary, along with a group of other businessmen. A week before at a summer cottage I heard about a group of well-known Canadian "players"—as developers often call themselves—studying plans for a multimillion-dollar development along the waterfront of a major Soviet city. Whatever happens to these particular deals, the vogue is evident. These days the money is going to the changing Soviet empire and its former colonies. Is it the smart money?

This question is harder to answer. Not only because it depends on many unknown and unknowable factors, but also because it depends on one's point of view. From the western investors' point of view, the main question is one of good (and safe) returns. The "smart" money is simply money that pays swift and secure dividends (though some investors also have a vision of a changing, cooperative world). For people in such countries as the Soviet Union or Hungary, it's a question of economic and political consequences. Will joint ventures raise the productivity of their hopelessly mismanaged economies? Will they raise people's living standards? Will they strengthen tottering tyrannies, or help bring about liberalization and democratic change?

For the governments and taxpayers of the West there are further questions. Can these ventures become liabilities? Can they be used to prop up oppressive and hostile regimes? Will they create stability or chaos in a volatile part of the world? Will they foster or hinder the cause of peace? On a purely economic level, won't such investments syphon off capital from western development? Won't they adversely affect western unemployment or the deficit? Won't taxpayers be required to bail out the bankers or backers of some of the bolder "players"? Are communist guarantees reliable? Will they play the game, or change the rules half way through with a stroke of a pen? So far, the indicators are mixed.

In China, for instance, it may have been the hasty and thoughtless influx of western business that brought about the sudden backlash of the hardliners. The regime felt threatened, probably with good reason, by demands for political change that came in the wake of a naive and greedy flow of western ventures and tourists which was flooding the country.

The famous "goulash communism" of Hungary, about which so much was written in the early 1980s, turned out to be a mirage. Not surprisingly, as it wasn't the result of a real economic renaissance but simply of $18 billion worth of western loans. Since the system remained essentially the same, this money wasn't invested, only dissipated by the socialist economy. Though some of it trickled down to the population, creating a temporary cornucopia by Soviet-bloc standards, it brought about no real development or change. Eventually, it left the country with nothing but a crippling debt.

As the 1980s draw to a close, Hungary's workers are faced with the anomaly of having to feel nostalgic about the pre-*glasnost* days. True, back then there was much less freedom of speech and no talk of elections or political parties, but there was also less inflation, no unemployment, and no direct income tax. The stores had more goods and they cost less money.

Countries like Hungary, Poland, and the Soviet Union today are suffering under the worst features of socialism and capitalism. *Perestroika* is still not working, but *glasnost* is working only too well. There's no more food in the stores, only more shouting in the streets.

Now there's labour unrest, strikes, nationalist and racial riots, just like in the West. There's unemployment and inflation. Only the gloss, glitter, and plenty are missing. There are none of the consumer goods, civil liberties, prosperity, enterprise, and productivity that characterize our part of the world. Soviet bloc countries are still stifled by the bureaucracy, overregulation, pecking order, and inefficiency of socialism. The KGB, though more subdued these days, still casts an ominous shadow.

It's doubtful if simply adding money to this mixture is of any use. It's a bit like adding gas to a defective engine. At best it's a total waste; at worst, it might go up in flames. It may bring about a backlash of hardliners as in China, or it may give free enterprise a bad name, as it's already doing in Poland and Hungary. For free enterprise to work, it has to be *free*. Without this fundamental change, it's only pouring good capitalist money down a bad communist drain.

1989

MEDICARE MADE PERFECT

People who oppose government insurance schemes (myself included) do not necessarily do so because they're mean-spirited, uncaring, antediluvian rednecks. They don't necessarily object to government insurance because they're in the pocket of wealthy doctors or big insurance companies. I've opposed all such schemes, from universal Medicare to "no-fault" car insurance, for one simple reason. I've always understood that whoever pays the piper calls the tune. Since the "tune" in this case is my freedom, I prefer to call it myself.

To stick with Medicare, one didn't have to be a prophet to foretell that some people would pretty quickly start resenting that they had to pay high premiums (as they saw it) for other people. Resenters would take their own habits and lifestyles for granted, but would waste no time demanding regulations for the habits and lifestyles of others. By now hardly a day passes without somebody threatening to cancel somebody else's OHIP unless he agrees to be regulated in this way or that. Even the newspaper for which I write, the *Toronto Sun,* came up with the gem the other day that motorcyclists who don't wear helmets should lose their OHIP privileges.

As I race bikes once in a while, I know enough not to dispute the usefulness of helmets. If the *Sun* had said that motorized or unmotorized cyclists who don't wear helmets have no brains to protect, I'd wholeheartedly agree. I'm only amused by the self-righteous ease with which people instruct others on how not to be a burden on society.

Anyway, for the benefit of those who may be interested, I've come up with the perfect suggestion for an equitable system of Medicare. It would place no unfair burden on anyone, yet would allow freedom for everybody. My scheme is simple. It would require OHIP-type premiums to be split into three schedules.

Schedule A would be the costliest. It could be selected by those who wish to do as they choose: summer or winter, day or night, whether or not others approve of their habits. This schedule would entitle people to go over Niagara Falls in a barrel if they like. They could drink, smoke, eat fatty foods, fly private planes, watch late-night TV, or play contact sports entirely at will.

Schedule B would be less costly. It could be selected by cautious souls who fasten their seatbelts and prefer playing chess to scuba diving, but who aren't quite prepared to promise that they'll never eat a hamburger with french fries or that they'll be in bed by 11 p.m. every night.

Schedule C would be the cheapest. It would be tailor-made for the stamp-collecting, early-to-bed, early-to-rise crowd. Naturally they'd let government inspectors visit their homes at midnight to make sure they're tucked in safely. They'd no doubt agree to report every six months to a public weigh-in bureau to prove they've varied no more than 4.5 kilos, plus-minus, from their ideal weight. Schedule C people would promise to refrain not only from smoking, drinking, downhill skiing, or hang-gliding, but also from arguing with their children (blood-pressure, you know) or allowing their cholesterol level to rise beyond two hundred. They'd walk at least ten kilometres or do twenty minutes of aerobics a day, fill in forms on their weekly intake of dietary fibre, eat only organic greens, stay away from DC-10s, and visit no countries that fail to conform to Canadian building codes or emission standards. They'd also undertake to practise only safe sex, of course, and never with more than one partner.

Speaking for myself, in such a system I'd gladly pay for Schedule A. I'm just a Schedule A type of guy, I guess. Teacher's pets and most members of Toronto's current city council would no doubt opt for Schedule C. For a further discount some might even undertake to spy on one another, or to distribute a pamphlet entitled "Cheating on your diet is cheating on the People" in schools.

Here's the funny thing, though. Schedule C people might not be doing the public such a great favor. True, they'd cost OHIP less, but on the average they'd also live twenty-five years longer. They'd hang around forever, drawing extra millions in pension funds. They'd require shiploads of medicine, acres of hospital beds, and decades of geriatric and social services. The post office would have to hire extra workers to deliver the Queen's congratulatory telegrams on their 100th birthdays. On public holidays gaggles of them would have to be taken for outings, where they'd dribble and wheeze, scare young children, and tie up traffic with their electric wheelchairs.

1989

THE ELEPHANT'S AWFUL LEGACY

Imagine an elephant sitting on you for forty years. Imagine also that by some miracle you survive. You choke, scream, wriggle, adjust, and somehow manage to stay alive. Then one day the elephant gets up and goes away. Just when you have given up all hope, he staggers to his feet and, almost from one moment to the next, he's gone. How would you feel?

Relieved, I imagine. Relieved and grateful—but also a little stiff. You'd be a bit sore, in both senses of the word. You wouldn't be ready for action just yet. You couldn't simply pick up where you left off forty years earlier. This is pretty much the condition of the countries of Eastern Europe after forty years of communism. The weight has been lifted. The relief is nothing short of spectacular. Still, every limb hurts. The people still feel weighed down, both in body and soul.

The aftermath had to be something like this. It was hardly necessary to travel to Eastern Europe to discover it, but two recent trips this year to Hungary confirmed it for me. It was confirmed both by what I saw and by what people told me: thoughtful, intelligent people from all walks of life. (It was, in fact, a Hungarian engineer from whom I borrowed the metaphor of the elephant.)

Non-metaphorically, the problems of Hungary—and by extension of Eastern Europe as a whole—can probably be summed up under four headings:

1) Communism has left the region economically devastated.
2) Communism has left the region spiritually devastated.
3) Communism has bequeathed to each country a legacy of stifling bureaucracy.
4) Since it was kept afloat for the last number of years by western loans, communism left behind a foreign debt of staggering proportions. In the case of Hungary about $23 billion, which is nearly two years' income for every wage-earner in the country.

The economic devastation is self-evident: a glance is enough to confirm it. Development had not only stopped in Eastern Europe after World War II, but it regressed. In terms of industry, technology, agriculture, consumer services, or environmental protection these countries are not just forty but more like eighty years behind the western half of Europe. In some ways, they're still in the mid-nineteenth century.

Still, the economic problems could be solved. The West could help solve them by a lot of investment. We could also reschedule East

Europe's crippling foreign debt—the money *we* threw at communism during the 1970s and '80s in an attempt to bribe it into "peaceful coexistence." We shouldn't put the whole burden of this debt on the fledgling democracies. In fairness, maybe we shouldn't ask them to repay it at all.

There isn't much we can do about the communist legacy of bureaucracy. East Europe's own new governments must dismantle that themselves. They'd better do it soon, or it will suffocate them. The serpents of red tape strangle all life, and not just under the hammer and sickle. They can strangle a country even under the maple leaf.

But had I listed them in order to importance, I should have started with the second item. It is the spiritual devastation that is the greatest obstacle to recovery in Eastern Europe. Unfortunately, there isn't much either the West or East Europe's own infant democracies can do about it. Throwing foreign aid at it won't help. Only time can cure it—perhaps.

Foreign aid won't help, because this spiritual devastation expresses itself in a paralysis of all initiative and self-reliance. Massive aid might only make it worse. It's a type of welfare syndrome, the legacy of an oppressive, omnipotent state. It is a malady that isn't easy to describe. Maybe one could call it the cynical beggar's disease. Its chief symptom is a nation sitting back and saying to its government: "A pretty mess, eh? Thank God it's none of our business."

"Yes, the old government was bad," many Hungarians say today, "and now they tell us that the new government is good. Well, that's nice. So what's the new government going to do for us?" People who say this don't understand that a good government doesn't necessarily *do* things for people; it simply lets them do things for themselves. Many East Europeans can't see this yet. For nearly two generations they have been conditioned to look to the government as the architect of things both good and evil.

Yet until they begin to see it, liberal democracy has little chance in the region. Until they see it, East Europeans will only feel trapped again. Trapped, this time, between the devil of tyranny and the uncharted deep blue sea of freedom.

1990

FEEDING THE TAX TAPEWORM

As most Canadians realize only too well, the Goods and Services Tax is upon us. I'm not raising the subject the day before Christmas because there's a sadistic streak in my nature; I'm mentioning it in order to make a point.

Most of us hate the tax, but most taxpayers have always hated most taxes, so this in itself is not remarkable. Is there anything that distinguishes the GST from other hated taxes? I think so, but before talking about it I'd like to make something clear. Much as I dislike feeding Ottawa's little red tapeworms, I accept the fact that some taxes are necessary. Simply put, they're payment for services I myself demand. As a citizen, I may want to write to the department of energy, mines, and resources for aeronautical charts. Maps cost money and so does the post office. The government has no money itself, so it must take some of mine to pay for the things I want.

Fair enough. The trouble begins when governments decide to use our money, not just to pay for the things that any of us may want or need, but for three additional purposes: 1) to build their own empires; 2) to finance their experiments in social engineering; and 3) to buy political support for themselves from special interest groups.

Someone may object that governments have always done these things, especially the first and the third. As for the second—"financing experiments in social engineering"—well, that's just a loaded way of saying "government policy," which is something all governments are supposed to have. Yes—but there's a big difference between a *little* empire building, a *little* social engineering, or a *little* catering to special interest groups, and making these things the heart and soul of government.

When I first came to Canada thiry-five years ago, things had not yet got out of hand. Government was spreading, but it had not yet run amok. And what was this country like thirty-five years ago? Well—a pretty good place, I'd say, by today's standards. For instance, inflation was minimal. The word "deficit" had hardly entered the political vocabulary. Most people could expect to own their own homes. As for *renting*—hell, some developers were offering two months free rent for the privilege of leasing you space. Far from experiencing a housing crisis, Toronto was a buyer's market.

The welfare state was already in full bloom, with most of the safety nets firmly in place, so there was adequate unemployment insurance. There were old-age pensions. It's just that government wasn't yet rampant. It didn't yet offer programs for multiculturalism, unrequited love, or creative bed-wetting. Sick people did get medical attention, even without universal Medicare. Except for a handful of bums—fewer, probably, than today—there were no beggars or starving people in the streets.

I'm not suggesting it was a perfect world thirty-five years ago. Canada had pockets of poverty. It had periodic unemployment as well as examples of discrimination and injustice. But even back then you could eat and keep warm, thank you very much. You could be free from persecution and have your day in court. You didn't have to be wealthy. Nor did you have to be a WASP. Penniless immigrants like myself, fresh off the boat, without even speaking the language, had no trouble finding jobs, housing, or social acceptance.

There was crime in Canada, too, but not on today's scale. No drugs in the schools, for one thing. I don't remember people having to worry about going for a late-night stroll in Toronto.

So what did thirty-five years of tax-sucking, rampant, all-pervasive government get us? Other than ever-increasing doses of deficit, inflation, crime, deadly diseases, drug addiction, housing crises, insurance crises, and ethnic strife? Other than a country ready to split into hostile fragments, not only between French and English or white and non-white, but even between men and women?

I'm not suggesting all of this has been the aim, or even the consequence, of our hare-brained social engineers. (Nobody could possibly foresee, say, the deadly epidemic of AIDS.) I'd argue, though, that three-quarters of our current troubles flowed naturally from Big Government's policies. They could have been predicted by anyone—and were, in fact, predicted by many people.

· So now, looking at the GST, I only see another tool in the social engineer's tool-box. A new screwdriver in the hands of government, the inept sorcerer's apprentice who has been systematically screwing up this country. For me, this is worse than the fact the GST takes another dollar out of my pocket or that it's a nightmarishly cumbersome tax that may cost more in bookkeeping than it brings in revenue. Those facts merely add insult to injury.

1990

11.

OLD VESSELS,
NEW WINE

Notes on Gorbachevism

WHICH WAY, COMRADE?

Which way is the Soviet Union going? A few years ago, when the late and unlamented ex-KGB chief Yuri Andropov was still at the helm of the Red Byzantium, a joke was making the rounds in the "People's Republic" of Hungary, the flexible land of goulash-communism. Andropov, U.S. President Ronald Reagan, and Hungary's ruler János Kádár are going to a summit meeting. The meeting is so top-level and secret that even the drivers of their limousines don't know the way. One by one, they come to a fork in the road.

"Which way Comrade Andropov?" inquires the Soviet driver.

"Stupid! Go left, of course."

Arriving at the same junction a few minutes later, President Reagan's chauffeur raises the same question.

"Turn right. Always right." replies Reagan.

Then Kádár's vehicle creaks to a halt. "Well, Chief, what now?" asks the driver.

Kádár looks around carefully. "It's simple," he says. "First, signal left. Then turn right."

Nowadays western pundits, looking at the Soviet Union from a great distance, their vision further obscured by deliberate smokescreens (and, in many cases, by their own wishful thinking), are trying to discern the direction in which Gorbachev's sleek new Kremlin may be turning. There seem to be all kinds of signals flashing, but it's not so easy to tell which way. It's even harder to tell whether or not any of those flickering lights signify the driver's real intentions. They could just as easily be a deception—or simply a short-circuit. Soviet electrics are not all that reliable.

Whatever the driver's intentions, the hardest thing to predict is whether or not he can carry them out. After nearly seventy years of solid momentum—the momentum of its ideology, history, and entrenched interests—the Kremlin may not be so easy to turn.

I don't claim to have better information than any other pundit— except for the odd snippet coming my way through ancient connections from a world I left thirty years ago. I'm bending over backwards not to let the things I've seen and experienced close my mind to anything new that I might see. I know that experience is a mixed blessing. Having been poisoned once makes you harder to poison again—but it may also make you needlessly suspicious of nourishment.

Taking all this into account, what can one make of the Gorbachevian "new wave" in the Soviet Union? What changes can one expect from his reshuffling of the Kremlin's bureaucracy, or from his new policy of "openness"? Is any of it real? Is any of it fundamental?

My answer to the first of these two questions is a cautious yes. To the second: I very much doubt it. The only thing "fundamental" would be turning the Soviet Union from a coercive into a more-or-less free society, and from an aggressively expansionist imperialism into a peaceful neighbouring state. I don't see any signs of either.

Tyrannies do calm down after a passage of time, once they have consolidated their power. This slow process of calming down has been part of Soviet reality, with some stops and starts, ever since Krushchev's 20th Party Congress in 1956. Gorbachev's desire to further eliminate the worst, the most cruel (and most inefficient) features of acute tyranny is probably real. It may also be successful, because it coincides with a natural tendency of human institutions in the long run. Only a fool would say that this makes no difference. Bad as a modern medium-security prison may be, who wouldn't prefer it to Devil's Island? But "fundamental" is a different question. Being incarcerated in either is still being in jail.

It is also possible that Gorbachev, who is in a good position to see the weaknesses and cracks in the apparent Soviet monolith, regards it as wiser to pull in his empire's horns a little. He may not regard the time as being right for picking too many fights, especially given the current mood of the West at the tail-end of the Reagan years. Times may be more propitious later.

The really interesting questions, I think, are independent of Gorbachev's conscious designs. They have to do with the unforeseeable *side-effects* of his policies. How will a more relaxed atmosphere affect Soviet men and women? *Vogue* is coming to Moscow; what will be the result of a western-type fashion magazine being available in Russia for the first time? In this sense, the clothes Raisa Gorbachev likes to wear may prove to be of more lasting importance than her husband's actual plans for his country or the world.

1987

GAMBLING ON GLASNOST

Remember the story about George Bernard Shaw and the beauty queen? The one in which the stunning lady suggested to Shaw that they ought to produce a child together because, as she said, their offspring would inherit *his* brains and *her* looks.

"But Madame," objected Shaw, "what if the unfortunate child inherits my looks and your brains?"

This, in a nutshell, is the problem of Soviet leader Mikhail Gorbachev—the problem of his twin policies of "openness" and "reconstruction." In a more general sense, it may also be the problem of our own mixed economy. It may be a fundamental problem of the welfare state. It may be the problem of every human attempt to combine the best features of any two systems, biological, political, or social. It is, bluntly put, the risk of ending up with the *worst* features of both.

Systems, like human beings, have good and bad features. Even if everyone agreed on the best and worst features of a given system (easy enough in the case of two biological "systems" like Shaw and the beauty queen), combining them could produce a wholly undesirable entity as easily as a wholly desirable one.

In practice, biological combinations tend to produce completely new entities with their own unique features, and often with little resemblance to their parent-systems. In socio-political combinations the resemblance is more pronounced. A new system may inherit some of the virtues of its progenitors and it is almost certain to inherit some of their vices. Whether the new combination will be "better" or "worse" is anybody's guess, and it is also anybody's guess whether or not it will be viable.

For future historians, the most characteristic feature of our times may appear to be how various "capitalist" systems attempted to incorporate quasi-socialist measures into their structures, while various "socialist" systems were trying to inject quasi–free enterprise notions into their statecraft and economy. These periodic attempts are not new on either side.

In the Soviet Union it was during the famous NEP era in the 1920s that Lenin first tried to rescue the hopeless tangle of socialism by a careful injection of private enterprise in a controlled experiment called the New Economic Policy. Maybe NEP did give a little boost to the Soviet economy, but it threatened to undermine the new ruling elite. Even a tiny bit of economic freedom ran counter to everything they stood for. Stalin speedily abandoned the experiment.

It's easy to say that Stalin doesn't count because he was a monster. He certainly was, but he did face two genuine problems. The first problem is that the best and worst features of any system are likely to be interdependent. You can't just pick out what you like and discard the rest. A system is more like a package deal. You can tinker with it, but only so much. Try altering it beyond a point, and the entire thing will come crashing down about your ears.

The other problem is that tinkering with a system may not make it *better*. On the contrary. You may end up adding, say, the periodic unemployment of capitalism to the inefficiency and low productivity of socialism. Or you may end up with expensive shoddy goods in place of cheap shoddy goods. To use a metaphor, look at free enterprise as a jungle and at socialism as a zoo. A zoo has some security and a jungle has some freedom. But bring a little jungle to the zoo and what have you got? A place where animals are caged just as tightly as before but are not fed as regularly and are subjected to occasional raids by hunters and predators.

Gorbachev has a problem and, just by reversing the metaphor, so do we. For many years now we have been building little socialist cages in our free enterprise jungle. The cages have done little to feed and protect us, but much to restrict our ability to feed and protect ourselves. A mixed economy can be a mixed blessing.

Having said all this, I'm delighted that Gorbachev appears to have won a round last week in the Politburo. If his policies can change the Soviet system for the better, all well and good. If not, they will at least hasten its internal decay.

1987

PERKS OF ABSOLUTE POWER

The former Soviet academician Michael Voslensky used the word "nomenclature." The old communist Milovan Djilas (who, until his fall from grace, was second in command to Yugoslavia's Josip Broz Tito) used the phrase "new class." Both were talking about the power elite of Soviet-type societies. I prefer older, more direct words—such an "aristocracy" or "oligarchy"—to describe these elite groups of power and privilege that are the true beneficiaries of the so-called dictatorship of the proletariat. Soviet-type regimes are really *their* dictatorships. They rule in the name of the proletariat in much the same way as feudal princes used to rule in the name of God.

The reason I prefer words like "aristocracy" or "oligarchy" is simple. Such words go to the heart of the matter. Being descriptive of feudal power relationships, they accurately express the neo-feudal nature of all societies created by Marxist socialism. In the Soviet Union this aristocracy or nomenclature (the word being derived from the Latin "list of names") is estimated at around three-quarters of a million people. They are the dukes, counts, and barons of communism. They are truly a new ruling class, set aside from ordinary Soviet citizens in both their private and public lives. Privately by their privileges, and publicly by their power.

In the private sphere, these privileges include choice residences or summer homes assigned to them by the state, chauffeur-driven automobiles (in some cities with reserved traffic lanes), access to passports and foreign currency, special shops stocked with western goods, and places for their sons and daughters in the best schools for future leaders. This last provision makes their privileges all but hereditary.

In the public sphere, their power includes deciding how their fellow citizens may live—in some instances, even for how long. Within limits, they can determine at what jobs and in which part of the country other people can work. Within limits, they can tell other people what to see, say, read, write, or think. Within limits, they can decide whom other people ought to marry. It is safe to say that in many areas of life their baronial powers meet, and in some areas even exceed, the powers of medieval liege lords over their subjects.

None of this is news. Djilas wrote about the new class more than twenty-five years ago; Voslensky published his writings about the nomenclature after his defection in 1980. Many other students of Soviet-type societies have analyzed the phenomenon of communist ruling elites before or since. I'm raising the subject here to make two specific points.

First, the rapid development of a new aristocracy after a revolution proves the essentially hierarchical nature of all human societies. It illustrates perfectly why egalitarian ideas, no matter how honestly held, are likely to be utopian and unrealistic. Upheavals may rearrange a given social order, they may even stand it on its head, but the new order will do little more than shuffle the players (and some of the rules). Then the new players under the new rules will emerge once again as top dogs and underdogs, insiders and outsiders, privileged and underprivileged, exactly as before.

This is not to say that revolutions or "new deals" never make any sense. Some social structures are clearly more humane, more equitable, or more efficient than others. In any case, certain social structures, having outlived their usefulness, may decay, explode, or evolve regardless of whether the structures that replace them turn out to be better or worse. The point is simply that the new structures will be no less hierarchical than the ones they replace. Revolutions, in other words, may make sense, but *not* if their purpose is to do away with hierarchies as such. That is the one thing they will probably never achieve.

The second point is that Soviet leader Mikhail Gorbachev's new policies of "openness" and "reconstruction"—which, as he always cautions, must take place within the essential framework of a *communist* society—have their natural boundaries. These boundaries are defined by the interests of the nomenclature, the roughly three-quarters of a million human beings who are the individual beneficiaries of the supposedly classless society. "Opening up" or "reconstructing" Soviet society means reducing their powers and privileges.

Gorbachev may defy the world, but he will find it much harder to defy—even assuming that he wanted to—the communist dukes, counts, and barons.

1987

THE GENIE'S RESTLESS

I've lived in Canada for the past thirty-two years as a direct result of *glasnost*. And *perestroika*, of course. I've tried for years to explain this to anyone who'd listen. I guess one more time can't hurt.

True, the words *glasnost* and *perestroika* had not yet been invented in 1956 when I escaped from a part of the world that President Ronald Reagan used to call the evil empire. More precisely, they had not yet come to mean what they mean today. Back in those days the rulers of the Kremlin were not yet concerned with either "openness" or "restructuring." Even such expressions as "reform communism" or "communism with a human face" emerged only with Dubček's Prague Spring, about twelve years later. In 1956 only a handful of dissenting intellectuals and worried party functionaries kept whispering about the concepts Mikhail Gorbachev is now proclaiming from the rooftops.

What Gorbachev is saying today is that certain fundamental reforms are necessary to save the Soviet system in Russia and its satellites, the so-called People's Democracies. Reforms as basic as *glasnost* and *perestroika*: openness and restructuring. Without such reforms the communist world can't survive, politically or economically.

In 1956 this was the very thing about which a handful of communist idealists tried to convince the Kremlin. Imre Nagy, an early reform communist, who during the short-lived revolution of 1956 was to become Hungary's prime minister, left a confidential memorandum at the Soviet embassy for Yuri Andropov. In it, he said that Soviet bloc countries can still "prevent a general crisis for their regimes by taking energetic measures of democratization. Tomorrow?" Nagy continued his memo. "If these measures are too late in coming it could happen that the very principle of a state-controlled structure will come under question."

Andropov—not yet KGB chief or Soviet leader back in those days, but only ambassador to Hungary—had probably discussed Nagy's memo with his comrades, including Nikita Khrushchev, himself a reformer of sorts, whose secret speech about Stalin's "mistakes" helped to prepare the climate for 1956. The top comrades must have concluded that it was thirty years too early for any openness or restructuring. Instead, they sent in the Soviet tanks, crushed the Hungarian reformers, and eventually hanged Nagy, the earliest proponent of *glasnost.*

They hanged him, but not because they disagreed with his essential goals. Khrushchev, Andropov, and their colleagues had much the same desire as the man they executed. They, too, wanted to prevent a general crisis for their regimes. They, too, wanted the principle of a state-controlled structure to remain unquestioned. Except, unlike Nagy, they did not think that energetic measures for democratization would achieve it. They put their faith in tanks.

What all Soviet leaders before Gorbachev believed was that fundamental reform—call it democratization, *glasnost,* or *perestroika*—were incompatible with the preservation of a Soviet-style regime. They noted, I think correctly, that any dictatorship, including the dictatorship of the "proletariat," would ultimately dissolve like a piece of cloth in the acid of genuine democracy. They even worried about the corrosive effects of too much *cosmetic* democracy on the fabric of tyranny. For them, *glasnost* would have been playing with fire.

Today Marxist-idealists, socialists, and left-lib sympathizers believe with Gorbachev (and his spiritual mentor Imre Nagy) that *glasnost* is not only harmless to communism, but can save it. Not just save it, but bring it to full fruition. They think that tanks and hangmen are not the essence of a state-controlled structure, only a Stalinist aberration.

Not being a Marxist or a socialist myself (or even a left-lib sympathizer), I'm more inclined to think that Gorbachev's predecessors—

Khrushchev, Brezhnev, Andropov, and Chernenko—were right. Loosen the cork a few turns and the genie of freedom might blow the top right off the bottle. So I'm all in favor of *glasnost*. It led me to Canada thirty-two years ago. Today, it can only have three results.

One, it can work as advertised, making life a little easier for people under communism. Good enough. Two, it can explode in the face of communism and sweep it away. Better still. And three, if the Kremlin has to re-cork the bottle hastily, if the tanks come again, followed by the hangman, if Gorbachev shares the fate of all reform-communists from Dubček to Imre Nagy, *glasnost* can still serve to reveal the true face of tyranny for another generation.

1988

THE VANISHING MARXIST

I often talked about the bankruptcy of Soviet-type socialism: its bankruptcy as an intellectual concept and a social model in those areas of the world where it is actually practiced. This is more important even than its economic bankruptcy. It is, perhaps, the most important development in the world as 1989 begins—though the development itself is far from new. Intellectuals both in the East and the West have doubted, criticized, or tried to tinker with the great Marxist experiment ever since it acquired a home base in Soviet Russia seventy years ago.

I'm not talking about those intellectuals who opposed communism from the word go. In Eastern Europe all such people were silenced, exiled, or killed by 1948, while in the West their influence gradually waned. By the mid-1960s we tended to view them (at best) as irrelevant. When I speak of intellectuals in this context I mean solely those writers, thinkers, and academics who started out either as Marxists or sympathizers, or could at least claim neutrality and detachment on the subject.

Only the doubts, questions, or disillusionment of such people was accorded any degree of respect in the West. They alone could legitimately tinker with the Marxist model or suggest ways in which it might be reformed. In the East, of course, only they had even a shadow of a chance to do so.

As the years went by, western intellectuals of this type would fluctuate between hope and despair. A few would eventually abandon Soviet-type models as being beyond redemption. Others would pin fervent hopes on every new Marxist twist and turn within the Soviet bloc or anywhere else in the world. Most simply continued keeping what they liked to call "an open mind."

In the East, intellectuals had to make tougher choices. Some chose silence, exile, or open dissent, with all the attendant dangers and hardships. Some, however, had genuine hopes of reforming the system. They sincerely believed that socialism might acquire a human face and often made heroic efforts to bring it about. In Hungary they tried in 1956. In Czechoslovakia they tried in 1968 and again in 1977. In Poland they tried in 1980. These are just the highlights; there were other attempts. These reform movements were conceived or supported by Marxist (or at least left wing) intellectuals. They were not designed to abolish the communist system, only to reconcile it with some ordinary notions of common sense and human dignity.

It probably wasn't until the 1980s that one could say, flatly and without exaggeration, that the Marxist-Leninist model as a viable *idea* has been abandoned by most serious writers and thinkers within the Soviet bloc. Hardly any East bloc intellectuals believe today that communism is capable of any real social, political, or economic adjustment or reform.

This is not a guess: it is a plain fact. In Poland or in Hungary one can read about it in just about any journal of opinion. In those countries it can be printed. In Czechoslovakia or East Germany (to say nothing of Romania) it has to be whispered or told to foreign interviewers. I'm not sure about Bulgaria, but I doubt if the situation is significantly different. In the East, as a political-economic idea Marxism is dead.

It certainly isn't dead as a power-structure, though, and this creates a major dilemma. In Eastern Europe people hope for little from

Mikhail Gorbachev's *glasnost* and *perestroika*. They may be new in the Soviet Union, but they have existed for a long time, especially in Poland and Hungary, without improving things. To some they seem signs not of liberalization, but of weakness and disintegration.

However, no one wishes to make trouble for Gorbachev. Not because of hopes that he'll do much good, but because of fear that he could be forced to do something bad.

People in the East are reluctant to tease a wounded tiger because it is dangerous, not because they expect it to change its stripes. The hope that the tiger might change its stripes exists today, if at all, solely in the West. In 1989 the old Iron Curtain is half torn down, but the illusions about what lies beyond are still on our side. It is probably in the West that people may be able to meet the last genuine Marxist one day, teaching at some Canadian university.

1989

CHINA FOLLOWS AN OLD SCRIPT

As I write this, the guns are silent in Beijing. It's possible that by the time it's printed, they will be firing once more. The Chinese communist government that uses guns against the people in whose name they pretend to rule, may or may not find it necessary to use them again.

In one sense it's impossible to predict events in China at this point. It is impossible to say if the voices for relative freedom and democracy have been silenced, or whether it will take more massacres to silence them. It seems a safe guess that the so-called hard-liners have succeeded. There's only a remote chance that the students of Beijing who asked for communism with a human face will continue the struggle, and that their challenge to the government will be joined by Chinese students, workers, and soldiers in other parts of the country. However, if so, there's a possibility that, after some bloodshed, the hardliners will have to give in to their demands and attempt to salvage their rule by some Chinese version of *glasnost*. I wouldn't bet on it, though.

As I say, in one sense the outcome is impossible to call, but in another sense it's easy. The events of the Beijing Summer of 1989 have been as predictable as those of the Prague Spring of 1968 or of the Budapest Autumn of 1956. They followed the script of the ritual conflict between two strains of the communist movement, a conflict that, by now, is at least forty years old.

One strain has been called "reform" or, more recently, "Gorbachevian" communism. The other is often described as "hard-line," "old-guard," or plain "Stalinist." Essentially it's a conflict between idealistic-romantic Marxists who believe communism can survive with a "human face," and pragmatic Marxists who call this a dangerous delusion.

Hard-liners say communism has to be the absolute dictatorship of the party, which is the "vanguard of the proletariat." For some hard-liners this is not just an excuse to hang on to their powers and privileges. They sincerely believe, with the touching honesty of ideological or religious fanatics, that in some historic future this inhumane dictatorship will bring about a kind of paradise on Earth.

They also say—probably quite accurately—that if their romantic colleagues try to "democratize" the communist state, relax the party's control, or mix it with bourgeois notions of civil liberties or free enterprise, sooner or later it will explode into their faces. Hard-liners warn that without total dictatorship communist systems must collapse.

Reformers usually share the hard-liners' faith in communism leading to some future paradise, but they argue that present-day Marxist systems are more likely to explode or collapse *unless* they're quickly democratized. This has been the view of such communist leaders as Hungary's Imre Nagy (who was hanged by his hard-line comrades) and Czechoslovakia's Alexander Dubček (who was merely sent to Coventry).

In the past, all arguments have been won by the Old Guard, but since the succession of Mikhail Gorbachev the star of the reform-communists has been waxing in some communist states—primarily in the Soviet Union, but also in Poland and in Hungary. This may have been good news for the millions suffering under their countries' brutal and bankrupt dictatorships, but it only confirmed hard-liners in their worst fears. Just as the Old Guard predicted, the formerly monolithic edifice of communism started swaying dangerously in the winds of reform.

From nationalist unrest in the Soviet Union to the defeat of government candidates in the Polish elections, all signs pointed to communism not being able to survive any genuine relaxation of its totalitarian reign. When, after Gorbachev's visit, the students of Beijing gathered to ask for *glasnost* in China—waving red banners and singing the communist *International*—the hard-liners called them "counter-revolutionaries" and ordered the army to open fire.

This may have surprised some Chinese students who, as young people everywhere, tend to be naive. It may have surprised those western observers or journalists who, incomprehensibly, still harbour illusions about communism. It didn't surprise anyone who could remember Kronstadt, Prague, Budapest, or Warsaw.

Communist systems can only survive as tyrannies. It's possible that some, having lost the stomach for bloody repression, may in time give up and gradually surrender to the will of the people. This may happen in Poland or in Hungary. For the time being, it's unlikely to happen in China.

1989

TOTALITARIAN TOOTH DECAY

Recent events in Poland and in China surprised no one who knew the nature and reality of communist systems. Given a chance, communist governments have always rejected their citizens; given a chance, citizens have always rejected a communist government. In China the process of rejection involved bullets. In Poland, much more happily, it involved only ballots. It involved ballots rather than bullets, not because communism in Poland has mellowed, but because, unlike their Chinese comrades, the Polish communists had no other choice.

What we are witnessing today in parts of the Soviet empire in Europe is, in the words of the Polish dissident writer Adam Michnik, "not socialism with a human face, but totalitarianism with broken teeth." The difference is enormous. Unless we understand it, we won't know how to deal with it.

Communism has been, and remains, a doctrine of complete strategic rigidity, but it's coupled with considerable tactical flexibility. Ultimately, communists always want total power and control—not because all communists are "power-hungry" in the ordinary sense, but because they have a quasi-religious belief in their historic mission. Those who weaken in this faith cease being communists.

However, in order to carry out their mission, communists have been ready for tactical compromises. Depending on circumstances, they have been prepared to put on the mask of sweet reason, talk peace, make liberal noises, or even form united fronts and temporary alliances with other political groups. The party has always been willing to play at democracy whenever the times did not seem right for repression. This has been at the heart of Leninist methodology.

In fact, communists have been eager to take advantage of ordinary (they would say "bourgeois") decency, fairness, and justice. They've always demanded it for themselves, while denying it to others. Though communists invariably preferred the finality of force whenever they had the teeth, as they did recently in Beijing, they were content to retreat or to give a little (as they recently had to in Poland) whenever their teeth were broken.

As the Czech-British writer Jacques Rupnik put it in his book, *The Other Europe*, "What the Communist regimes in the Soviet Union and in East-Central Europe have in common is a process of decay. At the periphery this decay is more advanced." I think that mistaking this kind of decay for "liberalization" is a grave error.

It's unlikely that people in Poland will make this mistake. The post-election stand of Solidarity is clear evidence they have no such illusions. Wisely, they are refusing the offer to enter into a coalition with the defeated communist government (whose defeat, without doubt, would have been complete if they had staked all their political power on this so-called election, instead of a mere thirty per cent of it).

It is typical of communist tactics to offer "power-sharing" at this point. It's as if a businessman, having squandered his capital—and also having retained his right to continue mismanaging the company—offered someone a full share of his debts. A coalition with those who've first hijacked, then ruined the country, would be tragic as well as ludicrous.

There's little danger that the leaders of the democratic movement in Poland are going to fall for such a ruse, but one can't be half as sure about the West. Our governments, to say nothing of our intellectuals and opinion-makers—and, lately, even some sections of our banking and business community—seem to wallow in a morass of bottomless illusions when it comes to communism.

In a way these people remind me of the Indian sage in Voltaire's fable, who kept rescuing a drowning scorpion from the river. Whenever he pulled it out, the scorpion stung him, then fell back into the water. Finally one of the holy man's disciples asked why he persisted in rescuing the venomous creature in spite of being stung by it every time.

"Well," replied the sage, "the scorpion can't help stinging me because it's a scorpion. And I can't help rescuing it because I'm a sage."

This bitter bit of Asiatic wisdom, served up in Voltaire's delicious French sauce, may be quite accurate. Perhaps we're all destined to act according to our nature. If so, the best we can hope for is that at some point during this endless cycle the scorpion will drown before it can poison us to death.

1989

No Place Like Home?

Twelve thousand East Germans can go to the West; maybe even 120,000 East Germans can go to the West; but East Germany as a whole cannot transfer to West Germany. This is obviously not the solution.

A few Chinese students can stay in Canada or in the United States; maybe even a few hundred thousand Chinese refugees can be accommodated, whether they fled from Hong Kong, Vietnam, or from across the Chinese border, but ultimately the whole of China cannot escape to the West. Neither can the population of much smaller countries, like Czechoslovakia, Romania, or Cuba—whether their socialist governments decide to throw open their borders or not.

In this respect it's immaterial whether refugees are "political" or "economic" or a mixture of both. It's immaterial whether they're trying to escape communism in Eastern Europe or right-wing dictators in Latin America. It's immaterial whether they're black, brown, or white. It's immaterial whether they're fleeing Salvadoran death-squads, North Korean secret police, Ethiopian famine, Mid-Eastern religious assassins, or the warriors of some neighbouring African tribe. The whole of the miserable, mismanaged, tyrannized, and overpopulated world cannot transfer to a handful of civilized and prosperous countries in Western Europe, Australia, New Zealand, or North America. It's not a question of selfishness or racism or any such nonsense. It just cannot be done.

Accepting refugees—though we should accept them, whenever possible, for humanitarian reasons—is a Band-Aid solution. The real solution is to help people tackle their problems at home. The real solution is for people to be able to live where they were born—which is, in fact, where most people prefer to live.

Aside from a few jet-setters, adventurers, professional cosmopolitans, or expatriates, most ordinary people desire to cross the borders of their native lands only for business trips or two-week vacations. Nearly everybody enjoys travelling, but almost nobody wishes to emigrate. People are usually forced to emigrate by circumstances. True, many make a success of it and feel quite settled in their new countries after some years (as I know from personal experience), but only a few would do so initially by choice.

Massive movements of population groups, though they've occurred in history often enough, have never been ideal. They weren't ideal even when most countries or continents were underpopulated. Population shifts have generally resulted in much hardship for newcomers and often even for the native population. Occasionally they've sown the seeds of some bitter struggle that has carried on through generations.

If this has been true of the half-empty world of past centuries, it's even truer of the overcrowded world of today. Large-scale population shifts could become touchy even in cases of perfect ethnic and linguistic harmony such as between East and West Germans. Naturally such shifts become far touchier wherever there are ethnic, cultural, and linguistic differences between the host population and immigrants. The greater the gap, the greater the potential touchiness.

That's why Hungary's fine gesture of letting a number of East Germans escape to West Germany, though important as a symbol, solves nothing. It may illustrate once again that socialism is bankrupt, and maybe that even socialist governments are beginning to recognize it, but it also underlines that a mere "relaxation" of communist regimes is meaningless. Sure, a few people can get the hell out—but as it's impossible for most people to do so, nothing much changes. For most people the solution is not to get rid of their passports or native lands, but of the tyrants or madmen who run them. The solution is for nations to wake up from ideological nightmares to the morning light of common sense.

The solution is to do what devastated Japan or underdeveloped and war-torn South Korea have done: business. It's a solution called freedom to work, produce, and sell. That's really all that Japan, South Korea, or Taiwan, countries emerging from a difficult historic past with lots of heavy cultural baggage and not too many natural resources, have done so brilliantly and successfully.

1989

I'M GLAD YOU ASKED...

Here are some of the questions people have asked me in recent days following the spectacular collapse of communist governments all over Eastern Europe.

Q: How come it happened so suddenly?

A: It didn't happen suddenly. I happened the way things often happen in history or in nature. The pressure builds up very slowly and gradually, then one day the volcano erupts. The eruption seems sudden to us because we have short memories and don't read small signs too well.

Q: Did it happen because of Mikhail Gorbachev?

A: Yes, undoubtedly, if you look only at the last link in a long chain of events. Gorbachev coughed, and the avalanche began. But the idea of change didn't start with Gorbachev. It probably started with Nikita Khrushchev, who officially dethroned Stalin at the 20th Party Congress in 1956 and later allowed Aleksandr Solzhenitsyn to publish his earliest stories on the Gulag. One of the first high-level memos calling for "democratization" in East Europe was circulated by Imre Nagy, the reform-communist who was hanged after the Hungarian revolution. These events occurred more than a generation ago. Gorbachev was hardly out of school then.

Q: But Khrushchev didn't go nearly as far as Gorbachev. He hanged Nagy and crushed the Hungarian uprising. Anyway, Khrushchev was soon deposed. He was succeeded by hard-liners like Leonid Brezhnev and Yuri Andropov. They came close to rehabilitating Stalin during the next twenty years. What happened in the 1980s to change the Politburo's mind?

A: Ronald Reagan. I'm not being facetious, though Reagan was obviously not the only factor. But by the late '70s many people in the western democracies got tired of being terrorized. They got tired of seeing the world taken over by cruel and primitive tyrannies, armed and supported by the Kremlin. They got tired of the loony left in their own countries. They'd had it with being shot, bombed, kidnapped, and bullied by savages yelling Marxist slogans.

So in the free world people started electing then re-electing politicians who might stand up to these forces—politicians like Reagan or Margaret Thatcher. The cardinals, truly inspired by the Holy Spirit for a change, elected a Polish pope.

Suddenly, in the East as well as in the West, resistance to evil had some new focus. Evil was finally *named* when Reagan called the Soviet Union an evil empire. Some academics and media-types snickered, but it was a vital statement.

Gorbachevism wasn't the Kremlin's first response. At first it just stepped up the pressure. It increased terrorism and sharpened its rhetoric between 1978 and 1985. It deployed more SS-20 missiles in Europe, shot a Korean airliner out of the sky, and brought martial law to Poland. It tried to assassinate the pope. It even attempted to revive Stalin's old "peace movement" in the West.

None of it worked. Thatcher surprised everybody when she sent the Royal Navy halfway around the world rather than let the Falklands go to a bunch of tin-pot dictators against the will of the Falkland Islanders. And Reagan, of course, responded with Star Wars. That's when the Kremlin finally decided to change its game plan and brought in Gorbachev.

Q: Assuming this is so, did Gorbachev then set out to really reform communism?

A: I don't think so. I'd say that initially Gorbachev wanted to make a few cosmetic changes, just enough to defuse Reaganism. He wanted us to go back to sleep, to disarm, to give him some credit. Communism was broke. He wanted to see if he could get us to re-finance it. I don't think he planned what actually happened. I don't think it was Gorbachev's idea to see communism collapse everywhere from East Germany to Romania.

Q: Why did it collapse?

A: Hard-liners always predicted it would if they relaxed their dictatorship beyond a certain point. Evidently they were right.

Q: Why didn't Gorbachev see it?

A: Search me. He probably did, but he thought that he had not gone beyond that certain point yet. He miscalculated. It happens. Gorbachev may have believed a pinch of free enterprise would make communism tastier. He may have thought people would be grateful for small mercies. After forty years, communism seemed sufficiently entrenched in East Europe. Maybe Gorbachev felt people hated Stalinism but they'd support "communism with a human face."

Q: And are you sure he was wrong? Now that people are free to chose in those countries, are you sure they won't choose communism?

A: Yes, I'm sure. I'm neither a prophet nor a gambler, but that's one bet I'd be happy to take.

1990

REDS ARE BETTER DEAD

Free elections are still to come in East Europe, but it's pretty clear that the nations of that region have rejected not only Soviet dominance and Stalinism, but communism of any kind. They've rejected it with *glasnost* or without it.

This, of course, was hardly surprising for anyone who knew anything about either East Europe or about communism. It was to be expected that, given a chance to choose, the people of Poland, East Germany, Hungary, Czechoslovakia, and Romania would not choose communism, whether or not it had a "human face."

I'd suggest, by the way, that the people of Yugoslavia, Estonia, Lithuania, Latvia, or Moldavia feel exactly the same way about communism. I doubt if people feel differently about it in the pre-war Soviet republics—in Ukraine, say, or even in Russia itself. What is different about those countries is that their population has not yet had an opportunity to make free choices.

This is worth stating only because in the West many people don't know the first thing about East Europe, have not had the slightest experience of communism, and still have very skewed ideas about the nature of recent events. In the media, especially, there have been voices suggesting that what is happening in Europe is a kind of triumph for Mikhail Gorbachev's reform-communism. This would only be so if the aim of Gorbachev's communism were to reform itself out of existence. Since I doubt if that has ever been Gorbachev's aim, what is happening in East Europe amounts not to a triumph of new-style communism, but to its total repudiation as a social model.

It goes without saying that people would prefer Gorbachev to a Stalin or to a Ceausescu if that were their only choice. In purely personal terms voters might even prefer Gorbachev to other politicians in East Europe—if he crossed the floor, as it were, and ran for office as a liberal democrat. But if Gorbachev stood for election as a communist, with democratic candidates opposing, he wouldn't get twenty per cent of the vote anywhere in East Europe. (A Ceausescu, of course, wouldn't even get two per cent.)

I'd go further. At present, even a democratic socialist party, like Britain's Labour or Canada's NDP, would have an uphill struggle forming a government in East Europe. Socialism has been thoroughly discredited there in the last forty years. If social democrats manage to form a majority or coalition government in a former "People's Republic" it will be because of some local circumstance—say, a very likable leader or some very poor rivals.

My own guess is that—assuming real and continued freedom—the leading political forces in East Europe will be liberal or Christian democratic parties that favor free enterprise. They'll promise to retain elements of the welfare state, but nothing else. The far right may try to raise its head in some countries, but I doubt if it'll have more popular support than the communists.

If this sounds like a pretty optimistic scenario for an inveterate pessimist, let me immediately throw some cold water on it. First, it depends on no last minute change of heart by the Soviet leadership, which is by no means assured. Second, it depends on no faddish, cocky or off-the-wall moves on the part of the U.S. administration, which is not assured either (especially after its recent adventures in Panama). Third, it depends on a stable economy in the West and on global peace. Given these conditions, within ten years the "miracle" of East Europe may rival the miracles of South Korea or Taiwan.

On a less optimistic note, even if all the Marxist-type tyrannies and the West's own loony left were to run out of steam together, mankind's totalitarian impulse still wouldn't come to an end. It's possible to do away with an evil empire; it's much harder to do away with evil. After Hitler blew his brains out, the world did not become a significantly better place. It may not become a significantly better place after the demise of Stalin's legacy, either.

Greed, fear, stupidity, selfishness, paranoia, intolerance, sloth, envy, and all our other deadly sins are here to stay. No doubt they'll find new flags in which to wrap themselves, new causes or ideologies to latch onto, even if communism is finally laid to rest.

The most likely new candidates for evil? I don't know, but after our experience of black, brown, and red fascism, I wouldn't exclude the greens. In fact, two varieties of greens: the fanatics of the environment and the fanatics of Islam. Nor would I exclude the fanatics of feminism. Our capacity for fads is unlimited, and we never lack true believers.

1990

Our Man in Moscow?

How important is Mikhail Gorbachev to us? How much should we do, how much can we do, to help Gorbachev stay in power? The popular answer, with negligible exceptions, is that Gorbachev is extremely important. He is the best hope for peace in our time. He is the best hope for a trouble-free transition from totalitarianism to democracy in the Soviet Union as well as in other parts of the world.

If you listen to the commentators, it would seem that outside of Gorbachev there's nothing for us but darkness and the gnashing of teeth. The only alternatives are a "hard-line" communist coup followed by a return to some form of Stalinism and the Cold War—or, conversely, a blind march to chaos, civil war, ethnic violence, anti-Semitic riots, famine, and disintegration inside the Soviet Union. Since these are the only two scenarios, we must do everything to help Gorbachev. If western pundits and politicians disagree on anything in the late spring of 1990, it's only on how much of the store we should give away to Gorbachev.

Some feel that giving away "everything" may be a tad too drastic. For instance, we might endeavor to keep a unified Germany in NATO. But others argue that communism is so bankrupt, the forces of the Soviet Union are so weakened—and the alternatives to Gorbachev are so unthinkable—that we shouldn't even insist on that. Why, let Germany stay neutral or even join the Warsaw Pact if old Gorbachev can make some hay out of it back home.

I'm exaggerating, but not by much. "Let's help Gorbachev stay in power" is a mood strong enough to be characterized as a hysteria. A bit of common sense returns only when a second question is asked: "Exactly how much *can* we do to help Gorbachev?"

This query tends to sober up both pundits and politicians. Well, let's see. Maybe there isn't a hell of a lot we can do to help him. Gorbachev's main problems are at home. They're not tied to his foreign policy successes. In fact, he'd hardly have any problems if his efforts were to be measured solely by how much he has managed to make everyone in the West fall in love with him.

Gorbachev's popularity may be at its zenith in the West, but it appears to be at its nadir inside his own country. Here he's fawned upon by an entire political spectrum from Margaret Thatcher to *New York Times* editorialists, but over there he's despised by an entire political spectrum from orthodox Stalinists to the followers of Boris Yeltsin.

Gorbachev may have brought us peace dividends and a liberated Europe, but he has brought his own people very little. Who exactly should love him in the Soviet Union, when he offers less food for the masses and fewer privileges for the elite? Maybe people can vote and complain a little more freely now, but you can't make a meal of votes and complaints.

So what can we do help Gorbachev? Obviously we can't feed the Soviet Union for him or rebuild its hopeless, shattered economy. Maybe we can help a bit on the margin, give the Red Army some money for new barracks when they withdraw from former Warsaw Pact territories. (This, incidentally, is not a joke. It's an actual suggestion.) But short of refinancing communism so its armies can keep their rockets, its cadres their dachas, while its population still gets enough cabbage to muddle on, there's really nothing we can do to restore Gorbachev's popularity at home.

And if we could, should we do it? I'm not so sure Gorbachevism represents a transition from totalitarianism to democracy. It may only represent a transition from a Politburo-type totalitarianism to a KGB-type totalitarianism, i.e. a deceptive, low-key system which is soft on rhetoric but still supplies MiGs to cluster-bomb children in Ethiopia. It could be more insidious and dangerous to the West than its previous models.

In any event, if Gorbachev's *perestroika* isn't a viable system, why should we help it survive? Why are we so certain that the alternatives must be a Stalinist coup or disintegration? Because Gorbachev says so? But that's what he *would* say if he wanted to make sure that we continue laying gifts at his feet.

Why are we so worried about a successful Stalinist coup (a remote possibility) that we would give away to Gorbachev what Stalin couldn't take from us by force? But most of all, why do we think the total disintegration of the Soviet system (a less remote possibility) would be so terrible? In the long run it may be the only hope for Russia or its subject nations for a decent and self-sufficient civilization.

1990

12.

WHERE FENCE
SITTING IS A
NATIONAL SPORT

Notes on Canada

COMING TO MY SENSES

Whoever said that I'm incapable of changing my mind? That I'm pig-headed? That I have no flexibility, and once I take the bit between my teeth I just run with my crazy notions contrary to all reason and common sense?

Well, I guess a lot of people have said that, including some of my closest friends. But, you see, they've been wrong. I *can so* change my mind. Give me the right arguments, and I'll see the error of my ways. Not only that, but I'll apologize. If pressed, I'll even sprinkle ashes on my head.

The Meech Lake Accord is a case in point.

Until a few days ago, had anybody asked me, I would have said that Prime Minister Brian Mulroney's dashing agreement of April 30 to bring Quebec into the Constitution stinks. Come to think of it, people *have* asked me, and that's exactly what I replied. I didn't even use a more prudent or cautious phrase. I didn't say: "Well, we should study it a little more closely." I didn't say: "We ought to look at all the implications." I just said: "It stinks."

Then, a few days later, I read former Prime Minister Pierre Elliott Trudeau's statement on the subject. I read it once, I read it again, and I read it a third time. For a while I stared into the middle distance. Then I rose, sprinkled some ashes on my head, and started phoning all the people I had earlier advised that Meech Lake stinks.

If this doesn't prove that, given the right arguments, I can change my mind, I don't know what does. All it took was one statement from Pierre Elliott Trudeau for me to make a standard 180-degree turn. Our former prime minister convinced me in a flash that Meech Lake might be the best damn agreement anyone has ever proposed in Canada in the last twenty years.

Quickly, before anyone accuses me of misrepresenting the views of our ex-monarch, Trudeau did not change my mind by supporting the Meech Lake Accord. *Au contraire,* he said that the agreement stinks. To use his exact phrase: "What a dark day for Canada was this April 30, 1987!" He evidently wasn't pussyfooting around either.

Now, it is perfectly true that I have a tendency for immediate second thoughts about any matter of public policy on which I may accidentally find myself in agreement with Trudeau. However, in this instance I did not succumb to some knee-jerk reaction. I did not simply say: "Ah, Pierre hates it, so it must be dandy." No: I carefully pondered the list of horrors that Trudeau thought would be consequent upon Meech Lake.

Here are a few examples: a dismantling of Canadian energy policy; a balkanization of social services; an end of the dream of multiculturalism and bilingualism; an impotent state, governed by eunuchs. "The political dynamic," writes Trudeau in his operative phrase, "will draw the best people to the provincial capitals, where the real power will reside, while the federal capital will become a backwater for political and bureaucratic rejects."

Wow! All this from Meech Lake? Could this really be true? Would real limits be placed on the relentless, centralized power of the federal bureaucracy? Would silly policies, from energy to multiculturalism, go by the wayside? Could social services be tailored to local conditions? Would provincial influence in the Senate or the Supreme Court create a greater division of powers? Would it become harder for future philosopher-kings to hijack the state or to govern by orders-in-council?

You see, until looking at Trudeau's statement, it didn't occur to me that Meech Lake could accomplish all this. I thought that, in practice, it would do nothing to check the growing tyranny of the unitary state, only it might offer the Péquistes (or their spirit) a side deal to establish a little special tyranny in Quebec on top of the federal one—say, a few more laws concerning language or immigration. Maybe Quebec would get some extra privileges or wriggle out of some obligations in compensation for the rude trick General Wolfe played on General Montcalm at the Plains of Abraham. That's precisely why I didn't think much of the Meech Lake Accord.

But maybe Trudeau is right. I bow to his superior olfactory sense in sniffing out the faintest whiff of a threat to monarchical powers. Maybe Meech Lake would turn us in the direction of the federalist State once again, as the founding fathers envisaged it, and away from the unitary monolith governed by an Ottawa mandarinate—in other words, the statist dream of Pierre Elliott Trudeau. Not by design, one hastens to add—dear Brian simply wants to be loved, and will give away the store to achieve it—but as an incidental result.

Gee, wouldn't that be nice. Pretty sharp fellow, our ex-PM. Long live Meech Lake.

1987

TAKING OUR RACIST PULSE

Are we a racist society for becoming upset when we wake up one morning to discover a number of illegally landed Sikhs wandering about in a Maritime village? I'm raising the question in these terms because it was the outraged reaction of many Canadians to this particular event that caused some other Canadians to suggest that we are racist.

Let's examine the proposition. Clearly, for a lucid answer, we first must look at what our likely reaction would be if one morning we discovered a group of illegally landed *Caucasian* people wandering about in a Maritime village. This has to be the most basic test, since Canadians are still predominantly Caucasian. If our reaction were substantially different, the accusation that we are a racist society could be well-founded.

Obviously, I have no way of stating for a fact what our reaction would be to an event that has not occurred. All I can make is an educated guess. My educated guess—some readers or commentators may guess differently—is that our reaction would be substantially similar. We would be outraged and upset, at least to some extent.

The precise extent to which we would be outraged and upset, I suggest, would be governed by a number of factors. If, for instance, the illegally landed people, or some of them, were suspected of being terrorists or supporters of terrorism in Ireland (whether on the side of the Ulster Defence League or the Provisional IRA) we would be quite upset. Our uneasiness would, in fact, closely match the uneasiness we exhibited upon the surreptitious landing of the Sikhs.

If, however, the illegal group comprised only members or supporters of the Solidarity union in Poland, we would probably be less disturbed. I don't think that we would be happy, mind you—I don't think that we would welcome any "queue-jumpers" with open arms these days—but we would be much less worried or outraged.

This is my guess. Assuming that it is correct (and I'd be willing to bet that it is), it would indicate to me that our primary reaction to illegal immigrants or refugees is not racially motivated. It is not even ethnically motivated, considering that the hypothetical Irish refugees would be ethnically much closer to one of Canada's founding groups than the hypothetical Poles.

In my opinion, our primary reaction would not be politically motivated either—though some Canadians, depending on their own politics, might be more tolerant of, say, Marxist refugees than others. But most Canadians would not care about politics any more than they'd care about ethnicity or race.

Most Canadians, I believe, insofar as they'd be prepared to overlook any queue-jumping at all, would base their relative tolerance solely on whether they thought that the illegals represented a danger to the peace and prosperity of Canada or not. Canadians would be worried in proportion not to the illegals' race or politics, but to whether or not they perceived the illegals as a potential threat to their own possessions and lives.

Viewed in this light, the choice is simple. Dissenting Polish groups blow up nothing these days, but some dissenting Irish or Latin American or Sikh groups do. There are groups that have rarely or never imported political violence into Canada, and there are other groups that have done so. Rightly or wrongly, these groups are now perceived as being capable of doing so again. It is this, I suggest, and *not* their race, that marks the dividing line for the tolerance of most Canadians.

Looking beyond the fear of political violence, it is probably true that most Canadians would prefer an immigration policy that is generally aimed at serving the interests of Canada. From this point of view, I think Canadians would find it less important whether prospective newcomers are "economic" or "political" refugees than whether their individual skills and attitudes are likely to enhance the quality of life in this country.

Who can blame those Canadians who find it easier to accept immigrants who wish to assimilate themselves to the Canadian way of life, than those who wish to impose their own "diversity" on Canada? I doubt if any Canadians care much where an immigrant comes from—but they may care to know where he is proposing to go. Canada is not an uninhabited land. We can make humanitarian gestures, but we can't solve the problems of the world. We welcome those who wish to join us, but not those who expect to draw us into their own struggles and grief.

1987

NOT IN CANADA YOU DON'T

I waited before commenting on the events surrounding Salman Rushdie's book. I waited, partly in the hope that the civilized world's response would be plain enough to require no comment, and also because I thought that with everybody commenting on the matter, sooner or later they'd say everything that could be usefully and intelligently said about the subject.

I guess what changed my mind was the American writer Norman Mailer saying that the Rushdie affair struck a deep chord in every American novelist's heart because novelists in the U.S. live with the fear that one day they'll be assassinated by members of the National Rifle Association, or some such thing, for a novel they've written.

Gee whiz. I'd have said that U.S. novelists in general, and Norman Mailer in particular, live with only one fear, and that is that nobody'll pay the slightest attention to them. That's the usual fate of U.S. novelists. There are nut-cases in America, but on the whole it is not a country of assassins. That distinction belongs to other lands.

Another thing that's causing me to comment was a message I received from a friend, expressing the hope I wouldn't comment on the Rushdie matter because it was too volatile. Maybe my friend said this because he has his eyes set on a career in the diplomatic service. Diplomats prefer not to comment on volatile matters. However, since I've always had my eyes set on a career in journalism, commenting on volatile matters is second nature to me.

Not that I have any comments to make on the book itself. The reason is simple: I haven't read it. Another reason is that the Rushdie affair isn't a literary or theological dispute.

Until the Ayatollah and his followers started their threat campaign, it would have made a big difference whether *The Satanic Verses* was a book written by a sensation-seeker who wished to shock people for notoriety and financial gain or not. In fact, without the terrorist threats this would have been the only issue. If this had been the issue, after reading the book I might have agreed with Rushdie's detractors, for all I know. I might have said, yes, this is scurrilous garbage. It's a book by a hysterical charlatan making a grab for the spoils of blasphemy.

But once the threats were made, this stopped being an issue at all. It no longer mattered one way or another. From that point the only issue that mattered was that Rushdie is Her Majesty's subject, and no one can put a bounty on a subject of the Queen. No one. If a foreigner does so, he commits a hostile, belligerent act. If a British or Commonwealth subject does so, he commits a seditious offence. If a person who owes allegiance to Her Majesty in Canada commits a seditious offence he is guilty of a crime punishable by fourteen years' imprisonment.

Once Moslem groups in Britain or Canada started saying they might follow other allegiances in conflict with the allegiance they owe to Her Majesty's law, they skirted the edge of treasonable talk. In Canada, by even hinting at acts of violence in order to intimidate Parliament or the legislature of a province, they came perilously close to being in breach of Section 51 of the Criminal Code, another offence punishable by fourteen years' imprisonment.

Perhaps this should have been pointed out to them. Perhaps the solicitor general should have said: "Just a minute! You may be touchy about books, but we're touchy about the Queen's peace."

Canada has welcomed many people of all faiths and from all corners of the globe. I have no quarrel with that. In my view most immigrants, certainly including Moslems, are excellent citizens whose faith deserves every respect. At the same time, it ought to be made unmistakably clear to all newcomers that this is not a country waiting to be remade in the image of other countries.

Canada has its own ideals and institutions, defended by blood in two world wars in this century. It is a secular, liberal democracy, governed by the rule of law. Newcomers are welcome to share it, but not to ruin it.

They can't threaten us with violence or repression. They can't start telling other Canadians what to say, think, or read. They may come here from the Middle East or Asia, but they can't bring the Middle East or Asia with them.

In calling for a government ban on Rushdie's book, a Moslem spokesman was quoted as saying that his group intended "to act within the law *first*." No sir. While you're in this country you will act within the law not only first but *always*. If you don't, you'll find that your first act outside the law has also been your last.

1989

DINNER WITH DRACULESCU

It happened on the second day of the uprising in Romania. Nicolae and Elena Ceausescu hadn't yet been executed; in fact, even their capture hadn't been confirmed. However, it already seemed likely that—what with the army solidly on the people's side—the revolution would succeed.

That's when Brian Mulroney came on TV. Asked to comment on the events in Romania, Canada's prime minister expressed the view that the Ceausescus ought to be tried by their own people. It was an impeccable opinion. It was certainly one with which I would wholeheartedly agree.

This was the very opinion I expressed from time to time—for instance, four years ago while Brian Mulroney was playing host to Nicolae and Elena Ceausescu. That's pretty much what I wrote while Mulroney was entertaining the despicable tyrants and warmly shaking their hands in Ottawa. I suggested that, far from selling nuclear reactors to the Ceausescu clan, we ought to have nothing to do with their bloody regime.

In fairness to our current PM, he wasn't the only statesman in the West to have the mass murderer and his wife to dinner. Former PM Pierre Elliott Trudeau did likewise, as did America's Jimmy Carter. As I'm writing this, there are two photographs in front of me: a solemn President Carter rising, with glass in hand, to toast a beaming Ceausescu, and Rosalyn Carter sharing a laugh with Elena Ceausescu. (True, for all Rosalyn knew about the world, she might have shared a laugh with Lady Macbeth.)

Even the Queen was persuaded by her government in Britain to pin some medal on "Draculescu"—as Ceausescu was nicknamed by his people. (This, by the way, so embarrassed some members of the royal family they started a quiet campaign to have the decoration revoked.) But the medal wasn't revoked. The "favourite nation" treaties and nuclear deals weren't cancelled either. Our politicians merrily played ball with the Ceausescus until about three days before the bitter end. Then, when the mad couple's palace was already in flames, western statesmen were quick to wash their hands of their erstwhile dinner guests. Our politicians didn't even have the decency to seem surprised. They didn't say: "Gee, we never knew Nick was such a bad guy." No; it was just Mulroney's unctuous baritone: "He ought to be tried by his own people."

Well, the Romanian people have tried the Ceausescus now, and their verdict has been swift and terrible. Perhaps it was a little too swift and terrible for our taste—though I don't know how swiftly or terribly we'd deal with tyrants who murdered, robbed, humiliated, and starved an entire generation, once we managed to get our hands on them. In Canada, thank God, we've never been put to that kind of test.

We've been put to a different test, though, and I suggest we've failed it. At least most of our politicians did, along with much of our media. It took no foresight or courage to condemn Ceausescu or to run exposés about his dictatorship once his palace started to burn. The time to do so would have been while he was firmly in power, starving and killing his own people. Except *then* we were selling nuclear reactors to him and apologizing for his murderous regime on air or in print. At best we kept quiet, pretending to see or hear no evil. The few exceptions—journalists or politicians who tried to speak out—were coolly dismissed as "ring wingers" or "cold warriors."

It wasn't a question of ignorance. Long before the images of mass graves appeared on our TV screens, our politicians and investigative reporters knew (or ought to have known) that Ceausescu trained and supported terrorists, traded human beings for cash, smuggled drugs, stole western technology and military intelligence, and used his much-vaunted "independence" from the Soviet Union to spy for the Kremlin—certainly during the Brezhnev years and possibly even under Gorbachev.

That's what our dinner guest and favourite trading partner did, in addition to enslaving his own people. Dozens of terrorists who blew up passenger jets or machine-gunned travellers at airports carried passports forged or stolen by Ceausescu. Everybody knew it by the time the bloodstained couple came to Ottawa—except, apparently, Brian Mulroney, Joe Clark, and the CBC's *The Journal.*

Well, I suppose, we should be grateful for small mercies. Finally our leaders and pundits have discovered it too, just as "Draculescu" and his wife were being shot through the heart in Bucharest. I only hope the soldiers who shot them remembered to use silver bullets.

1989

A Nation of Barricades

No shots have been exchanged between the Canadian army and the Mohawk warriors as I'm writing this. I share the hope of most Canadians that no shots will be fired by either side, now or in the future. However, I wouldn't bet on it.

Whether or not bloodshed will be averted in this particular instance, blood will be shed one day—almost inevitably, in my opinion—unless we fundamentally change the way in which we have chosen to look at ourselves in the past thirty years.

This is not an "Indian problem"—*that* problem is much older—so when the shooting comes it won't necessarily be between citizens of European and aboriginal stock. Though blood may flow between white

Canadians and members of our First Nations, as it already has in Oka, it may just as easily flow between Western and Eastern Canadians, Quebecers and English Canadians, native-born and naturalized citizens, WASPs and non-WASPs, blacks and non-blacks, Asians and non-Asians, heterosexuals and homosexuals, or maybe even between male and female Canadians.

Why? Simply put, because we view ourselves as an aggregation of hostile special-interest groups instead of a nation.

The process started around the mid-1960s, and it came about through a bizarre twist in the liberal position. This new, sick parody of liberalism, instead of seeking equality and justice for individual human beings, began seeking parity and even special status for entire groups.

First by slow degrees, then more and more rapidly, we abandoned all classical ideals of liberalism. We no longer tried to minimize our differences, but started emphasizing them. We no longer wanted equal opportunity for all human beings regardless of race, sex, ethnicity, lifestyle, or religion, but demanded special status and privileges for belonging to some minority. We no longer asked for a fair chance as individuals, but for a free (or at least subsidized) ride as members of a particular group.

Our "progressive" demagogues, inside as well as outside government, encouraged us to clamour for benefits for our own group and penalties for all other groups. They kept persuading us that we were entitled to such benefits because we had been "disadvantaged" or had suffered "historic wrongs." And as soon as a claim of some disadvantage—accurate or inaccurate—was made, all notions of fairness, due process, and common sense went out the window.

Some claims of historic wrongs were accurate enough—naturally, because the world has never been perfect. Canada may have been better than most places, but we have had many examples of exclusion and injustice. While liberals traditionally proposed to cure exclusion and injustice with integration and justice, our modern, post-'60s "liberals" have tried to cure them with separation and reverse or "affirmative" discrimination.

The cure has been worse than the disease. It has resulted in all groups feeling alienated, embittered, exploited, and ill done by. It has sent us into an orgy of hyphenation, fostered by prophets of bi- and multiculturalism, peddlers of so-called human rights, and preachers of class or gender-hatred. Naturally, this has re-kindled aboriginal nationalism as well.

By now, many of us have replaced pride in our shared citizenship with a pride in our separate identities, whether of ancestry, language, race, ethnicity, or sex. Many of us believe that we should be French or English or Indian first and Canadian second, if at all.

An entire industry has grown up around the forces that attempt to divide us. Bureaucrats, consultants, activists, and academics specialize in the politics of fragmentation. Our taxes are their sole source of income, so they keep demanding more. They have no other skills, but they often make a better living from trying to tear down this nation than the rest of us have ever made from trying to build it.

In this climate, I don't find it too surprising when Mohawk Warriors in Quebec declare that they're a sovereign nation and not subject to the laws of Canada. Why, the very province in which they live has made similar pronouncements. Sooner or later all groups in this country will have to seek special status. Those who don't will be the losers. They'll only be allowed to pay taxes and obey the laws.

It's another matter that, for the time being, the federal government must send troops to Oka. What else can it send, a bunch of anthropologists or human rights commissioners? Once a group armed with automatic weapons surrounds Montreal and announces that it's a separate nation—and a hostile one at that, blockading Canada's roads and bridges—the government can only resist or surrender. And surrender, while it may be coming, is not yet on the agenda.

1990

WHERE OUR MONEY GOES

A while ago I raised a question and recently a film director friend offered me an answer. Before I come to his answer, let me outline the question again. Why is Canada's per capita deficit larger than just about any other industrial democracy's in the world? I could never quite understand this. Where does our money go?

The debt-load problems of other nations may be hard to remedy but at least they're not hard to understand. Certain countries—the U.S., for instance, or Israel—have crippling military expenditures. On the other hand, some Scandinavian nations that spend little on defence have truly deluxe cradle-to-grave social security systems.

Then there are the countries that don't tax their citizens enough (especially their wealthier citizens). Naturally, they're debt-ridden. Other nations have been grievously underdeveloped or misgoverned. They may be so lacking in natural resources, capital, or infrastructure that the citizenry is simply unable to generate any wealth. In such countries the only thriving industry is corruption. Still other countries have been oppressed by external enemies or internal tyranny for so long that they've become economic as well as spiritual basket cases. It's no wonder they have nothing but debts.

But none of these reasons apply to Canada. At least, they don't apply enough to explain the size of our deficit. We're not lacking in natural resources. Our territory has never been devastated by war. Our citizens and businesses are taxed pretty damn hard—hard enough, in fact, for many to seek relief south of the border. And while our per capita deficit is larger than that of the U.S., our per capita military expenditure is smaller than Luxembourg's.

We spend quite a bit on social security, yes, but not more than many western industrial democracies, and less than some. We don't go deluxe. We certainly don't spend more than, say, Sweden or Denmark. Yet our per capita debt is larger.

Bad government? Well, our various governments may leave a lot to be desired, but they're not bloody or corrupt tyrannies. We can't explain the size of our deficit by the kind of misgovernment that has afflicted former communist countries (to say nothing of present ones). Even our worst politicians can't be mentioned in the same breath with their fellows in the Mideast, Africa, Asia, or Latin America.

Corruption? Sure we have corruption, but it's not world-class. In Canada, if a civil servant accepts a fridge it's a national scandal. I'm not saying we need more corruption in this country, believe me—only that it doesn't explain our national debt.

What, then, is the reason? We don't stand on guard for the free world. We make no big-power efforts, so why do we still burden our children with big-power debts? Our problems are not on a Third World scale, so why are we approaching a Third World scale deficit?

My friend's answer is that Canada—Canada as such—is a costly proposition. In many ways it isn't a natural entity at all. It isn't a nation but an act of political will. The *natural* flow of goods and ideas on this continent isn't east-west but north-south, according to my friend. Left to their own devices the economic waters of North America would follow the meridians. But we've artificially dammed them up at the 49th parallel, forcing them to run from the East Coast to the West Coast for the sake of an idea. This is the idea called "Canada." If it were a flower, it wouldn't occur in the wild. It is a hot-house creation, so it must be carefully cultivated and nurtured, which costs a lot of money.

My friend isn't critical of this, by the way.

"A while ago there was a meeting of Canadian film directors in Vancouver," he told me. "The government paid some thirty of us to fly thousands of miles to the West Coast and discuss the problems of Canadian identity. Do you think that's peanuts?"

Maybe my friend is right. We routinely pay for events of this kind—and not just in the field of culture. Others would call such efforts a waste, whether they involve film directors talking identity or a herd of bureaucrats discussing programs of regional development. But we're Canadians. We're not looking at these things in terms of dollars and cents.

Half of our policies make no sense, except in the context of hothouse flowers. In some ways, Canada as a whole resembles nothing as much as the Spicer Commission. We're a $26 million psychodrama, a marathon therapy session, in which we tell each other everything we already know and can't help anyway.

So what? Our children can pick up the tab. It'll save them from being mistaken for Americans.

1991

CANADA IS NOT LIKE YUGOSLAVIA

The other day I touched briefly on the topic of national self-determination in context of the recent events in Yugoslavia. A friend, who has long hoped to catch me in a contradiction, phoned me triumphantly the next morning.

"Well, old pal," he said, "I've just read where you come out for Slovenian and Croatian independence. You say that a distinct cultural, linguistic, and geographic entity is a nation, and it is entitled to the protection of the United Nations Charter with respect to national self-determination. So tell me, where does that leave Quebec?"

"It leaves Quebec just east of Ontario," I replied cautiously, "unless somebody figures out a way to move it someplace else."

"Come, come," said my friend. "You're on the record as a supporter of federalism. You like Canada as it is. You'd hate to see Quebec separate; you've said so many times. Well, how can you deny that Quebec is a distinct cultural, linguistic, and geographic entity?"

Unjust accusations wound me to the quick. "You little twerp," I said politely, "just where have I ever denied that Quebec is distinct? *Au contraire*, I think Quebec is distinct to the blooming core."

"Well, maybe you haven't denied it," my friend said, "but you're against Quebec leaving confederation. All I'm asking is how can you support Slovenia and Croatia splitting up Yugoslavia, yet argue for Quebec staying in Canada? Isn't that being hypocritical?"

"Tell me," I asked, "do you believe that every individual is a distinct entity? A sovereign being? A free agent?"

"Yeah, more or less," replied my friend.

"Do you, therefore, also believe that everyone should separate from his or her spouse?" I asked.

"What do you mean, 'therefore'?" said my friend. "The second proposition doesn't follow from the first."

"Precisely," I said. "I rest my case."

I'm not reporting this exchange because I see any similarity between the breakaway Yugoslav republics and a sovereignty-seeking Quebec. What worries me is that our federal government might see such a similarity and that this may account, at least in part, for our reluctance to recognize independent Slovenia and Croatia.

If so, Ottawa's concern is misplaced. There isn't the slightest contradiction in the position of anyone who favors federalism for Quebec, but independence for Slovenia and Croatia (or for Estonia, Latvia, Lithuania, Georgia, etc.).

The most fundamental difference stems from the way these federal states—Canada as opposed to Yugoslavia or the Soviet Union—came into being. Canada was born as a result of a contract, as in marriage. Yugoslavia and the Soviet Union came about as a result of coercion, as in abduction or rape.

True, Canada may have been born of a marriage of convenience rather than a marriage of love. Be that as it may, marriage is still a legitimate union. Abduction and rape are never legitimate.

Another fundamental difference is that Canada, much as it may wish to keep the union going, is not threatening violence if Quebec decides to break it up. Pierre Trudeau may have been right or wrong to respond with federal troops to a handful of terrorists who were kidnapping and murdering people twenty-odd years ago, but today no one threatens to send in the military if, in a free and democratic referendum, Quebecers choose to go their own way.

The independence-seeking nations of Yugoslavia and the Soviet Union have already had their referenda. They've already voted—and voted overwhelmingly—for sovereignty. *Their* federal governments responded by a show of force. I think it's ironic that Canada's government, which wouldn't dream of using force to prevent the breakup of this country, endorses other governments' use of force to prevent the breakup of other federal states.

Because, make no mistake about it, we *are* endorsing force whenever we refuse to recognize breakaway nations in Yugoslavia or in the Soviet Union. Even more ironically, we legitimize communist tyranny by our refusal to recognize emerging democracies. (We did recognize the Baltic countries in late August 1991, but not before the Communist Party was suspended in the Soviet Union itself. We never did anything to upset a tyranny while it was in power, except maybe vis-à-vis South Africa.)

But isn't nationalism petty and inefficient? Is it not in the long-term interest of small nations to work out their differences with other national groups and stay in a larger federation?

Well, maybe such an argument could be made in the case of Quebec, though not even this would justify forcing Quebec to stay. But no one in his right mind could argue that it's in Slovenia's or Croatia's interest to be in a Serbian-dominated confederation—and certainly not as long as the confederation is under communist rule.

1991

13.

APPRENTICE

SORCERERS

Notes on the United States

REACHING FOR THE STARS

Are there lessons to be learned from last week's shuttle disaster? Many people say no—except, obviously, technological lessons once the cause of the malfunction is established. Such tragedies are the by-products of man's exploratory nature. Accidents always have and always will occur as human beings test their skills and stretch the limits of their knowledge. The entire U.S., indeed the whole of mankind, mourns the courageous seven who gave their lives assisting humanity's embryonic venture into space. History will preserve their names in the manner of other explorer-martyrs like Captain Robert Scott. But their tragedy—so the argument goes—should not slow down the exploration of space any more than the death of Scott and his crew slowed exploration of the polar regions.

Many individuals risk their lives for scientific and technological progress, even apart from the great sailors or voyagers. Often they do it for much smaller causes than the crew of Mission 51-L. The conquest of the sea and the air—even of the roads, for that matter—would not have been possible if people hadn't been willing to lay down their lives for them. How could the sacrifice of the *Challenger*'s crew have been in vain, when test drivers risk their lives regularly just so the rest of us can drive our recreational vehicles in greater safety?

I do not disagree with any of this. All mammals are exploratory animals, and human beings are the most exploratory of all mammals. Probing our environment is as natural to our species as breathing. To some extent, we are explorers from birth.

I also agree that—considering the magnitude of the task—the U.S. space program has been conducted with a remarkable blend of courage and caution. No human venture into the unknown has been more audacious, none more successful, yet none achieved with a greater degree of relative safety. Learning how to fly to the moon cost us far fewer lives than learning how to take our cars around a corner.

Using the same statistical method of computation that the airline industry uses—accidents per passenger miles—space travel may be the safest method of human transportation, even after the shuttle tragedy. (Admittedly, this tells us more about the shortcomings of a statistical method than the safety of space travel—but that's by the by.) In short, there's much to be said for the view that—after honouring and mourning the heroic seven—we should simply figure out what went wrong, fix it, and get on with it. Every member of *Challenger*'s ill-fated crew would wish mankind to continue reaching for the stars.

Fair enough. I think, however, that we should consider one additional lesson. Some scientists have argued for years that the scientific value of sending human crews into space is very limited. In fact, they say, it only slows down the learning process about space and space travel. It makes it needlessly expensive. At this stage, we could learn more and learn faster from unmanned probes filled with instruments. Our insistence on human crews is romantic, old-fashioned, and unscientific. It's a throwback to the sailing ship of Columbus and doesn't fit the real requirements of the space age.

I don't know enough to have any opinion on this—but the mere fact that such views have been expressed by eminent scientists indicates one thing. Whether the sacrifice of the commander and the pilot aboard *Challenger* was worthwhile or not, the sacrifice of the brave school teacher Christa McAuliffe was utterly unnecessary.

In no way does this detract from her personal heroism, of course. The fault lies with those who sent her—and sent a senator and a congressman before her—into space. These fine people have been propelled aloft to prove the fatuous contention that "space is a natural environment for man." This may well be true one day, but it isn't true yet. As one astronaut put it on CBS-TV, these vehicles are still experimental. It is senseless to ask school teachers to assume a risk that normally only test pilots assume.

"Senseless" is, in fact, a mild word. "Cheap political stunt" may be more accurate. At this point, teachers and congressmen aboard a space vehicle are not payload but playload. Their presence makes no sense even from a publicist's point of view, for the needless death of McAuliffe is likely to harm the space program more than her successful flight could possibly have benefited it.

No doubt she would not have been aboard if the decision makers had not honestly assumed that the flight was, by now, routine. What they should have remembered is that routine flights are not televised on the nation's networks. This is a better test than any technological assurance of what is or isn't "routine." The next school teacher in space should be put on a flight the media no longer has any interest in covering.

1986

In Miami, Shoot First!

This is a small and rather amusing item from the news. It came from my phantom clipper in Miami, and I simply couldn't resist it. Last month the U.S. Customs Service unveiled its new tactical weapon for the continuing drug wars. The Service proposed a little escalation to raise the stakes for drug smugglers. Also for taxpayers, travellers, passers-by, and babes-in-arms. To raise the stakes sky-high, in fact.

U.S. Customs came up with a plan to shoot down private planes suspected of carrying illicit cargo. Shoot them right out of the sky. Honest. Wax their tail. That was the actual plan of U.S. Customs. Nothing more—but certainly nothing less.

Apparently the proposal was made in earnest. It was certainly taken seriously around the Gulf of Mexico. Seriously enough for several organizations to go into a bit of a tailspin, if you'll pardon the expression. Even the FBI said that it was a lousy idea. The Private Aircraft Owners' and Pilots' Association said—well, maybe I shouldn't print what the Private Aircraft Owners' and Pilots' Association said, but it was an expression of disapproval.

Perhaps in other parts of the continent they would have laughed at U.S. Customs' proposal, but in Florida people weren't laughing. That's *Miami Vice* country down there. Everybody watches the show (or at least they used to, until it ran out of steam) including the officers of U.S. Customs. In that state it seemed possible that when law-enforcement types announced that, dammit, they were going to wax the tail of private planes, they meant it.

I don't want to mislead readers: it is still quite safe to fly south of the Mason-Dixon line. Common sense prevailed even in Florida. The public reaction quickly indicated to U.S. Customs that their proposal was, well, a little premature. People weren't ready for it yet. They still preferred to watch *Miami Vice* in their living rooms rather than in the open skies above their towns and cities. As a result, U.S. Customs didn't get to put on their scarves and goggles like Snoopy after all. For the time being, they weren't allowed to play Red Baron over the Florida Keys. Still, the fighter jocks of Customs didn't yield with good grace. They kept muttering darkly about their guidelines.

After all, the Customs aces said, they wouldn't have been just shooting down private planes willy-nilly. They weren't going to shoot them down as if shooting down private planes was going out of fashion. They weren't going to run amok like a bunch of trigger-happy maniacs, as some folk suggested. No sir: they were responsible officers of the law. They would have followed meticulous guidelines.

This is what got to me in the entire story. It was at this juncture that I could no longer resist writing about it. Oh, the guidelines! Oh, the blessed guidelines of bureaucrats and policemen. Oh, for the Rules of Engagement of the U.S. Customs Service. Oh, for the Order of Battle of the Brussels Sprout Marketing Board.

How do you deal with people who, on being elected or appointed to public office, believe that they have acquired supernatural powers? Yes, supernatural, because they can devise guidelines to take every contingency into account. For instance, unlike any financial wizard, they can foresee the housing or the commodity market five years down the line. Hell, they can tell when a car is going to cross an intersection.

That's why civil servants, in or out of uniform, in Florida or in Ontario, are busy drawing up guidelines. They have plans for our economy and our health. They have plans for running red lights when chasing suspects. The fact that their guidelines have already destroyed the rental market in Toronto, or put a debt of $35,000 on the books of every Canadian household, or killed or maimed dozens of Canadians every year with pursuit vehicles, doesn't deter them.

It's always extreme cases that illustrate this government mentality best: the sincere belief that a "responsible" or "professional" bureaucrat can foresee where a crippled plane is going to crash. God himself couldn't foresee it—but a customs official can. He can draw up guidelines to provide for radio failures, or for someone in the plane being a hostage, or for the pilot being an undercover agent. (That's what *really* got the FBI worried, by the way.)

Well, I guess up here we don't go to such extremes yet. Maybe a few months of frost cools down our bureaucrats. In Ottawa, they're still content with having the highest income per household in the nation, without the urge to wax anybody's tail. That's why I don't envy Floridians their sunshine, as I note through my window a flock of fresh snowflakes settling slowly upon our brumal scene.

1988

WHITE HOUSE STAR SYSTEM

I see that everyone was fussed last week about Nancy Reagan consulting the stars about one thing or another. Some religious leaders, like Jerry Falwell, seemed especially aroused. At the risk of appearing to endorse rank superstition in general (or Nancy Reagan in particular) I would like to point out a few home truths.

To begin with, Nancy Reagan happens to be the first lady of a nation whose people are avid followers of astrological charts. I understand that astrology columns are as widely read as the weather forecasts in America's newspapers. (They're just about as reliable, too.) Anyway, I think it would be very snobbish of Nancy not to consult the same stars that the ordinary folk of her country consult all the time.

As for the press, I think it *is* snobbish (as well as hypocritical) for them to criticize Nancy for taking one of their regular columns seriously. If the newspapers think astrology is bunk, why do they keep printing the stuff? Is it possible that the media, our great disseminators of accuracy, enlightenment, and truth, have been feeding us baseless and misleading information all these years? Not only that, but have they done so *knowingly*?

When heaping scorn on the president's wife, does America's press mean to imply that Wednesday, May 18, may not be favourable for meeting a tall, dark stranger for all those who were born under the sign of Taurus? If so, why do they persist in putting it in the paper where it's liable to corrupt Nancy Reagan's mind?

As for religious leaders—well, I don't want to step on anybody's toes, so I'll put this carefully. The question is, what's wrong with astrology, tarot cards, or any other occult preoccupation, except that they are a bit irrational?

They *are* irrational, of course; there is no basis for them either in science or in common sense. They are purely matters of personal faith, supported by neither physical evidence nor deductive reasoning. Okay—but how are they different from any religion in this regard?

Don't misunderstand me. I respect all religions. I would fight to the hilt for anyone's right to believe in any metaphysical system of his or her choice. But people who pin their faith on something irrational are hardly in a position to criticize other people for pinning *their* faith on something equally irrational.

No one would criticize Nancy Reagan if it turned out that she prayed every night, or consulted the deity of her faith (or the deity's priestly representative) for spiritual guidance about the future of her nation. Nor would it be anything to criticize her about. Throughout history many greater leaders and their spouses have prayed, or consulted archbishops about the will of God. A great many have also consulted occult signals, including Canada's own Prime Minister William Lyon Mackenzie King.

Such devotions, while quite irrational, signify a degree of healthy humility to me. They show that the mighty are at least humble enough to acknowledge the limits of their powers. Consulting priests or fortune tellers symbolizes a useful understanding that human capacities are finite, including those of reasoning and intellect. In this regard, they symbolize a great truth. I'd rather be ruled by people who admit they don't know everything than by "scientific" socialists who think that they do.

As for the contention of Jerry Falwell and others that a belief in the occult is incompatible with Christianity, all I can say is that we must have read different history books. Most Christian princes—whose faith was at least as fundamental as that of the narrowest fundamentalist in America—used to have astrologers in their courts. Even princes of the Church had them.

The great sixteenth-century scientist Johannes Kepler started out as an astrologer and he never encountered the slightest objection from the Church as long as he was only casting horoscopes. The cardinals began to look critically at him only when he abandoned astrology and started dabbling in astronomy. Oh, and when he objected to his mom being burned at the stake. (Good Christians of his day just couldn't understand that. After all, the woman was a witch.)

I suppose all I'm saying is that we should be more tolerant of each other's faiths and superstitions, especially if we don't mind pocketing the money they bring in, whether via the collection plate or advertising revenue. As for political spouses, if we discourage their astrological ventures they might start consulting something far less reliable than the stars about the nation's affairs. Nancy Reagan in particular might start consulting her own mind.

1988

THEY GOT THE MESSAGE

Watching the U.S. election coverage on the big networks is like letting lukewarm waves of current fashion wash over one's brain. All issues are narrowed down to whatever appears to be of interest to the puny minds that put the programs together. Their answers are usually okay. It is their questions that are (with some honourable exceptions) fearfully hackneyed, mundane, or beside the point.

Their answers tend to be okay because top pros—and TV network journalists are nothing if not top pros—can generally find clever answers to silly questions. Answers require only resources, persistence, and skill. It's questions that also require some insight and intelligence, which are much harder to come by.

This, incidentally, is one of the problems with the TV debates of presidential (or prime ministerial) candidates. Just about everyone bemoans the low level of these debates, but few point out the abysmally low level of the reporters' questions that define the answers. What do you reply to a journalist who wants to know your views, of all the things, on the gender gap?

I bring up the subject because NBC saw fit to send its newsreader, Connie Chung, to investigate how the dreaded gender gap had plagued Vice-President George Bush. Up went a sign indicating that in a sample poll fifty-two per cent of women voted for Massachusetts Governor Michael Dukakis and only forty-eight per cent for Bush. This was followed by the poor girl having to talk to three women who voted for Dukakis and one who voted for Bush—which, of course, had the effect of neatly turning a four-point spread into seventy-five points to prove one (lame) point.

Well, I know you've got to put something on the air while the computers are counting up the returns, but really. It would have made as much sense—actually a bit more—to use the same data for suggesting that Dukakis was plagued by a gender gap since (according to NBC's own figures) he had a *ten-point* spread with forty-five per cent male votes against Bush's fifty-five per cent.

Of course, both suggestions would be unworthy of serious news analysis. They're examples of focusing on minor side issues to satisfy current journalistic preoccupations, while central issues remain unexplored.

Another example was the endless discussions on the effects of "negative campaigning" for Dukakis. To begin with, one need not be an expert on history to know that the 1988 presidential elections were no more negative in their general campaign rhetoric than most U.S. elections since George Washington's days (and much less negative than some). Next, one need to have only glanced at TV or the papers for ten seconds a day in the last six months to know that Republicans were no more negative about Dukakis than Democrats were about Bush.

The difference was that the Republicans could make it stick, or at least make it stick better than the Democrats. Moreover, they could make it stick not because they were better at selling, but because more

Americans were ready to buy. The question of "Where was George?" worried fewer voters than the question of "Is Mike a bleeding-heart liberal?"

Nor was it a matter of who had the better ad agencies or press aides, or any of the other side-issues that have been getting such a huge play in the media. Dukakis didn't lose because he couldn't "get his message across." He got his message across only too clearly. His problem was that Americans didn't care for his message in sufficient numbers.

While a majority of Americans may not have liked Bush much more than Dukakis, they liked Dukakis much less than they liked President Ronald Reagan. Since they couldn't elect Reagan for a third term, they chose the next best thing in electing his vice-president. In doing so they hoped, rightly or wrongly, that they might extend an era which they had enjoyed. Under Dukakis they would have been in a new ballgame. *This* was Dukakis' message, and he told it to the voters loud and clear. He got it across just splendidly—and it cost him the election.

Why did many Americans enjoy the Reagan era? For a some tangible reasons, no doubt, from relative domestic prosperity to an improved international climate. Reagan's "hard line" seemed to have done more for the prospect of peace, for disarmament, and even for turning the Soviet Union into a more reasonable society than all the appeasement and detente of his predecessors. But the main reason is, I think, simpler.

Reagan made Americans feel good about themselves. Quite a bit better, anyway, than they have in twenty-five years. For all his talk about caring for people, Governor Dukakis held out no such prospect.

1988

TIME IS OUT OF STEP

Last week's issue of *Time* displayed a smiling Raisa Gorbachev on its cover, with the legend underneath: "Raisa—A new image for the

Soviet Union's overworked, underappreciated women." Well, now, isn't that interesting?

Interesting on many levels, the first being that Raisa Gorbachev is about as symbolic of the average Soviet woman as Marie Antoinette was of the average Frenchwoman in the eighteenth century. I would have thought that whatever Raisa may be, underappreciated she is not. I doubt if any president's or general secretary's spouse ever is, at least in the ordinary sense of the word. Your average underappreciated woman rarely gets to wear three different fur coats in one day, as Raisa did on her last visit to Washington.

As a rule, rulers' wives symbolize only the overappreciated women in any society—and I'd be the last person to blame them. Why shouldn't they take the good with the bad? Life with Mikhail (or Ron or Brian) probably isn't a bowl of cherries. If you can cope with the downside of being a political spouse, you're entitled to the upside. Three cheers for Raisa's sables. She deserves them.

As for overworked, I could be persuaded that some political spouses, including Raisa, keep very busy and can hardly stand on their feet at the end of the day. I simply shed no tears for them. For ambitious people "overwork" of this kind is like oxygen is for the rest of us. I would neither blame nor admire anyone for breathing.

This is all by the by, however. The really amusing thing about *Time*'s cover is its innocent, American obtuseness. It's hilarious that, even when discussing a country such as the Soviet Union, the journalists of this naïve continent can only view it through the prism of their own trendy concerns—such as feminism, in this particular instance.

The Soviet Union, even by self-description, is a dictatorship. As all dictatorships (or oligarchies) it is deeply split between a general population and a ruling elite. The former are, indeed, overworked and underappreciated—but regardless of sex. Men or women, they consider themselves fortunate if they can keep out of the Gulag. The latter are the party bosses. They're overappreciated and often underworked—again, regardless of sex. (Incidentally, they also consider themselves lucky if they can keep out of the Gulag. In a dictatorship even the bosses aren't safe.)

To say that women in particular are underappreciated and over-worked in Soviet society is to latch onto the least important division in that society: a division that exists almost solely in the western observer's mind. Just how is the lady *apparatchik,* the lady functionary, the lady colonel in the KGB, underappreciated? And opposed to whom, the ordinary clerk or worker in the factory or on the collective farm?

True, Soviet wives may go out to work, then act as cooks at home without convenience shopping, microwave ovens, and other labour-saving devices. So what? Soviet husbands go out to work, then act as handymen at home without power tools and snowblowers. As consumers, even relatively affluent Soviet citizens may experience hardships North Americans would find intolerable, but men experience them as much as women.

Nothing reveals the silliness of *Time*'s preoccupation as much as the following petulant sentence from the cover piece: "Raisa. Even in this semi-enlightened age, prominent women are somehow reduced to first names: Maggie, Cory, Nancy." Talk about feminist injustice-collectors! To begin with, who is calling Raisa "Raisa" but the very (female) journalists of the *Time* cover story? If they don't like it, why don't they call her Mrs. or even Ms. Gorbachev? It's not going to unleash a nuclear war.

In any event, what is this arrant nonsense about prominent *women* being reduced to their first names? What about prominent men? I've seen more headlines referring to former president Eisenhower as "Ike"—or to former president Kennedy as "Jack"—than all the Maggies or Nancys combined. It's simply a style in popular western journalism.

But today's feminists have become such pompous asses, they carry such tedious chips on their shoulders, that they even object to being called by their actual names. And they get away with spouting these idiocies, in the pained tones of injured innocence, in leading magazines.

It's the political "analysis" of these minds from which the nation's readers are supposed to take their cue. No wonder Americans are among the most misinformed readers in the world.

1988

JUST CAUSE? WHAT A JOKE

I'm going to comment again on the U.S. invasion of Panama. It continues to trouble me. I realize that nothing succeeds like success. The president, far from receiving much flak, is being praised for his action even by traditional opponents. Within the U.S. not only the general population, but also people who go usually on automatic pilot in their condemnation of whatever a Republican president may do—Democrats, lefties, East Coast editorial writers, and so forth—are either approving of George Bush or at least subdued in their criticism.

Abroad, the usual assortment of injustice collectors keep a curiously low profile, not only in Canada or Europe, but even in Latin America. So are the Soviets (though right now they're so busy with their own problems that whatever they do doesn't really count). The silence worries me—perhaps it worries me more than the invasion itself. There must be something fundamentally wrong with what Bush has done if it upsets liberal intellectuals and reflex anti-Americans so little.

To avoid misunderstandings, I'll first outline some things that do *not* bother me about the invasion of Panama. I'm not opposing it because I have illusions about General Manuel Noriega, or because I think it's "just like Afghanistan," or because I cherish dictators, or because I think force should never be used to defend democracy, or because I feel the Americans are always wrong.

No, I'm troubled by the invasion for entirely different reasons. What troubles me, I guess, is that the grounds President Bush gave for the invasion—the Bush Doctrine, if you will—would justify almost any country invading almost any other country at almost any time.

What are Bush's grounds? 1) Noriega is a dictator. 2) Noriega is a suspected drug dealer. 3) Noriega has been indicted in Florida on criminal charges. 4) Noriega's government hurt or threatened to hurt American citizens. 5) As a result of Noriega's "declaration" of war, a state of war existed between the U.S. and Panama. 6) Noriega's acts posed a threat to the integrity of the Panama Canal treaty. 7) Most Panamanians voted against Noriega in the last election anyway, and are happy to be rid of him.

None of this is untrue, strictly speaking (except maybe that Noriega's declaration amounted to a state of war against the U.S.). Anyway, for the sake of simplicity, let's assume all of it is true. What does it do to our understanding of what justifies war—or what is a "just cause," to use Bush's own term?

There are many suspected drug dealers in the world: in Latin America, in Asia, in the Middle East, maybe even in Europe. They include high officials or heads of state. (Fidel Castro is one who springs to mind rather easily.) Getting a Florida grand jury to indict them would be a breeze. If they can't be extradited, would the U.S. (or any other country) be entitled under the Bush Doctrine to send in the Marines for them?

Many governments hurt or threaten to hurt the citizens of other countries, either directly or through the well-documented support of terrorist groups. True, the U.S. did bomb Libya for this reason once, but it generally objected when, for instance, Israel raided Lebanon on similar grounds. Will the U.S. object no longer? Will Bush send Marines to arms-supplying, terrorist-training Syria, Cuba, North Korea, Nicaragua, or Iran? North Korea would be the simplest, I suppose. Technically the U.S. is still at war with it.

Have all dictators become fair game under the Bush Doctrine, or only some? Once identified as dictators (say, by a Florida grand jury) are all other countries free to attack them, or only the U.S.? Is a CIA estimate that in an election the majority of citizens would vote against the head of state sufficient cause for a war against a country, or does it have to be supported by a CBS News–*New York Times* poll as well?

I apologize for lapsing into humour, but it illustrates the problem. Bush's reasons are a joke. Until now the U.S. has usually protested quite vociferously when other countries used force to protect their treaties—or protect democracy. In 1956 the U.S. condemned British-French-Israeli efforts to protect the Suez Canal against Egypt's Nasser, who was a far greater threat to Suez than Noriega was to Panama. Nor did America support Britain's war to save the Falklands from the dictators of Argentina, though it was clear that the Falklanders were praying to be saved. (I'm told that America aided Britain in all kinds of covert ways during the Falklands conflict. Be that as it may, the Reagan-Bush administration gave Mrs. Thatcher no public support.)

This time Britain was the first to support President Bush. Minimally, I think, good manners would require Bush to admit America's mistake and apologize to Margaret Thatcher.

1990